I0175922

The First Command

The First Command

IQRA—Its Impact on Global
Intellectualism and the Renaissance

M. JAMAL HAIDER

TOP

The Other Press
Kuala Lumpur

© M. Jamal Haider 2018

All rights reserved. No part of this publication may be reproduced, stored in a retrieval system, or transmitted, in any form or by any means, electronic, mechanical, photocopying, recording or otherwise without the prior permission of the publisher. Small excerpts from the book may be quoted only if properly referenced.

Published by
The Other Press Sdn. Bhd.
607 Mutiara Majestic
Jalan Othman
46000 Petaling Jaya
Selangor, Malaysia
www.ibtbooks.com

The Other Press Sdn. Bhd. is affiliated with Islamic Book Trust.

Perpustakaan Negara Malaysia   Cataloguing-in-Publication Data

M. Jamal Haider
    The First Command IQRA : Its Impact on Global Intellectualism and
    the Renaissance / M. Jamal Haider.
    ISBN 978-967-0957-22-7
    1. Knowledge, Theory of (Islam).
    2. Muslim scholars--Intellectual life.
    3. Islam and science.   I. Title.
    297.26

Printed by
SS Graphic Printers (M) Sdn. Bhd.
Lot 7 & 8, Jalan TIB 3, Taman Industri Bolton,
68100 Batu Caves, Selangor Darul Ehsan.

THIS BOOK IS DEDICATED TO MY GRANDFATHER

Nawab Badruddin Haider

AND FATHER

Nawabzada Kamruddin Haider

They were assiduously committed to the cause of
Muslim education and emancipation

Contents

SECTION TWO
Muslim Contributions to the Renaissance

SECTION THREE
Muslim Intellectual Regression

Acknowledgement

Knowledge is dynamic and human memory transient. For nearly a thousand years Muslims scholars were the stalwarts of all kinds of knowledge propagation—religious, scientific, philosophical, social-scientific, literary, *etc.* Their work has played a vital role in leading the world to where it is today. But the contemporary world has forgotten all their great achievements and contributions. Fortunately, there still remains a few scholars, both Muslim and non-Muslim, who are endeavouring to right this wrong by writing valuable books and by using eloquent oratory. They are the remarkable people who need to be acknowledged. My humble thanks and appreciation goes to them all.

On a more personal level, I have a number of people to acknowledge for support and encouragement. Dr Jan A. Ali of Western Sydney University for the support he has provided me over the years and Dr Khairul Haque Chowdhury of New South Wales Department of Education for reviewing and commenting on the initial manuscript. Thanks to Hotan Kheyrandish of Kuala Lumpur for editing the whole book and Rafi Ahmad of Sydney Darussalam for managing delivery and distribution of the book in Australia. Thanks also to The Other Press for finalising the layout of the book. Haji Koya, my publisher, has been remarkable in guiding me and giving professional suggestions throughout the publishing process.

I thank my children—Rakshanda and her husband Redhwan, Parisa, and Ryan—for pooling in and buying me a professional laptop, a surprise gift, so that I keep on writing and my wife Rubayyat for making enough space for me to make writing tranquil.

And thanks to Him Who holds all knowledge and gives to those He deems so. Thanks to Him for giving me a little drop of knowledge and the skill so that I could write this book.

> *And if all the trees of earth were pens*
> *And the ocean was ink,*
> *With seven oceans behind it to add to its supply*
> *Yet would not the words of God be exhausted;*
> *For God is exalted in power, full of wisdom.*

> — Qur'an, Luqmān 31:27

Introduction

Over the last two centuries there has been a niche of writers claiming that science actually came from the Muslims. In the Western world, from time to time, there have been considerable bias against Muslims so no one has actually paid much attention to it. In the Muslim world there have been many catastrophic reverses and the consequent ignorance has caused an inability or apathy towards really appreciating such a topic.

Nevertheless, by the first decade of the 21st century, the Muslim intellectual golden age has become more or less accepted. The age was the period between the 8th and 13th centuries CE when the early Muslim scholars made tremendous contributions to the advancement of science, social science and other disciplines. At that stage, the Muslims started to regress intellectually but would still remain at the top for a few centuries more till Europe surpassed them.

This acceptance of the golden age by the scholars was inevitable—there were too many historical records to be ignored. In recent times, both Muslim and Western scholars have written books on the same theme. But there still remains considerable misunderstanding as to how and why the Muslims became such great scholars. What were their contributions and how, precisely, did they influence the world in general and the West in particular? And having reached such an intellectual zenith, why have the Muslims regressed to the ignorant, almost illiterate, levels in recent centuries?

The acceptance by the scholars took time and happened grudgingly. Initially, some Western scholars claimed that the Muslims were just intermediary keepers of knowledge which they had inherited from the Greeks and had simply passed on that same knowledge to Europe. When the evidence of Muslim contributions to science became overwhelming, such scholars acquiesced stating that the reason Muslims became good at science was due to the Greek philosophy they had studied, and that they lost the sciences because they gave up studying philosophy. Thus, a large extent of the credit was still given to the Greeks, not the Muslims. The attempt to minimise the credit to the Muslim scholars was due to the unavailability of sufficient information or simply due to historic prejudice.

This book aims to correct that prejudice in a very logical and healthy manner. It uncontestably shows the great contributions of early Muslim scholars in all the disciplines—science, social science, philosophy, theology, literature and other areas of learning—that have profoundly affected Europe and the rest of the world. It would appear remarkable, but the Europeans inherited not just science with concepts like Newton's laws, optics and even evolutionary theory from the Muslims, but also subjects like sociology, economics and philosophy. Taking a historical approach, the book shows how the Muslims developed knowledge, when and who transferred this knowledge to Europe and, finally, what caused the intellectual regression among the Muslims themselves.

Following the prologue, which comes next, this book is chronologically set into three sections. Section one comprises six chapters starting with a brief historical background followed by the development of knowledge and intellectualism by the early Muslim scholars and their increasing international presence and influence.

Section two, in four chapters, gives a short background of comparative knowledge and intellectualism in Europe in that period and the Europeans contact with the Muslims' knowledge. Then, it discusses the disintegration of the early Muslim empires and the rise of Europe, leading to the Renaissance.

Finally, section three deals with the causes of intellectual regression among the Muslims that is evident in the present world.

Prologue

At the dawn of the 7th century, in a world stooped in ignorance and inequity, came down a divine command to the Prophet Muḥammad (ṣ):

> *Read, in the name of your Lord*
> *and Cherisher, Who created—*
> *Created man out of a clot that clings.*
> *Read! And your Lord is most bountiful,*
> *He Who taught the use of the pen,*
> *Taught man what he knew not.*

> — Qur'an, Iqra' 96:1-5

'Read' (*Iqra*) was the quintessential first command. It was the moment that gave birth to a new age and to a new class of humanity. They were fearless, relentless seekers of knowledge. They became a nation of morally upright scholars spreading brilliance. All else—the rulers, the warriors, the entrepreneurs— were to protect and support this path of illumination. For centuries, they enlightened the world and gave it the direction that it still abides by. They were the early Muslims. They chose to excel in every aspect of life.

Wisdom is the lost property of the believer. Wherever he finds it, he takes it.

— The Prophet, *Sunan at-Tirmidhi*, 2687

SECTION ONE

The Early Muslims and
Their Passion for Knowledge

The rise of the early Muslims and their quest for knowledge
is a most remarkable story. The driving force behind the
quest was the Qur'an and the Prophet of Islam,
Muḥammad, peace be upon him. From the very first verse
revealed, the Qur'an advocates and encourages the quest
for and the application of knowledge and intellectualism.
Throughout his life, the Prophet himself promoted the
importance of knowledge, which galvanised a passion
among the early Muslims.

This pursuit of knowledge among the Muslims was not
haphazard. It followed a definite pattern: First the ulemaic
or religious disciplines were perfected. This provided the
scholarly foundation. It was followed by disciplines like
history, theology, and liberal arts. This was the formative
phase for knowledge diversification. Finally came the
discovery and the study of philosophy, natural sciences and
social sciences which started the flowering of knowledge
that is still ongoing. Obviously, there were overlaps in the

study of these different disciplines but the pattern becomes distinct when the historical development of knowledge is studied in detail.

In the present day, it is confusing when trying to fathom the origin of the distinct science subjects—chemistry, physics, algebra, *etc.*—and the social science subjects— sociology, economics, historiography, *etc.* In the ancient civilisations, science as we know it today was unknown. Some discrete scientific 'ideas' existed within the sphere of philosophy, astrology or religious texts. When ancient Greek philosophers wrote about 'physics', it had nothing to do with empirical scientific studies. It was a 'philosophical' study into nature, all of which was theoretical. Empirical science and the scientific method was first discovered and practised by the Muslim scholars. They were the ones who first developed the above-mentioned subjects which were later inherited by the Europeans.

In order to understand the above premise, it is important to start with the very dawn of Islam.

CHAPTER 1

Historical Context

The World at the Advent of Islam

Towards the end of the 3rd century CE, Emperor Diocletian divided the vast Roman Empire into two administrative regions which, over the next century, would lead to the formation of the Western Roman Empire and Eastern Roman Empire (Byzantium). Further west, Europe consisted of a large number of small kingdoms and chiefdoms, most of which were barbaric, tribal and pagan. In 313 CE, after centuries of persecuting Christians, Imperial Rome finally accepted Christianity as an official religion of the Empire. The Western Roman Empire, which included the city of Rome, fell to Germanic barbarians in 476 CE.

By the late 6th century, just before the advent of Islam, the two main powers in the world were Christian Byzantium and Zoroastrian Persia. The Persian empire was older than the Roman Empire and had existed even prior to the classical Greeks. These two empires, Romans and Persians, were in perpetual military conflict.

In the Far East, the great Han Dynasty of China had disintegrated by the end of the 2nd century CE. After that China went through a period of internal conflict and division for a few centuries. The state-sponsored Confucianism became less influential. By the 6th century, Buddhism was firmly entrenched in China, having acquired many Chinese features in the process. In India, the end of the Gupta Empire in c. 550 CE left a melee of minor Hindu and Buddhist revivalist kingdoms.

In the late 6th century, there were a few minor kingdoms in Southeast Asia and Africa. Christian kings ruled Abyssinia (Ethiopia) and Coptic Alexandria (Egypt). The Americas and Australia were yet to be discovered and were populated by indigenous tribes, many nomadic, with no established intellectualism.

Thus, it was a time when most of the civilisations had collapsed and whatever remained no longer pursued knowledge with an intent or capacity that would progresses humanity. The great accumulation of knowledge by the Greeks was over and the knowledge itself was 'lost' (*see* appendices 1 and 2 for more information on pre-Islamic civilisations). In such an environment was the advent of Islam, which came with a full commitment to 'Total Knowledge'.

Periods of Muslim Intellectualism

The intellectual development of the early Muslims and the later regression of Muslim societies can be divided into six historical periods:

1. The Prophetic Period (610-632 CE).

    This period covers the time of the prophetic mission of the Prophet Muhammad (ṣ). He was born in 570 but the first revelation came to him in 610 after which he started his mission. The Prophet was based first in Makkah but due to persecution he and his followers migrated to

Madinah in 622. The Prophet died in 632. During this period the Muslims received knowledge from two sources:

- the revelations (verses) of the Qur'an to the Prophet.

- the Prophet's teachings or Tradition (*Sunnah*).

The prophetic revelations were memorised and written down during the Prophet's lifetime. The collection of all the revelations formed the Qur'an. The formal compilation was completed in about a year after his death. The Prophet himself was the teacher of the Muslims. The teachings and tradition of the Prophet, which are separate from the revelations of the Qur'an, are known as the *Sunnah*. It comprises the sayings, advices and way of life of the Prophet. Each of these sayings is known as a ḥadīth.

The Qur'an and *Sunnah* provided the integrated intellect from which other disciplines developed starting with jurisprudence followed by theology and rationalism in later periods. During this period, Muslims were instilled with a remarkable passion for knowledge.

2. Rule of the Rashidun Caliphs (632-661 CE).

After the death of the Prophet, Muslims were ruled by four Rashidun Caliphs (meaning righteous representatives of the Prophet)—Abu Bakr, Umar ibn al-Khattab, Uthman ibn Affan and Ali ibn Abi Talib. These caliphs were selected-elected by the Muslims in Madinah. Following the footsteps of the Prophet, the caliphs, one after another, encouraged and sponsored the pursuit of knowledge.

During this period, *tafsīr* (interpretation and exegesis of the Qur'an), ḥadīth (sayings or traditions of the Prophet) and *fiqh* (jurisprudence) were researched and developed by the ulema (orthodox religious scholars) and came to be known as the ulemaic disciplines. The academic foundation of the Muslims was laid down by them. These disciplines would continue to further develop in the following periods.

3.   Period of the Early Muslim Empires (661-1258 CE).

The early Muslim empires are represented by the Umayyad (which includes the Spanish Umayyad), Abbasid and Seljuk dynasties which followed one another over the centuries. Along with the Seljuk there were also some Persian and Shi'ah Dynasties including the Fatimid who claimed to be decendant of Fatima, daughter of the Prophet.

During this period the disciplines that developed were the following:

- Further research and development of *tafsīr* schools of the Qur'an.

- Further development of *fiqh* schools based on Qur'an and *Sunnah*.

- Complete compilation of ḥadīth—all the ḥadīths were compiled, authenticated, categorised and finalised.

- The development of theological schools.

The passion for knowledge caused the flowering of many disciplines in this period. Great academic institutions were set up investigating into a variety of disciplines. A network developed between all these institutions bringing forth an illuminated domain. The passion was greatly sponsored by all Muslim rulers who provided incentives and sponsorship for the scholars.

As the orthodox religious scholars toiled and taught the ulemaic disciplines, the literacy and the intellect of the masses increased and they started to study other disciplines as well. This led to:

- The development of rational sciences.

- The development of Muslim philosophical schools.

- The development of the Sufi discipline.

By this time period, knowledge from pre-existing civilisations, like those of the Greeks, Persians and Indians, was also incorporated by the Muslim scholars. The Muslims became the most advanced intellectual society in the world.

4. The Tri-Military Events (c. 1000-1200 CE).

The early Muslim empires had disintegrated, forming fractious sultanates and emirates, towards the end of the previous period. Then the divided and weakened Muslim domains were invaded by external powers. Three of most destructive of these invasions were the Spanish *Reconquista* (followed by the Inquisition), the Crusades and, finally, the Mongol invasion. Muslims suffered death and destruction extensively during this period leading to far-reaching consequences. Much of the six centuries of intellectual institutions built by the Muslims were destroyed leading to the start of intellectual regression from the mid-13th century onwards.

Fortunately, during this period a large amount of knowledge of the early Muslims was translated to mainly Latin. Scholars from Europe came to the Muslim domains, studied there and translated books on science, social science, philosophy, theology, *etc.*, and took those books and learning's back to Europe.

5. Latter Muslim Empires and the Renaissance (c. 1300-1800 CE).

   After the devastations of the above-mentioned Tri-Military period, the Muslims revived and reasserted, giving rise to great new empires—Ottoman, Moghul, Safavid—and other dynasties. The yearning for knowledge was still present but rational knowledge was eventually lost.

   Europe inherited not just the knowledge from the Muslims but also the passion that led to the Renaissance and further into industrialisation.

6. The Colonial Period (1800-1950 CE).

   Europe industrialised and transformed to modern nation states. In contrast, the Muslims regressed due to intellectual stagnation. The Europeans colonised most of the world, including much that belonged to the Muslims. This was the time that the Muslims regressed as a civilisation to its lowest ebb.

The early Muslims belong to the first three periods mentioned above—the Prophetic period, the Rashidun Caliph period and the period of the early Muslim empires. During these periods the Muslims, most of all, were a nation of scholars. As Islam advocates a pursuit of 'Total Knowledge', the early Muslims relentlessly and passionately pursued all types of knowledge and became the best in the world at all the known disciplines. During these periods, the Muslim scholars belonged to different ethnicities and races. Among the political leaders Umayyad and Abbasid rulers were Arabs, while the Seljuks were Turks, and other leaders of Persian origin would also emerge. But Arabic was the medium of instruction for all and all of these rulers, without exception, sponsored knowledge extensively.

While the rulers were the most powerful and the warriors the most heroic, it was the scholars who were the most respected in the Muslim societies. Even at a later stage, when the large empires had disintegrated to smaller sultanates and emirates, the new Turk and Persian rulers maintained sponsoring the high-standard pursuit of knowledge that had been exemplified by the previous Arab rulers. To understand this phenomenal rise of knowledge among the early Muslims, it is necessary to understand the first three periods in further details.

The Prophetic Period and the First Command

The prophetic period is the first period that marks the growth and intellectual development of Muslims. Islam started off as a small peaceful monotheistic activist movement in Makkah in 610 CE under Prophet Muhammad (ṣ). The ruling Quraysh tribal leaders of Makkah cruelly suppressed this movement by killing and torturing the new Muslims. In fear for their lives the Muslims fled to the desert oases of Madinah in 622. Here, as well, they came under attack of the Quraysh army and their confederates but managed to fend them off with great bravery. The Muslims established an illuminated state in Madinah open to all who wanted to join them. Vast number of tribes became highly impressed by the social justice and knowledge quest of this state. By the time of the Prophet's death, in 632 CE, all of Arabia had given allegiance to Madinah.

Both the Persian and Byzantine empires held occupied 'Arab' lands under their imperial rule and tried to suppress, covertly in the initial stage, the nascent Muslim nation. Muslims took up arms against them and drove them away from the occupied lands and then progressed into Persia. Within a few decades Islam had spread to North Africa in the west and to Central Asia up to the borders of India and China in the east. The learning centres in Persia and Egypt came under their rule. While battles were fought against aggressive and imperial forces, the spread of the religion itself was by an exemplary way of life. It was a religious edict that no one be forced to accept the religion.

This spread of the Islamic civilisation was accompanied by the massive development of knowledge. The inspiration and initiation of the knowledge quest came from the Qur'an. At the very start of his prophethood, while in Makkah, the Prophet received the first revelation. He was in a cave high up on a mountain when the revelation was announced to him by the angel Gabriel. It consisted of five verses:

> Read in the name of your Lord and Cherisher,
> who created—Created man out of a clot that clings.
> Read! And your Lord is most bountiful,
> He who taught the use of the pen,
> Taught man what he knew not.

The very first word of the very first verse of the very first revelation—the first command—revealed to the Prophet was 'Read'. The second verse mentioned a 'clot that clings'— indicating the ovum, which, when fertilised, forms a clot that clings to the uterus. This verse mentions embryology, a scientific notion. The third verse asked to 'Read!' again emphasising the importance of reading and literacy. The fourth verse referred to the use of the pen, inspiring writing. And finally, the fifth verse referred to God, who 'taught man what he knew not', *i.e.*, knowledge. Thus, the very first command to the Muslims was to read, write and acquire knowledge.

Over the years, knowledge was stressed over and over again in the revelations to the Prophet. Its importance can be ascertained from the fact that it is mentioned more than 800 times in the Qur'an. A passion had been instilled, a new direction to illumination bestowed. The first revelation of the Qur'an was the defining moment at which the essence of the modern era was born.

The Prophet made the acquisition of knowledge mandatory for all men and women.[1] He took every opportunity to encourage education. During the battle of Badr, the Muslims captured many prisoners. In those days, throughout the world, prisoners of war were highly prized for the ransom they fetched. Their relatives would come and pay money for their release or they could be sold as slaves. But the Prophet gave the prisoners a different option. He said that anyone who teaches ten Muslims to read will be given freedom, no ransom required.[2]

The Prophet was 40 years old when the first revelation, mentioned above, came down to him. After preaching for 13 years in Makkah, he, along with the Muslims, migrated to Madinah to escape persecution. He established a state there and lived for 10 more years. For those 23 years in Makkah and Madinah, revelations came to him intermittently. Whenever a revelation came to him he recited it to his Companions, the famous *Ṣaḥābah (radi'allahu unhum)*, and some of them memorised the verses while others wrote them down.

The education of the Muslims started with the Prophet. He was the 'teacher' in both Makkah and Madinah. In Makkah the revelations were mainly related to eschatology, which explained concepts including matters of faith, heaven, hell and the Day of Judgement when good deeds will be rewarded and bad deeds will be punished. In Madinah, the revelations became more social and legal in focus. The Prophet interpreted and explained the

---

[1] Ḥadīth 224, Sunan Ibn Mājah.
[2] Siddiqi, Muhammad Zubayr, 1993, p. 26.

revelations to the Companions. All these revelations together comprise the Qur'an. The revelations of the Qur'an, written down and memorised by the Companions, were compiled together in about a year after the Prophet's death. Approximately within 15 years of that compilation, copies of the Qur'an were sent to all the Muslim domains.

Along with the Qur'an the second most important source of Islamic scripture is the *Sunnah, i.e.,* the sayings of the Prophet. These included his advice and instructions. The individual sayings of the Prophet are known as '*ḥadīth*'. There are numerous ḥadīths that interpret the Qur'an and clarify eschatology, while other ḥadīths deal with different topics such as prayers, knowledge, family laws, leadership, good manners, physical training, cleanliness, hygiene, good diet and many different aspects of life.

Education during the Prophetic Period

The Prophet's mosque was not just for praying, though that was a mandatory function, but was also a socio-political and educational centre. The Prophet taught *dīn* or 'religion' and subjects like manners, ethics, spirituality and *tajwid* (proper recitation of the Qur'an) in the mosque. There was a shaded extension of the mosque like a veranda on one side, which was the shelter or housing for the poor homeless Muslims who had come from various regions and who were known as *Ahl al-Suffah* (People of the Verandah).

But this space was also used for study and pursuit of knowledge. Some of the great scholars—such as Abu Hurayrah, Ubaydah ibn al-Samit and Abdullah ibn Sa'd ibn al-As—were dwellers of this place.[3] Abu Hurayrah became the greatest ḥadīth scholar in Islam, Ubaydah became a renowned teacher in

---

[3] Danner, Victor, 1985, p. 245.

Palestine during the time of Caliph Umar, and Abdullah became another famous teacher in Madinah.[4]

The main theme of study in Madinah was 'religion'. But from its very onset Muslim education also included 'practical' disciplines along with 'religious' ones, The Prophet allowed the study of poetry and numeracy, poetry being taught in the *suffah*[5] probably as part of linguistic development. He also asked some of his Companions to learn Hebrew and Syriac to be able to discuss and debate with Jews and Christians who came to visit him.[6]

As the literacy rate increased, towards the end of the Prophet's life, he had twenty-four scribes for the Qur'an, including Abu Bakr, Uthman, Ali and his personal secretary Zayd. Professional documentation also developed among the Muslims due to the Qur'an. For example, the Qur'an encouraged the writing down of contracts:

> *You who believe, when you take on a debt*
> *for a specific period, write it down*

—Qur'an, Al-Baqarah 2:282

One of the early written legal documents was the Madinah Charter or the Constitution of Madinah as agreed between the Prophet and the residents of Madinah including the Jews. Jurisprudence started to develop from the Qur'an and ḥadīth. Another discipline that developed early is *tafsīr*, *i.e.* the interpretation (exegesis) of the Qur'an.

The Prophet introduced two methods of teaching—the *halaqah* and the *rihlah*. The *halaqah*s were 'classrooms' where the teacher would sit against a wall or a pillar and the students would

---

[4] Hossain, M. Amjad, 2013, p. 11, see 'Note on Books' after appendices.

[5] Hossain, M. Amjad, 2013, p. 13.

[6] *Ibid.*, p. 23.

be seated on the floor in a semicircle around him. The teacher would sit in a higher place so that he could be seen by all the students. During the time of the Prophet there were at least nine mosques in Madinah which held such study circles. The Prophet had encouraged *halaqah*s in local mosques so that the central mosque would not become overcrowded.[7] The central mosque was the most advanced one and considered the 'university' of Madinah.[8]

The *rihlah* was long-distance education by travelling to places of learning. People would come to Madinah and study under the Prophet and go back and teach their family and their people. The Prophet also sent his trained Companions to distant areas to teach the local people. The *rihlah* would be adopted by scholars of later periods, as well, to do field surveys or acquire knowledge from distant lands, which led to the development of subjects like geography and botany.

By the time the Prophet died he had established a political state with its capital in Madinah. The knowledge base of the state came from two sources, the Qur'an and the Prophet's *Sunnah*, which along with its interpretation (*tafsīr*), principals (*uṣul*) and creed (*aqa'id*), formed the *integrated intellect*. From this integrated intellect would develop other epistemologies, starting with jurisprudence (*fiqh*) and followed by theological, rational and spiritual disciplines. This integrated intellect dealt with every aspect of life—political, military, social and individual—which emancipated society. At the root of this emancipation was a passion for knowledge. Muslims had developed an insatiable thirst for unbounded knowledge.

---

[7] Hamidullah, 1997, p. 202-206.
[8] Makdisi, George, 1981, p. 293.

Knowledge during the Rashidun Caliphate

The rule of the Rashidun Caliphs lasted from 632 to 661 CE. There were four Rashidun Caliphs—Abu Bakr, Umar ibn al-Khattab, Uthman ibn Affan and Ali ibn Abi Talib. Their ascension to the caliphate office was not on the basis of family inheritance or tribal affiliation. They were selected and elected to the caliphate office by the people in Madinah.

The Muslims defeated the Persian Empire during the early part of the Rashidun period. They also took over the Levant region—the land along the Eastern Mediterranean—which was under the occupation of Roman Byzantium. During the latter part of this period there was a civil war among the Muslims. Though the battles caused significant fatalities, the effect of these wars were limited only to the battlefields and the combatants. There was no destruction of townships or societal institutions. The Qur'an and the Prophet had redefined 'war', in which non-combatants, the general public, could not be harmed and their possessions could not be confiscated. Thus, even during such military or political upheavals, the rapid pursuit of knowledge continued unabated. Social development and military efforts were in completely separate arenas. One did not affect the other significantly, and society as a whole kept on progressing. The passion for knowledge remained intact.

The Rashidun Caliphs dynamically progressed the education system that the Prophet had initiated. The ulemaic disciplines—*tafsīr*, ḥadīth, *fiqh*—along with its derivatives and applied subjects, were being studied with intensity everywhere in the Muslim domain. In Madinah itself, the Companions of the Prophet formed a committee that supported the caliphs in jurisprudence and legal matters as well as in political and economic decision-making.

The reign of Abu Bakr was only for two years and initially he was busy protecting Madinah from the apostate tribes. After that he took the fight to the imperial forces of Persia and Byzantium as they had occupied Arab lands under their control and were also covertly planning mischief against Madinah. Had he not taken appropriate action Madinah would have been destroyed. But the greatest achievement of his reign was the first compilation of the Qur'an. After its compilation the complete manuscript was given to the caliph for safekeeping.

The second caliph, Umar, set up schools for both children and adults in the mosques throughout the extended Muslim domain. He maintained that students had to be taught poetry, history and social disciplines, which were needed for the successful development of society. Along with the curricula, teaching methodology was also improved. Short breaks were provided during class studies so that the students did not become tired (proposed by the Companion Abdullah ibn Abbas). They also introduced a review system with discussions and interviews to monitor students' progress (proposed by Caliph Ali).[9]

In time, some of the Companions, including men and women, spread out to different cities like Kufa, Basra, Damascus and Jerusalem and became eminent scholarly teachers. Umar supported the teaching profession by setting up a government salary for them. He also setup judges in courts of different towns who dispensed justice using the Qur'an, ḥadīth, *qiyas* (deductive analogy) and *ijtihad* (personal research) further progressing jurisprudence. It was also during this time that the famous medical academy of Jundi-Shapur in Persia was taken over by the Muslims. It continued to receive support from subsequent caliphs. Initially, the hospitals in the Muslim domain were modelled upon the Jundi-Shapur facility.[10]

---

[9] Hossain, M. Amjad, 2013, p. 14.
[10] *Ibid.*, p. 33.

During the reign of third caliph, Uthman, the Qur'an manuscript that was compiled during the time of Abu Bakr was reviewed, copied and sent to different regions of the Muslim domain. This was a major achievement, as it ensured the proper uncontaminated continuation of a unique Qur'an. The fourth caliph, Ali, initiated the study of Arabic grammar and sponsored Abu al-Aswad al-Duwali to carry out the work.[11] The caliph himself was also a remarkable poet.

Knowledge during the Umayyad Dynasty (661-750)

Following the death of the fourth Rashidun Caliph, Ali, the early Muslims were ruled by royal dynasties—the Umayyad, the Abbasid and the Seljuk. During the time of the Umayyads, as the empire grew rapidly, more and more scholars were needed to educate the population throughout the Muslim domain. Not only were more scholars needed but new types of scholars were also required. For example, the *abids* were trained professionals who would become administrators, accountants and clerks in the royal courts, courts of justice, the governor's offices and copyists for book publishers. Caliph Abd al-Malik ibn Marwan in 690 made it mandatory to use Arabic in administration throughout the provinces of the empire. Caliph Umar ibn Abd al-Aziz (in the early 8th century) encouraged the study of the *Sunnah* and *fiqh* (jurisprudence). It was his recommendation that led to the compilation of the *Muwatta* by Imam Malik, one of the first formally published collections of ḥadīth, and the compilation of the six major ḥadīth collections that was to follow.[12]

Education developed not simply due to the support of the caliphs but also due to the evolution and spread of a vast number of scholars and teachers into an independent networked system.

---

[11] Makdisi, George, 1990, p. 123.
[12] Hossain, M. Amjad, 2013, p. 40.

Some of these scholars had distanced themselves from the political office when the caliphal rule became dynastic-hereditary under the Umayyads. They were against the change from the selective-elective governing system practised under the Rashidun rule and as a whole they considered political office to be debasing to scholars. The whole of Islamic jurisprudence by the four great imams developed in such a politically independent manner. But the political wariness was not universal and other scholars did grace the caliphs' courts and the caliphs did continue to support scholars.

Primary literacy classes for children and secondary education for adults had been started within the mosques from the time of the Prophet and later supported by Umar. By the time of the Rashiduns, these classes had become external extensions to the mosques. Imam Malik (710-795) was probably the first to move the classes to separate rooms attached to the mosque in Madinah. By the Umayyad time these classes separated from the mosques, becoming independent schools.[13] The classes were called *kuttab* or *maktab* interchangeably. These may have been different types of schools initially. The *kuttab*s were the revolutionary new education system spreading out of Madinah, while *maktab*s were the Arabised successor of some Byzantine manner of schools. Both coalesced to form one elementary school system but with a wider range of subjects being taught—Qur'an, ḥadīth, *adab* disciplines (basic reading and writing, manners, etiquette, *etc.*), poetry, grammar, language and some 'sciences'. The teachers came to be known as *mu'allim*s.[14] Mathematics was taught along with both the ulemaic and *adab* disciplines in the *kuttab*.[15]

Grammar and language holds a special place among the

---

[13] Hossain, M. Amjad, 2013, p. 32.

[14] *Ibid.*, p. 48-50.

[15] Makdisi, 1990, p. 49.

disciplines studied at this early stage. The impetus came from the exegesis (*tafsīr*) of the Qur'an. The scholars needed to understand the revelations. They studied each and every word in multifarious ways delving into detailed linguistics. The development of lexicography and philology were soon to follow.[16] The Muslims were the first to truly write huge lexicons. The *adab* studies evolved to include grammar, lexicography, poetry, prose, history, genealogy and similar subjects.[17] The professionals graduating in *adab* studies were the *adib*s. At the same time there was also a demand for private tutors known as *mu'addib*s. They taught mainly the children of the rich, aristocrats and royalty.[18]

As the Umayyad reign progressed, all the Companions of the Prophet died with age. They had known the context of the revelations of the Qur'an and the purpose of the Prophet's ḥadīths because they were eyewitnesses to all the events and teachings. With their death it was deemed important that the interpretation and context of revelation be recorded and the Prophet's ḥadīths be formally compiled using a methodology that would ensure its authenticity. As a result, books on the interpretation of the Qur'an, *tafsīr*s, were written. Soon the compilation of ḥadīths also started. The text of a ḥadīth (saying of the Prophet) known as the *matan*, along with the authoritative sources of the ḥadīth, a reference system known as *isnad*, were recorded.[19]

An elementary scientific academic pedagogy also developed and progressed during the Umayyad period. The Prophet had encouraged good health and personal hygiene and had tried natural medication in case of sickness. This was later collected in the form of a book titled *Tibb al-Nabawi* (*Medicine of the*

---

[16] Hossain, M. Amjad, 2013, p. 55.
[17] Makdisi, 1990, p. 52.
[18] Hossain, M. Amjad, 2013, p. 51.
[19] *Ibid.*, p. 57-58.

Prophet). This inspired the Muslims to study medicine. Al-Harith ibn Kaladah (d. 634), a Companion, had studied medicine in Jundi-Shapur, Persia. The Prophet used to refer people with medical problems to him.[20] Mu'awiyah, a Companion of the Prophet and founder of the Umayyad Dynasty, invited the Christian Arab doctor Ibn Athal to translate a medical book into Arabic.[21] The Umayyad Prince Khalid ibn Yazid sponsored the translation of medicine and alchemy text to Arabic. Alchemy soon developed into chemistry.

Initially, when people had started to accept Islam, the existing physicians were mainly Christians, Jews or Zoroastrians. Masarjawayh, a Jewish physician, translated the *Pandectae Medicinae* of Ahron from Greek to Arabic. After Arabic became the established language, a large number of Muslims embraced the medical profession and soon became the vast majority among the practitioners of medicine. Medical institutions were developed modelled upon the facilities in Jundi-Shapur in Persia and Alexandria in Egypt.[22] Thus, the first scientific discipline that Muslims investigated was medicine followed by chemistry.

The five-times prayer had become mandatory since the time of the Prophet. People were encouraged to attend the prayers in the mosques on time. This led to the understanding of time division. Women were given some leeway so that they could pray at home. This enabled them to carry out chores like looking after the children. But apart from this leeway, they were also encouraged to attain knowledge and scholarship and they responded with a passion for becoming experts in the fields of ḥadīth and jurisprudence. Female education and scholarship was one of the prominent features of Islam.

---

[20] *Ibid.*, p. 58-59.
[21] Hossain, M. Amjad, 2013, p. 40.
[22] *Ibid.*, p. 58-59.

CHAPTER 2

Knowledge during the Abbasid Dynasty
(750-1258)

The Abbasid period is *a milestone* in the development of knowledge and *the milestone* in the development of science in the world. Early during this stage, the pursuit of knowledge bloomed in an explosive manner. The increase in the number of scholars along with the specialisations and diversification of disciplines continued, and by the time of the early Abbasids the tertiary institutions were producing highly specialised scholars of many different types. These included a range of great scholars and extraordinary works in *tafsīr*, law, ḥadīth, pure sciences, social sciences, *tasawwuf* (Sufism), *kalam* (theology) and philosophy. The passion for knowledge reigned supreme. It gave birth to the scientific spirit and was the golden age of knowledge of the world.

The foundation of knowledge was earlier laid down by the ulema. Extensive scholarly skills of reading, writing, researching and investigation had been developed by the ulema working on *tafsīr* of the Qur'an, compiling the ḥadīth of the Prophet, and legislating jurisprudence. These skills were next applied to the study of all other disciplines. Thus, at the root of this progress were the ulemaic disciplines, which are discussed below first.

The Ulemaic Disciplines

The Qur'an

As the verses of the Qur'an were revealed, the Prophet would recite it to his Companions, many of whom would memorise it or write it down on various objects like papyri (writing material made out of papyrus leaf), parchment (made of dried animal skin) and bones. The usage of papyri is known to have been common in Arabia. Some have been found from as early as 642 CE. Adolf Grohmann estimated that there are about 16,000 Arabic papyri in various collections in Europe.[23]

The written and memorised verses would be recited back to the Prophet for verification. The memorisation of the Qur'an led to the establishment of the school of the *huffaz*. Each member of the *huffaz*, known as a *hafiz*, would memorise the entire Qur'an. This school started from the time of the Prophet and continues to the present. There are tens of thousands of *huffaz* at present who can reproduce the Qur'an verbatim from memory.

Zayd ibn Thabit was the principal secretary to the Prophet. He, along with others, used to record the verses. This is mentioned in the Qur'an itself.

> *It is in Books (sheets) held greatly in honour,*
> *Exalted in dignity, kept pure and holy,*
> *Written by the hands of scribes*
> *Honourable and pious and just.*

> —Qur'an, 'Abasa 80:13

During the caliphate of Abu Bakr, Zayd ibn Thabit, working with members of the *huffaz* and other Companions, engaged in a corroborative work of compilation to produce the *mushaf*—the

---

[23] Grohmann, A., 1952, p. 2.

first official manuscript of the Qur'an. In about 15 more years, during the caliphate of Uthman, this *mushaf* was reviewed again by a board under Zayd, copies were made and sent to all the Muslim domains.

Since the very initial days, the Qur'an has always warranted absolute sanctity and has presented a complete code of life. In *Lectures on the Reconstruction of Religious Thought in Islam*, Dr. Muhammad Iqbal states, "The main purpose of the Qur'an is to awaken in man the higher consciousness of his manifold relations with Allah and the universe". The text further states, 'It is in view of this essential aspect of the Qur'anic teaching that (Johann Wolfgang von) Goethe, while making a general review of Islam as an educational force, said to (Johann Peter) Eckermann: "You see this teaching never fails; with all our systems, we cannot go, and generally speaking no man can go, farther than that".[24]

Tafsīr: Interpretation of the Qur'an

The first discipline, in addition to the *huffaz* school of the Qur'an memorisation, that rose out of the study of the Qur'an was the school of interpretation and commentary (exegesis) of the Qur'an, known as *tafsīr*. The discipline of *tafsīr* was initiated by the Prophet himself. He explained the verses of the Qur'an to the Companions.

> *And We have sent down unto you the Message,*
> *That you (O Prophet) may explain*
> *clearly to men what is sent for them,*
> *And that they may give thought.*

—Qur'an, Al-Naḥl 16:44.

---

[24] Iqbal, M., 1974, p. 9.

A few famous schools of *tafsīr* developed following the death of the Prophet. The main ones with the largest student followings developed in:

1. Makkah under the authority of the Prophet's Companion Abdullah ibn Abbas,

2. Kufa (in current day Iraq) under the authority of the Prophet's Companion Abdullah ibn Mas'ud,

3. Madinah under the authority of the Prophet's Companion Ubayy ibn Ka'b.

The *mufassirs*, scholars of *tafsīr*, explained, clarified, expounded and commented upon every verse of the Qur'an. Many *tafsīrs* were written, the oldest known attributed to Ibn Abbas (d. 687). Other books of *tafsīr* include the works of Zayd ibn Ali (d. 740) and Mujahid (d. 722).[25] By the Abbasid period, *tafsīr* had been tenaciously developed and refined and became a highly respected discipline. The oldest complete *tafsīr* which is still extant is by Abu Ja'far Muhammad ibn Jarir al-Tabari (d. 923).

Al-Tabari, from Tabaristan, Persia, was an exceptional scholar who wrote voluminously. His two most important works are the *Jami al-Bayan fi Ta'wil al-Qur'an* (*Tafsīr al-Tabari*) and *Tarikh al-Rusul wa al-Muluk* (*History of the Prophets and Kings*). The full English translation of his *tafsīr* consists of 30 volumes, with each consisting of a few hundred pages. The older *tafsīrs* are no longer extant but have been mentioned in different texts. His *Tarikh* is an even larger piece of work and consists of history from the beginning of the world to the 10th century CE, *i.e.*, up to the period he lived in.

The next major classical *tafsīr* is by al-Qurtubi (1273), a great

---

[25] Hossain, M. Amjad, 2013, p. 57.

scholar from Muslim Spain (al-Andalus). His *tafsīr* has a legal basis, *i.e.* his commentaries could be used to derive legal rulings. In later years, commentators formulated books on 'applied *tafsīr*', which included various types of rules that enabled Arabs and non-Arabs to interpret the Qur'an. One such book is *al-Kashshaf* by Abu al-Qasim Mahmud al-Zamakhshari (d. 1144). In his *tafsīr* he also quoted from Arabic poetry and dwelled on the rhetorical beauty of the Qur'an. He was a Mu'tazili, *i.e.*, a rationalist scholar.

Fakhr al-Din al-Razi (d. 1209), a renowned Ash'ari theologian, named his commentary *al-Tafsīr al-Kabir*. He held an ideological position between the rationalist scholars and the traditional ulema. His commentary was an Ash'ari response to the rationalist al-Zamakhshari's *tafsīr*.[26] Abdullah ibn Umar al-Baydawi (d. 1282) made improvements on the al-Zamakkshari commentary and named it *Anwar al-Tanzil wa Asrar al-Ta'wil*. He removed or reinterpreted some of the controversial interpretations that was in it. Some Sunnis consider this improved *tafsīr* to be one of the best commentaries.[27]

Among the popular commentaries to date is the ten-volume abridged *tafsīr* of Ibn Kathir (d. 1343). His method was to explain the verses of the Qur'an by correlating with other verses of the Qur'an or by using explanations given in the ḥadīth. Many other *tafsīr*s, each significantly massive work, were written by different scholars and some are still being written.

There have developed two major types of *tafsīr*. The first type is by the traditionalists or the orthodox ulema. They have used the interpretations of the verses of the Qur'an by the very initial scholars as one of the main criteria. First, they would explain the verses of the Qur'an by correlating with other verses of the Qur'an with similar meaning. Second, they used ḥadīth in explaining

---

[26] Hasan, M. 2004, p. 609.
[27] *Ibid.*, p. 610.

Qur'anic verses. Finally, they would look into the previous interpretations by the scholars among the first three generations of Muslims—the Companions, the *Tabi'un* and the *Tabi' al-Tabi'in* —for interpreting the Qur'anic verses. They further included interpretations using the biblical and Judeo-Christian traditions. Al-Tabari and Ibn Kathir fall in this group.

The second type of *tafsīr* is by the ulema who used rationalism in their interpretations. This group while using the transmitted interpretations of previous scholars also included opinion or reason while interpreting the Qur'an. They had developed a detailed 'reason-based' method that used various tools like linguistics for interpretation. This group did not use Judeo-Christian traditions. Fakhr al-Din al-Razi and al-Zamakhshari fall in this group.

Law and Jurisprudence

Lawmakers or jurists were another group of scholars who excelled at about the same time as classical *tafsīr* writers. The Umayyad and the following Abbasid empires had grown very extensive and at one stage became the most powerful empires in the world. Wide-ranging laws were needed to run such empires.

In the 8th century CE, around a hundred years after the Prophet, initially a large number of legal schools developed. But four of these schools attained great prominence. These were the schools founded by Imam Abu Hanifah, Imam Malik, Imam Shāfi'ī and Imam Hanbal. They developed massive legal systems. They are called imams with due respect, though, in today's vocabulary these imams can also be considered professors of law and founders of legal guilds.[28] They were not just brilliant scholars, they possessed indomitable integrity. They would not

---

[28] Hossain, M. Amjad, 2013, p. 40-41.

allow any political authority, including that of the caliph, to influence their law-making. For that reason they faced political duress and imprisonment. These four imams are the greatest individual lawgivers that the world has ever seen.

Noel Coulson in *History of Islamic Law* states, "Islamic jurisprudence had in fact been essentially idealistic from the outset. Law had not formed out of the practice of the courts or the remedies therein available as the Roman law had developed from the *actio* or the English common law from the writ, but had originated as the academic formulation of a scheme, alternative to that practice; its authority did not lie in the fact that it was observed but in the theoretical arguments of the scholars as to why it ought to be observed".[29]

In fact, the imams used the Qur'an and the Prophet's ḥadīth as the basis of legal formulation and being experts on the verdicts issued by the Rashidun Caliphs have used those as legal precedence as well. Calling these men great and brilliant scholars would be an understatement. Each one of them formulated legal systems by which empires would be run; they were legal architects of empires.

Imam Abu Hanifah and his students wrote a large number of books. Some of his books are as follows:

- *Kitab al-Athar* (a compilation made after the study of 70,000 ḥadīths).

- *Alim wa al-Muta'allim.*

- *Al-Fiqh al-Akbar.*

- *Jami al-Masanid.*

- *Kitab al-Radd ala al-Qadariyyah.*

---

[29] Coulson, N. J., 1964, p. 82.

The students of Imam Abu Hanifah also became famous imams. Abu Yusuf and Muhammad ibn al-Hasan al-Shaybani were the foremost among them. Apart from *fiqh* and ḥadīth, Abu Yusuf also wrote a book named *al-Kharaj*, which contained topics on economics such as classification of land depending on productivity, tax and tribute. Muhammad's famous work is the *Mabsut*, which he co-authored with Abu Yusuf. His other books include *Al-Siyar al-Saghir*, *Al-Siyar al-Kabir*, *Al-Jami al-Saghir*, *Al-Jami al-Kabir*, *Al-Hujaj* and *Al-Ziyadat*.

The best-known works of Imam al-Shāfiʻī are:

- *Al-Risalah* (jurisprudence coming down from the Companion).

- *Usul al-fiqh* (the study of the origin, sources and principles on which Islamic jurisprudence is based).

Imam Malik's books are:

- Al-Muwatta

- Al-Mudawwanah al-Kubra.

There existed other hadith compilations by different scholars before the *Muwatta* which were used by individual schools and scholars but were not well-known or authorative.

Imam Hanbal's famous work is the *Musnad*, which is a collection of more than thirty thousand ḥadīths.

Ḥadīth

The study of ḥadīth underpinned three different disciplines having three different functions:

- Religious scripture.

- A co-required subject in jurisprudence (*fiqh*) and exegesis (*tafsīr*).

- A Civics and Ethics discipline.

While the importance of jurisprudence and exegesis is easily grasped the part that ḥadīth played needs some elaboration.

The study of ḥadīth did not mean only memorising the sayings of the Prophet. It was a very important part of the overall education system. Essentially, ḥadīth was and remains the second most important scripture in Islam. Secondly, it gives context, meaning and details to many of the injunctions in the Qur'an. It was a co-requirement in the study of jurisprudence and law making and exegesis or *tafsīr* of the Qur'an. It would be difficult to understand the principles of jurisprudence and *tafsīr* without understanding the application of ḥadīth in it. Thirdly, it also was the 'civics' and 'ethics' subject for the Muslims as it provided, and still provides, information on civic and ethical nature for all in the society. It provides guidance on aspects like rights, roles, duties, responsibilities, hygiene, manners, etiquette, *etc.* Its study also included its social implementation (*amal*).

To prevent any faulty proliferation of ḥadīths, the caliphs Abu Bakr and Umar had set up very strict rules against mentioning a ḥadīth without evidence or witnesses. Hadīth was taught in both oral and written forms. A number of the Companions—including Abdullah ibn Amr, Ali ibn Abi Talib, Jabir ibn Abdullah, Abu Rafi, Ibn Abbas, Itban ibn Malik al-Ansari, Samurah ibn Jundub and Abu Hurayrah—wrote down the sayings of the Prophet. These collections were known as the *Sahifat*.[30]

There was a temporary injunction by the Prophet that forbade the writing of anything besides the Qur'an. This makes many scholars think that was why the writing of ḥadīths may have been stopped during the time of the Prophet. But the injunction was temporary, probably so that at the early stage the written

---

[30] Hossain, M. Amjad, 2013, p.22.

scrolls of the Qur'an would not get mixed up with other writings. It is important to recall that at the time of the Prophet the written Qur'an was in loose sheets of papyri rather than in book form. So, writing ḥadīth or other texts on similar sheets would have made it easy to mix up written Qur'an with written ḥadīth especially by those who were not so literate.

It is not known exactly when the prohibition was lifted but it may have lasted up to the time when the Prophet instructed that written messages be sent to rulers of Persia, Byzantium and Coptic Egypt or, at most, up to the opening of Makkah when, according to another ḥadīth, the Prophet asked his address be written down. This would have abrogated the 'not writing' instruction.[31] It is obvious, as the Qur'an encourages writing, that this 'not writing' had to be temporary for specific reasons.

Hence, there existed written ḥadīth on different materials like papyrus, bones and stone tablets[32] from the time of the Companions.[33] Students also memorised ḥadīth and when they became teachers they would pass it on to their students. Soon, the Qur'an had been compiled and distributed and Muslims, in general, became literate. Hadīth could then be documented without the fear of it being mixed up with the Qur'an.

The history of ḥadīth-learning starts with the Prophet. He had asked those Companions, whom he sent to different regions away from Madinah on official duty, to rely on the Qur'an and the ḥadīth (*Sunnah*) in the running of public affairs. Thus, ḥadīth was used extensively from the very beginning. After the Prophet's death it was a common subject of study among scholars and in their schools. They had their own collections which they preserved with commitment and dedication. Over generations,

---

[31] Hossain, M. Amjad, 2013, p. 22-23.
[32] Web Reference: WR10.
[33] Hossain, M. Amjad, 2013, p. 57.

scholars taught ḥadīth in a formalised manner to their students, who would then become ḥadīth scholars themselves and then teach the next generation.

It was the Umayyad Caliph Umar ibn Abd al-Aziz (682-720) who first asked the scholars to start formally compiling all ḥadīths. The first person to formally compile ḥadīths was Ibn Jurayj[34] which was followed by Imam Malik's *Muwatta*. This led to extensive works on ḥadīth collection and compilation from all the ḥadīth centres and scholars and the final production of massive compendiums.

It was during the early Abbasid period that a significant number of books on ḥadīths were written. Six of these compilations were recognised as the 'authentic' ḥadīth books for their comprehensiveness and the very detailed methods used in authentication of the compiled ḥadīths. The distinguished writers of the six *ṣaḥīḥ* (authentic) compendiums are al-Bukhari (b. 810), Muslim (b. 817), Abu Dawud (b. 817), al-Tirmidhi (b. 824), Ibn Mājah (b. 824) and al-Nasa'i (b. 830). These scholars spent their entire lives collecting and corroborating ḥadīths from different schools and different scholars.

To ensure that no mistakes crept into the ḥadīth books or no fabrication were accepted as authentic, the ḥadīth schools formulated a very stringent and detailed methodology to test its authenticity. They divided the ḥadīth into two parts: a reference system or chain of narrators of the ḥadīth known as the *isnad* and the ḥadīth text itself known as *matn*. The following is an example of a ḥadīth from al-Bukhari:

Isnad: Al-Bukhari narrated on the authority of al-Humaydi Abdullah ibn al-Zubayr on the authority of Sufyan on the authority of Yahya ibn Sa'id al-Ansari on the authority of

---

[34] Hossain, M. Amjad, 2013, p.58.

Muhammad ibn Ibrahim al-Taymi on the authority of
Alqamah ibn Waqqas al-Laythi, who said I heard Umar ibn
al-Khattab saying from the pulpit:

Matn: 'I heard Allah's Messenger (ṣ) say: The reward of
deeds depends on the intentions, and every person will get
a reward according to what he has intended. So, if someone
emigrates for worldly benefits or for a woman to marry, his
emigration will be for what he migrated.'

The *isnad* comprises the ḥadīth's chain of narrators.
According to the *isnad* of the above ḥadīth, al-Bukhari collected
this ḥadīth from the scholar al-Humaydi, who learned it from his
teacher Sufyan, who learned it from his teacher Yahya and so on
till the chain ends with a Companion, in this case Umar, who
heard it personally from the Prophet. This was not the end of
isnad methodology. The biography of each and every one of the
narrators of each ḥadīth were examined. If the integrity of all the
narrators was perfect, only then the ḥadīth would be declared
authentic depending on further corroboration of the text, the
matn, itself with the Qur'an. If even one of the narrators was
unknown or deemed not of perfect character, the ḥadīth would
not be characterised *ṣaḥīḥ* or 'authentic'. All such biographies of
the narrators were documented. There are books with the
biographies of tens of thousands of these narrators. The *isnad*
itself became a major discipline of study.

The particular ḥadīth mentioned in the example above is
about intentions. It states that actions are judged and rewarded by
its intentions. There is an interesting story behind the mention of
'marriage' in this ḥadīth. The Muslims were undergoing
persecution in Makkah, so they migrated to Madinah—the *Hijrah*.
There was a man who proposed marriage to a woman called
Umm Qays. She refused to marry him until he made the Hijrah.
So he made Hijrah and married her. His intent to migrate was the

woman, not to establish a progressive and just political state in Madinah as was the intentions of all the Muslims who had migrated. So, that is why this mention of marriage in the ḥadīth.

It was very important to the scholars that the *isnad* and *matn* be authentic. Thus, from the very start, the ḥadīth scholars had employed the *rihlah* or 'travelling from one scholar to another even in distant regions' to correct, corroborate and collect ḥadīths. An example of those who travelled for such knowledge is Urwah ibn al-Zubayr, the nephew of Aisha, the Prophet's wife. He was the teacher of al-Zuhri, who was employed by Caliph Umar ibn Abd al-Aziz to compile ḥadīths. Al-Zuhri is another person who travelled for forty-five years on this same quest. Muhammad ibn Ishaq, a student of al-Zuhri absorbed the works of the ḥadīth scholars and based on them wrote a historical book on the genesis of creation, the life of the Prophet and the military exploits of the earliest Muslims.[35]

The above-mentioned methodology is just an ideal and simple example. The methodology used by the ḥadīth collectors was multifaceted, detailed and thorough. Many different ways of checking the ḥadīths were established and many categories of ḥadīth were made—not just authentic and non-authentic. Such stringent methods had not been employed in the collection of any of the scriptures of any other religion or any philosophy of any ancient civilisation.

Shi'ah ḥadīth, in addition to the Prophet's sayings, adds what the Shi'ah imams did or said.[36] They do not accept many Sunni ḥadīths, especially those narrated by caliphs Abu Bakr and Umar. Their ḥadīth collectors are Muhammad ibn Ya'qub al-Kulayni (d. 939 CE), Muhammad al-Hummi (d. 991), Tahir al-Sharif al-Murtada (d. 1044 CE) and Muhammad Tusi (d. 1067).

---

[35] Hossain, M. Amjad, 2013, p.73.
[36] Hasan, M., 2004, p. 613.

Female Scholars

The women of Islam have from the outset been no less passionate about knowledge than the men. They have been scholars, teachers and builders of great academic institutions. Aisha bint Abi Bakr, the Prophet's wife, became one of the greatest ḥadīth scholars ever among the Muslims and is known to have taught a significant number of students that included the Ṣaḥābah (Companions of the Prophet). There is no book of ḥadīth, *fiqh* or *tafsīr* which does not directly mention her name. Her contribution to ḥadīth became fundamental in the development of jurisprudence that was to rule nations and empires for a thousand years. A quarter of that jurisprudence comes from Aisha[37] including most of the family laws. The Prophet himself had been her teacher and she had been a very inquisitive student.

The Prophet had arranged education for women. When the women of Madinah asked the Prophet if he could set a day every week to educate them, he agreed. He also sent other Companions to teach the women.[38] He assigned al-Shifa bint Abdullah to teach reading and writing to his wife Hafsah.

Women could take part in law-making in Madinah. When Caliph Umar tried to fix the upper limit of the dower that women receive during their marriage to four hundred *dirhams*, a woman among them objected and provided evidence from the Qur'an that there should be no upper limit. Umar acknowledged her decision and said she was right and he was wrong[39] and her point was accepted as the law.

The setting of such examples inspired the women in Islam to become very advanced academically and they became the most educated women in the world. Education and knowledge became

---

[37] WR 23.
[38] Khan, Mohammad Muhsin, 1984.
[39] al-Mubarakpuri, Shaykh Saifur Rahman, 2003, p. 411.

a right of women as of men. There are many women who have been mentioned in Muslim annals in relation to their scholarly aptitude, especially in ḥadīth and the development of jurisprudence. Dr. Mohammad Akram Nadwi's *Al-Muhaddithat: The Women Scholars In Islam* is a prefatory to his 40-volume biographical dictionary of thousands of female Muslim scholars.[40]

In the early Islamic period, female scholars had high public standing and authority. They travelled intensively for knowledge. At that period of time the Muslim domain appears to have been safe for women to undertake such travels. They routinely attended the most prestigious mosques and *madrasahs* across the Islamic world. There is detailed documentary evidence of women scholars who were teachers of revered ulema. They used to give the *ijazah*, that is, they certified the students who had become masters or scholars themselves and were ready to transmit or teach ḥadīth.[41] It was a graduation ceremony for the students.

Women scholars have also been the tutors of famous male Muslim scholars and contributed to the development of great men. Sayyidah Nafisah, a great grand-daughter of the Prophet, was one of the early teachers of Imam al-Shāfi'ī. One of Imam Malik's tutors was a woman named Aisha bint Sa'd ibn Abi Waqqas. The father of the famous Imam al-Bukhari died when he was a child. It was his mother and sister who supported and financed his studies. Muhammad ibn Qasim, the famous Umayyad General, was educated by his mother. She and tutors she hired supervised his education.

Muslim females were also scholars of literature. There have been female poets in the Muslim world over all the ages, like al-Khansa' (d. 646 CE), Safiyyah al-Baghdadiyyah (12th century CE), and Umm al-Sa'd bint Isam al-Himyari (d. 1243 CE). Rabi'ah al-

---

[40] Nadwi, M. A., 1913.
[41] *Ibid.*, 2013, p. 171.

Basri (714-801 CE) became one of the most renowned Sufi scholars and poet in the 8th century CE. There are many such names spread over the ages, some of them legendary.

Muslim women were not just scholars and teachers, they also established academic institutions. Al-Qarawiyyin, one of the first natural science universities in history, was established by a rich lady of Fez named Fatimah al-Fihri in the mid-9th century. According to UNESCO[42] and *The Guinness Book of World Records*,[43] it is the oldest existing,[44] continually operating and the first degree-awarding educational institution in the world. The Sankore University of Timbuktu, which consisted of a number of big institutes, was funded by a wealthy Mandika lady in the late 10th century.[45] In the 13th century, a combined hospital-medical-school-*madrasah* was built in Keysari in Anatolia. The hospital was built by Gevher Nesibe, sister of Seljuk Sultan Ghiyath al-Din ibn Qilij Arsalan, while the adjacent madrasah was built by the sultan.[46] These are just examples; the contributions of Muslim women are manifold.

Schools of Islamic Theology (*Kalam*)

Theology can be considered the philosophy of religion. It is a study of the nature of God and a systematic analysis of religious beliefs and the development of religious theories. Islamic theology, also sometimes known as 'Islamic scholastic theology', is called *ilm al-kalam* in Arabic.

The main body of the religion of Islam and its articles of faith were established within the lifespan of the Prophet through divine

---

[42] WR14.

[43] WR15.

[44] Verger, Jacques, 2003, p. 35.

[45] Al Hossaini, 2007, p. 56.

[46] Hossain, M. Amjad, 2013, p. 122.

revelations and the Prophet's interpretation of the revelations and his teachings. After the Prophet, the *tafsīr* experts or exegetes (*mufassir*s) preserved the Prophet's interpretation of the Qur'an. Thus, theology did not play any part in establishing the basic tenets of Islam. It played a role, later, needed for political justification in sect-formation, debate or defence of finer religious viewpoints.

Early in Muslim history there appeared different types of political movements. These movements needed to defend their credence theologically. That gave the initial impetus for the development of theological schools. In the 7th century, there was a *fitnah* or 'civil war' among the Muslims, which became a conflict between the supporters of Caliph Ali and Mu'awiyah, leader of the Umayyads.

During this conflict, another group formed which did not support either of the warring groups. They were a relatively small anti-establishment faction and came to be known as the Khawarij (secessionists). They were critical of both the sides in the *fitnah* and were basically fundamental and strict in their beliefs. They declared that anyone committing a major sin went out of the fold of Islam and was no longer a Muslim. Countering them theologically were the Murji'ah, who believed that faith was sufficient to consider a person to be a Muslim and only God has the authority to judge who is a true Muslim and who is not so.[47] They considered acts of piety and good works of prime importance but faith to be indispensable. This was one of the earliest theological debates.

The 7th century civil war fought between the Alids and Mu'awiyah's Umayyads led to far-reaching consequences. After the death of Ali, the Umayyads established dynastic rule and took over the title of the caliph. The Alids were permanently expunged

---

[47] Izutsu, Toshihiko, 2001, p. 55-56.

from political power. But they did not accept the Umayyad
Caliphate and countered that leadership has to remain within the
family of the Prophet. Ali's offspring by Fatimah, the daughter of
the Prophet, were the foremost representatives of the house of the
Prophet. Over historical time, the Alids' struggle turned from a
political movement to a legal entity with its own jurisprudence
(*fiqh*) and theology and finally into a religious sect known as the
Shi'ah. Such sects would also engage into theological discourses in
favour of their beliefs.

Besides politics, as time went by, finer religious issues and
queries cropped up that required debates, discussions and
clarifications. Such actions also produced theological groups. One
of the early queries was about the apparent incongruity between
concepts of predestination and free will. Some people believed
that everything that happened in this world was predestined while
other believed that individual had free will and thus their acts
were their choice. If the action of people were predestined by God
then why would they suffer punishment? There developed a
bipolar spectrum among the believers with predestination and
free will at opposite ends. People took a variety of positions within
the spectrum, some being nearer to one or the other of these two
views. Schools of thought thus developed based on this particular
issue.

The Mujbirah (*Jabriyyah*) school were absolute determinists
or believers in predestination, that everything a person does has
been decided upon by God, not by the individual. To them free
will was an illusion, while the Qadari school postulated that action
was contingent on free will and thus people had true choice and
could be rewarded for good deeds and punished for bad deeds.
This debate raged during the Umayyad period and moved away
from its original scholarly stance, taking on a political hue. A large
section of people was still critical of the Umayyad 'usurpation' of
power and their harsh treatment of the Alids. The Mujbirah,

apparently, had the political support of some Umayyad rulers because if everything was predestined by God, then any mistake or wrong-doing the rulers had committed was not their fault and thus they could escape penance. The Qadaris opposed this hypothesis on the basis that humans possessed free will and were thus responsible for their actions.

The rational Mu'tazili school belonged to the free will end of the spectrum. They believed that due to 'free will' people were the 'creators' of their deeds and thus deserved rewards and punishments. The Mujbirah considered this 'creation of deeds' that was at the core of the Mu'tazili view to be a plurality of creation, giving it a polytheistic affinity. To them God was the sole 'Creator' at all levels.

Such theological discourses led to the formation of groups with different sets of beliefs or creed (*aqidah*). Over historical time a number of theological schools developed. The orthodox scholars did not want such theological debates to spread to the layman as that would cause confusion. Imam al-Shāfiʿī[48] and Imam al-Ghazali[49] maintained that theology was not to be practised by all and sundry but by specialist scholars only. They believed that the general individual trying to grapple with theology would end up confused.

One very interesting aspect of the Sunni Muslim state is that though the state religion remains Islam, the political governance is secular, not theocratic. Islam itself is secular in political and judicial matters. That is, people of different religions can stay in such a state and practise their own religion and be equal in the eyes of the law.

---

[48] Macdonald, Duncan Black, 2008. p. 187.
[49] Bennett, Clinton, 2012, p. 119.

Major Kalam Schools

The Mu'tazili School

The Mu'tazili school emerged around the 8th century during the Umayyad dynastic rule. It flourished during the early Abbasid period and gradually declined after the 10th century. They maintained that the injunctions of God are accessible to rational thought and inquiry. Thus, 'reason' is an effective approach to determine what is just and obligatory in religion.[50]

The first known Mu'tazili was Wasil ibn Ata, a student of the famous Tabi scholar Hasan al-Basri (Tabi means belonging to the generation after the Companions of the Prophet). Wasil got involved in a debate about the status of a Muslim who has committed a grave sin. He claimed that such a person was a *fasiq*, someone between a believer and non-believer.

The initial Mu'tazilis espoused a variety of rational views including those held by the free-will Qadari school. As time went by they started to consolidate and develop a more cohesive set of principles. When they came in touch with Aristotelian Greek philosophy, it appealed to their rational sense and they incorporated it among their rational views. This rational Islamic school later studied logic, early Islamic philosophy, ancient Greek philosophy and Neo-Platonic philosophy. But they were critical of the metaphysics of those systems. For instance, Mu'tazilis adopted unanimously the doctrine of *ex nihilo* (out of nothing) creation of the universe, contrary to the Greek and some Muslim philosophers who had supported the eternity of the world in one form or another. Their main conflict with the orthodox ulema was in believing in the 'createdness of the Qur'an', which meant that the Qur'an was not eternal.

---

[50] Arabi, Oussama, 2001, p. 27-28.

The theology of the Muʿtazili was centred on the concepts of divine justice and divine unity.[51] They disagreed with any degree of anthropomorphism and unqualified predestination. They considered belief in only *mutawatir* ḥadīths (*i.e.* ḥadīths that had come down via multiple chains of narrators) as central to the Islamic faith. But for formulating laws or jurisprudence (*fiqh*) the Muʿtazilis accepted non-*mutawatir* ḥadīths, *i.e.,* those ḥadīths which are known from only one chain of narrators. They also attempted to resolve complex theological and philosophical concepts like causality and theodicy.

Causality is a philosophical concept that defines the relationship between events and causes. In general, it states that causes produce events. For example, cotton placed in fire will burn. So, placing cotton in contact with fire is the 'cause' that triggers the 'event' of burning. Muʿtazilis believed that to be morally coherent, divine reward and punishment was based on predictable and real causal laws. They, probably the later Muʿtazilis, agreed with the Ashʿari view that the world is comprised of the smallest possible atomic particles. According to them, atoms and their motions are related causally and these particles persist through time, having a continuous existence. They differentiated between God's and human's actions by considering that God's acts were direct, while human acts were generated.

Theodicy, another contentious issue that they attempted to resolve, is a theological attempt to understand the presence of evil in the world. The Muslim theologians had naturally been unanimous in denying that God could be unjust, but then why was there evil in the world? Why did people suffer? This was a crucial issue that the Muʿtazilis and other theologians, including non-Muslims, faced. Muʿtazilis believed that good and evil are

---

[51] Fakhry, Majid, 1983, p. 46.

intrinsic properties in human beings and when they cause evil it is not God who can be blamed. Good and evil are rational concepts which can be understood through reason.[52] At the same time, God is also bound to act within that system of good and evil values. Thus, their system actually constrained God's action within a system.

They further developed a notion that every suffering in the world has to receive a due compensation. So, if a person is hurt even accidently, the person will receive compensation later in the world or in the hereafter. They also said that animals will go to heaven, as animals also suffer in this world, so they will also get compensation. On the contrary, the orthodox ulemaic view stated that though kindness to animals is a part and parcel of Islam, as animals do not have the ability to choose between good and evil, they will not be resurrected for judgement.

In the 9th century, during the time of Caliph al-Ma'mun, there was an intellectual conflict between the Mu'tazilis and the orthodox scholars known as the *Mihnah*. The conflict started over the status of the Qur'an. The orthodoxy considered it was the *eternal uncreated* word of God. The rationalists also considered it to be the word of God, but created, not eternal. After years of conflict the orthodoxy won. The rationalists lost some of their prime positions in the imperial court but rationalism remained strong, supporting science and producing great scientists over the subsequent centuries.

Though the Mu'tazilis are called the rationalists, all the other theological schools of Islam also had some degree of in-built rationalism. Even 'literalists' like the Hanbalis, who said that the scripture must be interpreted literally, are rational to a significant degree, as the fundamental scriptures, the Qur'an and ḥadīth, encourages rational inquiry. Thus, the element of rationalism

---

[52] Fakhry, Majid, 1983, p. 47.

existed in all the schools, and if there were times in which rationalism was negated, it was an individual and temporal choice.

Hanbali Theology and Its Effect

At one stage, the Mu'tazili theologians and also philosophers like al-Kindi and al-Farabi started to apply some precepts of Islam in interpreting the Greek philosophical ideas. Metaphysical speculation gained significant ground in intellectualism. This resulted in 'reason' being considered the sole basis of truth even when it came in conflict with religion. This alarmed the orthodoxy and a powerful reaction set in.

Some of the ḥadīth experts and jurists, like Imam Hanbal, refused any change to tradition and supported only a literal interpretation of the Qur'an and the *Sunnah*. Even verses of the Qur'an like '*God rose to his throne*' were to be taken literally; whether it had any metaphoric implication was inconsequential. Imam Malik had earlier clarified, 'God's settling Himself firmly upon His Throne is known. The 'how' of it is unknown; belief in it is obligatory'.[53]

The Ash'ari School

At length, the 'rationalism' in the Qur'an and ḥadīth appealed to other theologians. They took a middle position in between the extreme rationalist and the strict literalist views in interpreting the precepts. Gradually, this movement gathered strength and established a number of middle-course theological schools in the 10th century. The three most influential ones were led by Abu al-Hasan al-Ash'ari (d. 941 or 945) in Mesopotemia (Iraq), Abu Ja'far ibn al-Tahawi (d. 942) in Egypt, and Mansur al-Maturidi (d.

---

[53] Sharif, M. M., 2016, p.221, see 'Note on Books' after appendices.

944) in Samarqand (of Uzbekistan).[54]

All three of them produced a theology similar in scheme only differing in details. In the interpretation of scriptures, their premise lay between absolute literal interpretation (like the Hanbalis) and ultra-rational interpretation (as of the Mu'tazilis) and also tended to remain aloof from metaphysical speculation (as of the philosophers). They placed significance on reason at slightly varying degrees.

Initially, the Ash'aris would become the most influential of the three schools. The great period of Ash'arism was the 12th and 13th centuries. Some of the most famous Ash'aris were al-Shahrastani, al-Suyuti, al-Bayhaqi, al-Nawawi, Izz al-Din ibn Abd al-Salam, Ibn Asakir, Ibn Hajar al-Asqalani, al-Qurtubi, al-Ghazali and al-Subki. A classical work that assesses the foundation of theological sciences is the *Nihayat al-Iqdam* (*Summa Philosophiae*) by al-Shahrastani.

The Ash'aris believed that the world was composed of the smallest particles—atoms. (In fact, the Ash'aris were the first to understand 'atoms' as minute particles comprising matter. Philosophical mentions of 'atom' in ancient Greek, Indian and Chinese philosophies were not actually 'atomic' but meant the natural elements fire, water, earth and air, along with ether, *i.e.* sky). Unlike the Mu'tazilis, the Ash'aris believed that there is no natural causality in the world. Events that are seen as cause and effect are only illusory. For example, if paper is put into fire, the burning is actually not caused by the fire. The paper burns because God makes it burn. Another way of saying this is that God caused fire to burn. This concept came to be known as 'occasionalism' in later European philosophy.

Unlike the Mu'tazilis, who believed that good and evil intrinsically exist in human beings, the Ash'aris believed that there

---

[54] Sharif, M. M., 2016, p. 222.

is no intrinsic reality to good and evil. According to the Ash'aris, actions are good or bad only because God considers them to be so. To the Ash'aris, the Mu'tazili doctrine introduces a compulsion on God or actually constrains God to act within a system of right or wrong. Such compulsions are inventions of the limited human intellect, which in itself has been given by God and does not have the ability to decide what is and is not possible for God. Imposing human understanding of good and bad on God causes one to end up in absurd paradoxes.

The Maturidi School

Abu Mansur al-Maturidi's school of systematic theology is close to the creed (*aqidah*) of the Ash'ari theology. There are minor differences, for example, the Ash'aris said that 'faith' increases and decreases according to the degree of piety achieved but the Maturidis believed that 'faith' in individuals does not increase nor decrease with action, it is rather piety (*taqwa*) which increases and decreases.

In certain cases, the Maturidis placed slightly more emphasis on reason. They said that the unaided human mind is able to cognise that major sins, like murder, are evil and immoral without the aid of divine revelation. The Ash'aris, on the contrary, said that the unaided human mind is unable to determine whether something is moral or immoral without the direct aid of revelation. Both the Ash'aris and Maturidis believed in 'occasionalism'.

The Maturidi school became popular in places where the Hanafi school of law was followed, particularly in the lands of the former Ottoman and Moghul empires, *i.e.* Afghanistan, the Balkans, Bangladesh, Bashkortostan, the Caucasus, the Levant, Central Asia, northwest China, India, Pakistan, Tatarstan and Turkey.

The Tahawi School

Al-Tahawi (853-933) established his school in Egypt. It was significantly influenced by Imam Abu Hanifah. It also supported a middle-line theology between reason and absolute literal interpretation of scriptures. All these three schools rejected the Mu'tazili application of extreme reason that put constraints on the all-pervading will and power of God. Tahawi's theology was also counteractive to the philosophical insights of al-Kindi and the later al-Farabi.

Shi'ah Theology

The Shi'ah Muslims share the same core belief as the Sunni and follow the same Qur'an. The main difference was initially political which gradually transformed into theological. They believe that the descendants of the Prophet through his daughter Fatimah and his son-in-law Ali are each an imam (*khalifah ilahiyyah*) of the Muslims. They believe that the divine guidance of the imams comes not from revelation but through inspiration. Their inspired knowledge enables the imams to be the guide to the people.

This concept of *imamah* is a fundamental belief of Shi'ah Islam and is based on the premise that God would not leave humanity without access to divine guidance. They believe that the *imamah* descended from the Prophet to Ali,[55] that the divine spirit that dwelled on all prophets was transferred to Ali after the death of the Prophet. The Twelver sect (*Ithna 'Ashari*) are the dominant group among the Shi'ah who believe that there were twelve such imams. Ali was the first imam and the following eleven were his descendants. The twelfth, Imam Muhammad Ibn Hasan, who had vanished, was placed in a *spiritual hidden state* by God but is living and will return to redeem the Muslims and be the ultimate

---

[55] Sharif, M. M., 2016, p. 733.

Savior, the *Mahdi*, when the world will need him the most.

The Shi'ah Muslim disagrees with the caliphate of Abu Bakr, Umar and Uthman and believe that Ali should have been the first caliph. The theological-political position of the orthodox Shi'ah are, thus, based on three points:[56]

1. The divine right of the descendant of Ali and Fatimah to succeed to the *imamat*.

2. The sinlessness of all the imams.

3. The return of the twelfth imam as the *Mahdi*.

Theologically, it means that the state is a theocracy where the main leader cannot be elected or deposed even though the first four caliphs of Islam including Ali were elected. As the imams are sinless they cannot be blamed. The twelfth imam will return as the *Mahdi*, who will bring an end to the tyranny, suffering, despotism and sinfulness that people are suffering from and will usher in a new era of prosperity bliss and happiness such as never experienced by humanity. During the period before he returns people will be ruled by *mujtahids* who are righteous, erudite, competent, learned and virtuous.[57]

The other Shi'ah sects—Isma'ili, Zaydi and Bohra—believe in a different number of imams and in a different path of succession of imams, and similar to the Sunnis, do not consider Muhammad ibn Hasan to be the *Mahdi*. The Shi'ah, especially the Zaydis, have been influenced by the Mu'tazilah school of rationalism. The extreme Shi'ah (*Gulah*) believed that Ali was the reincarnation of the Prophet.[58]

The Shi'ah were also dedicated to knowledge. For example, Egypt under the Fatimid Shi'ah rule (10th-12th century) was a

---

[56] Sharif, M. M., 2016, p. 736.

[57] *Ibid.*, p. 737.

[58] Sharif, M. M., 2016, p. 732.

centre of learning and knowledge where libraries, observatories and academic institutions were established, of which al-Azhar University is an example.

The Sufi Discipline

The core of Sufism comes from *tasawwuf*—the spiritual essence of religion. It deals with the purity of the heart and nearness to God. There are verses in the Qur'an that ask the believers to purify their hearts and souls, as that is the basis of achieving success in life and eternity.

> *By the sun and its glorious splendour,*
> *By the moon as it follows,*
> *By the day as it shows the glory,*
> *By the night as it conceals it,*
> *By the firmament and its wonderful structure,*
> *By the earth and its wide expanse,*
> *By the soul and the proportion and order given to it,*
> *Truly he succeeds that purifies*
> *And he fails that corrupts it.*

—Qur'an, Al-Shams 91:1-10

Muslim scholars give great importance to the purification of body, mind and soul. To the Sufis, the purification of the soul and heart (which traditionally also means the mind) is at the root of religion. They sought communion with God influenced by verses of the Qur'an like:

> *Whichever way you turn, there is the Face of God.*

—Qur'an, Al-Baqarah 2:115

And produced poetical verses like:

Everywhere I look, I see Your winning face
Everywhere I go, I arrive at Your dwelling-place

They found the overwhelming immanence of God in verses like:

Surely your Lord encompasses mankind.

—Qur'an, Al-Isrā' 17:60

Indeed, I am near.

—Qur'an, Al-Baqarah 2:186

Some of the Sufis projected this concept of spiritual-seeking of God to a 'union' with God. Sufi scholar al-Hallaj claimed his union to such an extent that according to him he had blended with the Godhead. Such Sufis may have been influenced by the ancient Persian Zoroastarian tradition of *Amesha Spenta,* which progresses the self to a divine immortality (*Ameretat*). Al-Ghazali, who investigated all the knowledge of his time including Sufism, did not agree with the 'union with God' concept. According to him the aim was nearness to God, which could be attained.[59]

Sufism is a knowledge sphere that includes a great degree of creative intellectualism. It is not mere mysticism, for a real Sufi is first and foremost a great scholar. Sufis of the past were highly intelligent and educated people. Some of them established schools of purification and devotion that would take the practitioner near to God. Over time, these schools developed into Sufi Orders (*Tarika*). Historically, as there were great luminaries in the Sufi world, there also were false scholars claiming to be Sufis. Any

---

[59] Sharif, M. M., 2016, p. 623.

Tarika that goes outside of Sharī'ah is deceitful. Any person claiming to be a Sufi (*pir* or dervish) and is not an eminent scholar is a charlatan.

One way to understand Sufism is to realise that it is *a quest for God, not to comprehend God as that is humanly impossible but to experience or 'feel' God. As rational thought led to the study of science, Sufi creative intellectualism led to the study of arts and culture.* Sufism led to the development of profound poetry, literature and culture on the one hand, and an understanding of human psychology on the other. Later Sufis had aspects of delicate psychology ingrained in their poetry, such as in the verses of Jami, a 15th century Sufi poet-philosopher:

> *Brother, you are 'thought' wholly*
> *Rest is bone and muscle solely*
> *If your thought is a rose, a rose bouquet you are*
> *If your thought is a thorn, fuel for fire you are.*

> —Whinfield, E. H., and
> Kazvini, Muḥammad Mirza, 2010, p. 13.

By the 10th century, as *ijtihad* (personal research and analysis, especially in jurisprudence) was banned, the juristic schools of the great imams gradually turned into dogmatic sects. The caliphate had also become highly politicised. Confined by these two powerful and rigid forces the scope for the free-thinking people become highly restricted. Sufism became an intellectual rebellion against the religious and political dogmas. At one stage, the Sufis clashed with the orthodox ulema, but would subdue themselves after the execution of the Sufi al-Hallaj in the 10th century, then re-invent themselves as the architect of popular culture that would influence the world, such as the works by poets Jalal al-Din al-Rumi and Nizami and the legendary humour of Nasreddin Hodja .

People like Hasan al-Basri and al-Ghazali who are highly respected by Sufi scholars and the original Sufis like Ibn Arabi, Abd al-Qadir al-Jilani, Jalal al-Din al-Rumi and Nizami were all men of the highest literacy and foremost in knowledge about science, philosophy, psychology, theology, literature and linguistics. They had absorbed and assimilated vast amounts of knowledge and using an incredible thought process produced works full of wisdom. They wrote books and opened up schools. A few of the famous books of the 10th century are:

Book	**Author**
Food for the Hearts (*Qut al-Qulub*)	Abu Talib al-Makki
Book of Flashes (*Kitab al-Luma*)	Abu Nasr al-Sarraj
The Doctrine of the Sufis (*Kitab al-Ta'arruf li Madhhab Ahl al-Tasawwuf*)	Abu Bakr al-Kalabadhi

Many books were written by Sufis over the following centuries. They were too much dedicated in their field of knowledge to care about or have time for worldly matters and thus their asceticism or *zuhd*. Sufi asceticism was not a vogue or escapism but a practical measure of a well laid methodology. Their asceticism was always accompanied with cleanliness and purity. The Sufis can also be considered as a type of spiritual philosopher in conflict with atheistic philosophy. Jami would write in his *Lawa'ih* (*Flashes of Light*):

> *Philosophers devoid of reason find*
> *This world a mere idea of the mind;*
> *It is an idea—but they fail to see*

The great Idealist Who looms behind. [60]

Sufis are considered mystics who were never involved with scientific pursuits. But rationalism was not absent from their diversity of thought. Jami even when dwelling on spiritualism digresses into the rational:

> *The essential modes in earth and heavens*
> *Are facets of Him who is a veiled Immanence.*
> *Hence, inquirer, learn what is essence,*
> *What is attribute, cause, and consequence.*

The schools that the Sufis opened were different from the standard ones. These schools developed methods of indoctrination for its disciple-students. Each school developed a methodology by which human emotional weaknesses—animal instincts, material attachments, desire, hatred, *etc.*—were removed leaving the Sufi-initiate liberated. Then, their full mental capacity could be applied in the pursuit of knowledge and the seeking of nearness to God. From the 12th century, the more popular of these schools persisted over time turning into Sufi orders. A list of Sufis and recognised orders are listed in the appendix 3.

The 13th century produced three great Sufi luminaries—Ibn Arabi, Ibn al-Farid, and Jalal al-Din al-Rumi—whose works are still very popular. Ibn Arabi, a great scholar, proposed the theory 'God is the only reality and existence.' This is based on the Sufi statement 'To whatever side I turn, I see nought but Allah,' which, again, is based on a verse of the Qur'an, '*Whichever way you turn, there is the Face of God*' (Al-Baqarah 2:115). Ibn Arabi wrote a number of books including *Al-Futuhat al-Makkiyyah* (*Makkan Revelations*) and *Fusus al Hikam* (*Bezels of Wisdom*). There are 800 works attributed to him.

---

[60] WR4.

Ibn al-Farid postulated the theory of the 'Perfect Man'. According to him a perfect man is the miniature of reality. He is the microcosm in whom is reflected all the perfect attributes of the cosmos. The Prophet was the Perfect Man. Ibn al-Farid was a mystic poet. His *Nazm al-Suluk* (*Poem of the Way*) is the longest Arabic poem written in praise of the Prophet. This concept of the Perfect Man would persist over time. About 600 years later Friedrich Nietzsche would write of a similar, but anti-religious, 'Superman' after studying the works on Zoroaster. He expected transcendent men to replace the nihilistic moral vacuum of Europe of his time. Hitler took up this call and remoulded it to his racially superior Aryan identity. George Bernard Shaw wrote his 'Man and Superman' expounding his philosophy that humanity is the latest stage of evoulution into higher beings which is same as the view of poet Rumi (details in later chapters).

The fame of the poet and mystic Jalal al-Din al-Rumi has remained legendary over the centuries. He still remains one of the most widely read poets in the world. A UNESCO Medal was issued in his name in 2007. His epoch-making work is the *Mathnawi*, a literary masterpiece presenting a panoramic view of the Sufi Gnosis, love and attainment of Communion with God in poetic form.

Quietness.

You've no idea how hard I've looked for a gift to bring You.
Nothing seemed right.
What's the point of bringing gold to the gold mine,
or water to the Ocean.
Everything I came up with was like
taking spices to the Orient.
It's no good giving my heart and my soul
because you already have these.

So—I've brought you a mirror.
Look at yourself and remember me.

The Gift of Water.

Someone who doesn't know the Tigris exists
brings the caliph who lives near the river
a jar of fresh water. The caliph accepts, thanks him,
and gives in return a jar filled with gold coins.

'Since this man has come through the desert,
he should return by water.' Taken out by another door,
the man steps into a waiting boat
and sees the freshwater of the Tigris.
He bows his head, 'What wonderful kindness
that he took my gift.'
Every object and being in the universe is
a jar overfilled with wisdom and beauty,
a drop of the Tigris that cannot be contained
by any skin. Every jarful spills and makes the earth
more shining, as though covered in satin.
If the man had seen even a tributary
of the great river, he wouldn't have brought
the innocence of his gift.
Those that stay and live by the Tigris
grow so ecstatic that they throw rocks at the jugs,
and the jugs become perfect!
They shatter.
The pieces dance, and water...
Do you see?
Neither jar, nor water, nor stone, nothing.
You knock at the door of reality,

shake your thought-wings, loosen
your shoulders, and open.

—*The Essential Rumi*, Coleman Barks

The Rational Disciplines

As the Muslims studied and became scholars in the ulemaic disciplines, jurisprudence and theology, they also opened up to the rational disciplines. There are two very important reasons that led them to the study of the sciences:

1. The upsurge of literacy and knowledge among the Muslims.

2. The encouragement for scientific pursuits in the Qur'an.

The above two points are elaborated below.

Upsurge of Literacy and Knowledge among the Muslims

Following the Prophet's injunctions to read and follow the Qur'an, all men and women were induced to read. Initially, young people were taught in the mosques. Next, small schools developed adjacent to mosques. The first systematic style of schooling for the young people were developed for the study of the Qur'an and the Arabic language. Soon, a large number of schools were established for all in the empire. For the first time in the history of the world, literacy came to the common masses in a society. By the 9th century, a significant proportion of the population was literate.

With academic progress, jurisprudence was one of the first to become a separate discipline within religious studies. This new discipline attracted a large number of students who wanted to earn their livelihood as a jurist, judge or teacher. Bright students could master enough jurisprudence in a few years to get a job. On the other hand, studying ḥadīth or *tafsīr* (exegesis) of the Qur'an was a long and onerous job and took an entire lifetime. Hadīth and *tafsīr* were more attractive to the students who wanted a life of dedication and research.

The masses dedicated themselves to the pursuit of knowledge. The *adib* litterateurs soon developed a hunger for the practical and the systematic. Over time more and more disciplines were added to the curricula. Gradually, the curricula of the schools evolved to include philosophy, history and geography that came out of a litterateur's or *adib*'s studies and, unlike the past, these subjects developed their own methods of enquiry and style.

The other product of the litterateur's learning were the clerks in the royal courts. The Umayyads did not have any *wazir* or 'prime minister'. They had powerful 'clerks' who carried out the executive orders of the royals. Under the Abbasids the 'chief clerk' emerged as the prime minister (*wazir*) and became more powerful than Generals and nobilities.

Soon there were different types of schools: the primary schools, the readers' school (which mainly taught the Arabic language and Qur'an recitation), the hadīth schools and medical schools.[61] As schools developed out of mosques so did universities and libraries. In fact, *jami'ah*, meaning university, is linguistically the feminine of *jami*, which means a large or central mosque. In the Islamic context the place of high learning is tied to religion. Three examples of such mosque-universities are the al-Azhar University of Cairo, al-Qarawiyyin of Fez in Morocco and University of Sankore in Timbuktu.

Al-Azhar which still exists as a university had the famed physicist of the 10th century Ibn Haytham as one of the alumni and the great sociologist and historian of the 14th century Ibn Khaldun as a teacher.[62] Al-Qarawiyyin, one of the first natural

---

[61] Al Hassani, 2007, p. 51.
[62] Enan, Mohammad Abdullah, 2007, p. 53.

science universities in history was established in Fez, Morocco. The Sankore University constituted a number of institutes, which by the 12th century had 25 thousand students and taught diverse subjects like Islamic studies, medicine, surgery, law, literature, astronomy, physics, chemistry, philosophy, geography, history, *etc.* It became the intellectual centre of Mali, Ghana and Songhay. The universities also offered oratorical and poetical competitions and apprentice classes in farming, fishing, construction, tailoring, shoemaking, navigation, *etc.*[63]

With the extensive development of schools and universities, the demand for books was correspondingly high. Besides universities, libraries also cropped up in every mosque of any significance and were called *dar al-kutub* (house of books). The general public were allowed to borrow books from these libraries. Makdisi states that besides private study and research many activities such as reading, copying, debates, discussions and disputation took place in the libraries. In exceptional cases, teaching facilities were also available. A professor is known to have taught *kalam* (theology) in the Basra library.[64]

Besides the mosques, the nobilities and general public also took pride in private collections. The first command in the Qur'an is to *'read'*. Thus, Muslims developed a passion for reading books. Stories of book-lovers among the early Muslims are quite popular. Among the well-known examples are the 8th century scholar named al-Jahiz, a court aristocrat named al-Fath ibn Khaqan, and a *qadi* (judge) named Isma'il ibn Ishaq.

Al-Jahiz loved books and read every book that came his way. At the age of 92, a pile of books fell on him in his library and he died a true bibliophile's death.[65] His quote on books became very

---

[63] Al Hassani, 2007, p. 56.
[64] Makdisi, 1981, p. 25-27.
[65] Al Hassani, 2007, p. 62.

famous:

> "The book is silent as long as you need silence, eloquent
> whenever you want discourse. He never interrupts you if
> you are engaged, but if you feel lonely he will be a good
> companion. He is a friend who never deceives or flatters
> you, and he is a companion who does not grow tired of
> you."

Al-Jahiz studied in Baghdad and wrote 200 books in fifty years
including the seven-volume *Book on Animals* which included a
discussion of the social organisation of ants and communication
between animals. Such scholars would have been influenced by
the verse of the Qur'an:

> *There is not an animal on the earth,*
> *Nor a being that flies on its wings,*
> *But forms part of communities like you.*

> —Qur'an, Al-An'ām 6:38

Al-Fath Ibn Khaqan had special sleeves (pockets) made in his
robes to carry books, so that he could read them whenever he had
free time. Isma'il ibn Ishaq was famous as an avid reader of all
kinds of books—theology, philosophy or literature.

Historian Edward Gibbon tells the tale of a book lover who
refused the invitation of the sultan of Bukhara as he could not
leave his books behind. It would have taken 400 camels to carry all
his books.[66] Even a court marshall in Baghdad left behind, in 924,
books worth 2000 *dirham*.[67] Sultan Adud al-Dawlah had a
separate building for his library with books from every branch of

---

[66] *Ibid.*, p. 62.
[67] Khudabaksh and Margoliouth, 1996.

learning, sorted into categories in shelves.[68]

In the 10th century, all the three great rulers of the Islamic world—Spain, Egypt and Baghdad—were lovers and readers of books. Al-Hakam of Spain had his agents scour the East for any new books they could acquire. There were 200,000 volumes in his library.[69]

The rulers or political leaders of the Muslim domains spent sufficiently to make the Muslims most advanced in knowledge. Their love for books and reading led them to a massive quest for knowledge. This quest, over centuries, by the early Muslims was so total and so intense that it would have historical ramification for the entire world.

The Encouragement for Scientific Pursuits in the Qur'an

The quest for knowledge by the Muslims starts with the Qur'an. The 'First Command' in the Qur'an, 'Read...', directed the Muslims to read, write and acquire knowledge. The rationalism in the Qur'an along with its repeated mention of aspects that are of scientific nature led to the initiation of a massive quest for knowledge which caused, over historical time, the assimilation and improvement of pre-existing knowledge, the development of the scientific methods and discoveries of new fields of knowledge and its dissemination to all the societies of the world.

In the Qur'an, knowledge has been mentioned more than 800 times. It questions and encourages questions to be asked and impels rational thinking. The Qur'an repeatedly mentions 'thinking' and 'contemplation'. The word 'intellect' is mentioned about 50 times and phrases like 'people of intellect' and 'people of discernment' have been mentioned several times in the Qur'an. Professor Oliver Leaman states, 'The Qur'an does indeed display

---

[68] Hossain, M. Amjad, 2013, p. 15-16.
[69] Khudabaksh and Margoliouth, 1996.

an unusual commitment to argument and logic and its self-explanation'. Quite interestingly, the first Christians who had observed Islam, for example John of Damascus, considered Islam inferior because 'of its emphasis on reason and its apparent disinterest in mystery'.[70]

In many chapters of the Qur'an a variety of scientific notions have been expressed and affirmed. These notions acted as catalyst for the Muslim scholars to delve into concepts of science and attempt to understand them. There are many such verses of which a good example is Surah al-Rahman. This Surah (Chapter 55) starts with the following verses:

Most Gracious,
Taught the Qur'an,
Created humanity
He taught eloquent speech.

This states that God the Most Gracious taught the Qur'an, knowledge, to the humanity He created. Human beings were given the ability to communicate which fosters knowledge. The verses that follow are:

The sun and the moon move by precise calculation.

Here the Qur'an is dwelling on a notion of astronomy.

And the stars and the trees prostrate.

Everything, from stars in the heavens to the trees on the ground all prostrate to Him. This is allegorical, stars and trees do not have heads and hands like human beings that they can bow down. Here prostration means they constantly obey the command or processes set by God. A fuller explanation of the verse can be

---

[70] WR8.

that the stars obey all the laws of thermodynamics, gravity and force, which are the commands of God. The trees obey their own processes—using photosynthesis to produce its own food and bear fruits and flowers—as they are set to do.

And He has raised the sky and imposed balance.

The mention of imposing balance in the high sky makes this verse extraordinary. In astrophysics and astronomy one knows how well the forces of gravity of the stars, the solar systems and the galaxies are all balanced. If there is any imbalance a catastrophe would tear away the celestial bodies from their orbits. But due to the balance of forces everything follows its path.

Do not transgress the balance.

This is a counsel not to transgress the balance, for imbalance causes disturbances and chaos. Balance is not restricted only to the celestial bodies. The human world and society also require their own kind of social balances.

And observe the weights with equity
and do not upset the balance.

The weights mentioned in this verse refer to the salesman's standard measuring weights used for weighing and selling goods. The verse says not to cheat while weighing or selling. There are balances in daily life, law and order that are not to be broken. Social imbalance causes chaos in society, political instability and wars leading to economic ills. Thus, as the Qur'an points towards astronomy and its physical laws, it also mentions social behaviour.

And the world he has spread for the creatures, and
in it are fruits and palm trees with sheaths (of dates).
And grains having husks and scented plants.

Here biology, fauna and flora, is being mentioned. The verse not only mentions palm trees or plants but also narrates some characteristics like sheaths and husks and scents. People are to be 'aware' of the details of the world they live in, not ignorant. A few verses later, the Qur'an states:

> *He has let free the two bodies of flowing water,*
> *meeting together;*
> *Between them is a barrier which they do not transgress;*
> *Then which of the favours of your Lord will you deny?*
> *Out of them come pearls and coral.*

Initially, scholars were not sure what exactly these verses meant. What were the barriers between waters? But, in recent times, scientists have discovered boundaries between water bodies. When two large natural water bodies, like currents of seas and oceans, meet they do not readily mix even after coming together. There is a time delay till a certain barrier—caused by differences in salinity, temperature and density between the water bodies—is overcome. One example is where the Mediterranean meets the Atlantic, the two bodies of water stay separate for considerable time even after they come in contact.

Another such barrier is the thermocline found in large water bodies. In its vertical profile the ocean can be divided into three very thick layers. The top, a relatively thinner and warmer layer, the lowest cold layer and the middle layer. This middle layer acts as the barrier between the top and lower layers of water. The middle layer is the thermocline which rises and lowers with the seasons. The thermocline affects the condition in the sea-shelf where coral is formed, and in the coral reef can be found the pearl oysters. These are all connected as can be seen in the above verses. Thus, here the Qur'an narrates about the thermocline, ocean currents, corals and pearls—this is oceanography and marine life.

There are many verses in other chapters which advocate scientific ideas and facts that are quite amazing and have much influenced the Muslim scholars since the time of the Prophet. Dr. Maurice Bucaille, a French physician-scientist, in his book *La Bible, Le Coran et la Science*, writes that all the compiled citations of scientific nature mentioned in the Qur'an are compatible with modern day science. Among all the religious scriptures this is a unique quality of the Qur'an. He[71] further states:

> "In view of the level of knowledge in Muhammad's day, it is inconceivable that many of the statements in the Qur'an which are connected with science could have been the work of a man. It is, moreover, perfectly legitimate, not only to regard the Qur'an as the expression of a revelation, but also to award it a very special place, on account of the guarantee of authenticity it provides and the presence in it of scientific statement which when studied today, appear as a challenge to explanations in human terms."

Following are some of the verses of scientific nature of in the Qur'an:

- Astrophysics postulates that after the very initial formation of the universe the primordial universal matter consisted of gaseous masses of hydrogen and helium formed by nucleo-synthesis of the big bang. Scientists now claim that initially the universe was all in a gaseous, smoky or cloud-like form. More than fourteen hundred years ago, when this was completely unknown, the Qur'an stated,

Moreover, He (God) comprehended in His design the sky
And it had been (as) smoke: He said to it and to the earth,

---

[71] Bucaille, Maurice, 1995, p. 164.

'Come you together, willingly or unwillingly.' They said,
'We do come (together), in willing obedience.'

—Qur'an, Fuṣṣilat 41:11

- Over a time period of billions of years this uniformly spread gaseous matter separated out into huge fragments and coalesced. This divided interstellar galactic matter formed nebulae in which the coalescing matter came together to form galaxies of stars and planets.

Do not the believers see that the heaven and earth were fused together before we clove them asunder?

—Qur'an, Al-Anbiyā' 21:30

- In recent times, with information received from powerful telescopes and related scientific sources, it has been proven that the universe is expanding. Amazingly the Qur'an states,

The heavens We built with power and
We are expanding them.

—Qur'an Al-Dhāriyāt 51:47

- There are balance, equilibrium, laws and patterns in the universe. These are reflected in a number of verses of the Qur'an.

God created everything in due and proper measure.

—Qur'an, Al-Furqān 25:2

It is not permitted for the sun to catch up with the moon,
Nor the night outstrip the day.

Each swims along in its own orbit.

—Qur'an, Yā Sīn 36:40

He draws the night as a veil over the day,
Each seeking the other in rapid succession.
He created the sun, the moon and the stars,
All governed by laws under His command.

—Qur'an, Al- A'rāf 7:54

- It has now been proven that there are many other planets in different galaxies. The Qur'an also mentions worlds, not just one world.

*Praise be to God, the Cherisher and Sustainer of the **worlds**.*

—Qur'an, Al-Fātiḥah 1:2

- Like multiple worlds the Qur'an also speaks of multiple heavens which may indicate the existence of multiple universes.

*And God created the **heavens** and the earth in truth.*

—Qur'an, Al-Jāthiyah 45:21

- In the earth, life first formed in water, then amphibians went on to the land and finally the animals occupied the land.

We made from water every living thing.
Will they not then believe.

—Qur'an. Al-Anbiyā' 21:30

- Anthropological studies claim that humanity started off

from a unique place in the world and then multiplied, migrated and spread out. About the migration of humanity after being created, the Qur'an states that the first to be created were Adam and Eve:

And of His signs is that He created you from dust (clay);
then behold, you are humans scattered far and wide.

—Qur'an, Al-Rūm 30:20

- Archaeological findings show the continuous existence of several civilisation at the estimated time of Noah which indicates that Noah's flood was not global. Had it been global all the people would have been destroyed at the same time. The deluge in the Qur'an is not global but rather local affecting only the people of Noah.

*And the **people of Noah**—*
When they rejected the messengers,
We drowned them,
And We made them
A sign for mankind.

—Qur'an, Al-Furqān 25:37

- The world evolved through geological periods. Both the Bible and the Qur'an state the formation of the world in six days, *i.e.* six stages. Both teach in parables and metaphors. The Arabic and Hebrew for 'day' is *yawm* and *yom*, respectively. But the meaning of '*yawm*' can be a day or it can be an eon, an age or a period relative to the context it is stated in. This 'relative' usage of *yawm* is clarified in the Qur'an.

The angels and the Spirit ascend to Him in a day (yawm) the measure of which is fifty thousand years.

—Qur'an, Al-Ma'ārji 70:4

- Similar verses indicate the relativity of time.

*A day (yawm) with your Lord is equivalent to a thousand
years in the way you count.*

—Qur'an, Al-Ḥajj 22:4

*He rules all affairs from the heavens to the earth.
In the end will all the affairs go up to Him
On a day whose space will be a
thousand years of your reckoning.*

—Qur'an, Al-Sajdah 32:5

- The Qur'an speaks of vegetation and water, indicating the
hydrologic cycle and its effect on vegetation, in a number
of verses. One example is given below.

*Don't you see that God sends down rain from the sky,
And leads it through springs in the earth?
Then he causes, therewith, products of various colours.*

—Qur'an, Al-Zumar 39:21

- The 20th century concept of plate tectonics and orogenic
movements—by which mountains rise and then are
weathered, eroded and again flattened and pass away in
time—is depicted in the following verse:

*You see the mountains and see them firmly fixed.
But they shall pass away as the clouds pass away.
Such is the artistry of God,*

Who dispossess of all things in perfect order.

—Qur'an, Al-Naml 27:88

- Studies in physical geology have established the fact that high mountains have 'roots' in the earth. The crust under the mountains goes deeper into the earth's mantle like pegs.

> *Have We not made the earth as a wide expanse,*
> *And the mountains as pegs?*

—Qur'an Al-Naba' 78:6-7

- Zoological studies have led to the understanding that not only humans but animals also have communities with work and social organisation. For example, the working organisation of ants and bees consists of groups and subgroups. Tigers divide regions in the forest for preying without disturbing each other. Birds migrate, flying in organised groups.

> *There is not an animal on the earth,*
> *Nor a being that flies on its wings,*
> *But forms part of communities like you.*

—Qur'an, Al-An'ām 6:38

- Physiology and biochemistry show that in animals the nutrients in food contained within the intestine passes to the systemic circulation, *i.e.* the blood circulation that acts as the conduit for these nutrients to the organs. This nourishes the organs including the mammary glands that produce milk.

From what is within their bodies
Coming from a conjunction of intestines and blood
We produce, for your drink, milk
Pure and agreeable for those who drink it.

—Qur'an, Al-Naḥl 16:66

- The process of human reproduction is captured in accurate details in the Qur'an. The Greeks had some knowledge of the reproduction that was a mix of wild speculation and some facts. The embryological information in the Qur'an is precise.

Human reproduction starts with fertilisation of the ovum that has detached from the ovary of a female. It is fertilised by a sperm from a male formed internally by the *mingling of fluids* originating from different glands like the testicles, the seminal vesicles and the prostate gland. The Qur'an describes this, saying:

Verily, We fashioned man from a
small quantity of mingled liquids.

—Qur'an, Al-Insān 76:2

- After fertilisation, the egg descends down the fallopian tube in the female and lodges in the body of the uterus where it implants itself. Of this, the Qur'an says:

We cause whom We will to rest in the womb
for an appointed term.

—Qur'an, Al-Ḥajj 22:5

- The egg develops villosities, which are like roots in the

soil, that cling to the uterus and draw nourishment.

Was man not a small quantity of sperm which has been
*poured out? After that he was **something which clings**;*
then God fashioned him in due proportions.

—Qur'an, Al-Qiyāmah 75:37-38

- Soon, the foetus becomes large enough to be observed
  with the naked eye. It is a small mass of flesh without any
  features and grows in progressive stages.

God fashions you in stages.

—Qur'an, Nūḥ 71:14

- The foetus develops first like a clinging irregular piece of
  flesh which soon grows to an intact lump. Bones develop
  and are covered by flesh.

Then We made the sperm into a clot that clings.
Then out of the clot We made an intact lump.
Then We made out of the lump bones
and clothed the bones with flesh.
Then we developed out of it another creature.

—Qur'an Al-Mu'minūn 23:14

- As the embryo starts to take form, some parts of it—the
  head, limbs and body—are initially out of proportion.

We fashioned you ... into a lump of flesh partly in
proportion and partly out of proportion...

—Qur'an Al-Ḥajj 22:5

- Then the embryo develops the senses.

> *There came over man a long period of time*
> *When he was nothing—not even worth mentioning.*
> *Verily We created man from a drop of mingled sperm,*
> *In order to try him: so We gave him*
> *the gifts of hearing and sight.*
>
> —Qur'an Al-Insān 76:1-2

In 1976, addressing the French Academy of Medicine, Maurice Bucaille reasons,

"Our knowledge of these disciplines is such that it is impossible to explain how a text produced at the time of the Qur'an could have contained ideas that have only been discovered in modern times."[72]

It is only recently that the scholars are starting to see the connections between the verses of revelation and the recently established facts of science. In the past, when science had not uncovered much of the facts, verses like those mentioned above needed explanations. Some scholars would attribute esoteric meanings to these verses. But al-Tabari, in the 10th century, having noticed ambiguities in attempts by other scholars to explain the then inexplicable verses, commented, 'It is our duty to keep silent when we don't know.'

Although scholars remained silent over such verses, they were still motivated to find out what actually these verses indicated. Numerous other verses which contain phrases like *'Don't they think', 'Don't they see', 'Don't they hear'* and *'Don't they reflect'* encouraged investigation. The scholars started to think, see, hear, study, analyse and, in the process, discover. If now some

---

[72] WR17.

scholars are using such verses as proof of authenticity of the Qur'an, in the past, such verses had directed the Muslims into an incredible quest for scientific knowledge that had lasted over centuries.

The above examples suffice to show that the Qur'an speaks of both 'religious' and 'worldly' knowledge, leading the early scholars to study and investigate both. The Qur'an teaches Muslims to take interest in both their hereafter and this world as well:

'But seek, through that which Allah has given you,
***the home of the Hereafter; and (yet),* do not forget your share of the world**. *And do good as Allah has done good to you. And desire not corruption in the land. Indeed, Allah does not like corrupters'*

—Qur'an, Al-Qaṣaṣ 28:77

The Qur'an encourages praying for both this world and the next:

*'Our Lord, give us good **in this world** and good **in the hereafter**…'*

—Qur'an Al-Baqarah 2:201

Thus, acquisition of knowledge for both the hereafter and for this world is encouraged, in fact, commanded. While the spiritual knowledge allows humanity to be successful in the hereafter, rational knowledge gives the ability to build a better present world. There is a need to ponder on all types of verses in the Qur'an.

Do they not carefully consider the Qur'an Or are there locks upon their hearts.

—Qur'an Muḥammad 47:24

CHAPTER 3

The Quest for Science

"God, help with your grace. The soul craves for facts and not for theories. And for that reason the preface is restricted to these very words. God willing, the book will demonstrate the aim of its publication. We seek God's help and blessing."

—Ibn Nadim, in the preface of the *Fihrist*,
a huge index of books, composed in 987

During the time of the Prophet and the Rashidun Caliphs the focus of knowledge was, obviously, on the ulemaic disciplines. As literacy and knowledge progressed the Muslims began to the study other disciplines including the sciences as well. This happened along with the gradual development of academic methodology and institutions.

Search for Science during the Umayyad Period

During the Umayyad period, the *kuttab* (primary school) had been separated from the mosques. After finishing study in the *kuttab* classes, higher education fell under three categories—the ulemaic disciplines, the *adab* disciplines and the natural-philosophy or 'science' disciplines. They were taught in three types of 'schools'—mosques, chancery schools, and private institutions including libraries.

Mosques were used as the school for higher education of mainly the ulemaic disciplines. But other subjects including poetry, grammar, and theology were also taught there. Much of the Muslim intellectual life revolved around the mosque. The Damascus booksellers market was near the famous Umayyad Mosque. Lectures, debates, discussions on a wide range of religious, scientific and philosophical issues of the day were common in those houses of worship.[73]

The main school for *adab* studies were the chancery (state departments) schools. By the Umayyad period the Islamic empire needed professionals who could work as clerks and administrator in the governmental bureaucracy concerned with finance, taxations and the legal system. Among other subjects they were taught language, poetry, history, social studies, and arithmetic. These schools were patronised by the caliphs, sultans, princes, chancery heads and high functionaries of the society.[74]

During the Umayyad time, natural sciences and philosophy were taught in private institutions and libraries.[75] Science started off with the study of medicine. Two hospitals (*bimaristan* or 'place for the sick') were setup in Damascus and Cairo. By the Abbasid time hospitals also provided the functions of medical schools for students. The students learned by apprenticeship. This was the first time when hospitals took the shape of modern hospitals.[76]

Libraries became very important during this period. While the initial library contained books of ulemaic discipline, some of

---

[73] Lyons, Jonathan, 2009, p.59, see 'Note on Book' after appendices.

[74] Hossain, M. Amjad, 2013, p. 65-66.

[75] *Ibid.*, p. 61.

[76] *Ibid.*, p. 67-68.

the library collections came to the Muslims as legacy of the Byzantine Romans (Alexandria in Egypt) and the Persians. The initial translation of ancient manuscripts started during this time. The translation and development of ancient disciplines was supported not just by the rulers but by the ulema as well.[77] The Umayyad ruling dynasty also owned some of the first small library collections. In the 8th century, Prince Khalid ibn Yazid ibn Mu'awiyah initiated some translation work.[78] He gave up the throne to study chemistry.[79]

Soon, the Umayyads built their first large libraries with reading rooms and copying materials in Damascus. These libraries included not only the Islamic disciplines but also other sciences like the old works on alchemy and medicine by the Greeks and Christian scholars.[80] During the time of the Umayyads the ground work for scientific enquiry has been laid. In the following Abbasid period, with all manners of sciences being studied, the libraries would grow extensively.

The *rihlah* or 'the travelling quest for knowledge' continued through the centuries. Botanists, for example, travelled from places to places in search of flora, especially those of medicinal value, and then listed the plants and described their affects, properties and usage in proper medical texts.[81] Rihlah also played a major part in the corroboration and compilation of ḥadīth from various sources. The initial compilations were used in the development of jurisprudence.

---

[77] Hossain, M. Amjad, 2013, p.70.

[78] *Ibid.*, p. 69-70.

[79] Al Hassani, 2007, p. 72.

[80] Lyons, Jonathan, 2009, p. 58.

[81] Said, H. M., 1991, p. 21.

The Umayyads of Spain

In Damascus, the Umayyads were overthrown by the Abbasids in 750. Al-Saffah, the Abbasid leader, became the caliph and carried out a purge. One of the Umayyad royalties who escaped the purge was a prince named Abd al-Rahman. He escaped to the Berbers tribes of North Africa who were related to him through his mother. From there he went to Spain (al-Andalus), which was already a Muslim domain since Tarik ibn Ziyad had conquered it. He set up an emirate in Cordoba which would extend and become the Western Caliphate under a great descendant of his with the same name, Abd al-Rahman.

The Umayyads of Andalusia were contemporaries with the Abbasids of Baghdad in the east. They set up a rich tradition of social, intellectual and cultural progression along with religious tolerance, a hallmark of all Muslim domains. Muslims introduced irrigation, agronomy, botany, pharmacology and meteorology, making Spain the most advanced European country of their time.[82] Europe's first observatory was set up in Seville under the supervision of mathematician Jabir ibn Aflah. Their royal courts imported books and attracted scholars from the Muslim East.

Muslims also introduced refined culture—songs, the use of toothpaste, underarm deodorant, fine dining with coursed meals—to Spain and Portugal. Ziryab, a famous cultural icon, came to Spain from Baghdad to introduce popular cultural trends and fashion.[83]

Search for Science during the Abbasid Period

As the Umayyads continued to progress knowledge in Spain, the Abbasid caliphate, in the east, had established itself over a vast

[82] Lyons, Jonathan, 2009, p. 148.
[83] *Ibid.*, p. 146.

zone extending from North Africa to central Asia and up to India. They ruled over this large expanse which had shared values, outlook and opportunity.

After the death of al-Saffah the reign of the Abbasid Caliphate passed on to his brother Abu Ja'far al-Mansur. Al-Saffah had been an utterly successful revolutionary, his brother turned out to be one of the great visionaries in the annals of history. He ruled an amazing empire and built a new capital city from scratch and said, 'It will become the most prosperous city in the world'.[84]

Al-Mansur designed his city, Baghdad, after the round shape of Madinah with a mosque and the caliph's palace and offices in the centre (in Madinah, the Prophet's mosque and the Prophet's house were in the approximate centre) and even had named it *Madinah al-Salam* after Madinah. He planned the city with a diverse range of skilled craftsmen and engineers. It had the design of a ringed Persian citadel imposed on it for reliable defence. In a short period of time, it did become the world's greatest city and al-Mansur's imperious prediction was vindicated.

A hundred years later, a scholar named al-Ya'qubi in his *Kitab al-Buldan* (*Book of Countries*) wrote,

"I mention Baghdad first of all because it is the heart of Iraq, and, with no equal on earth either in the orient or the occident, it is the most extensive city in area, in importance, in prosperity, in abundance or water and in healthful climate … No one is better educated than their scholars, better informed than their authorities in tradition, more solid in their syntax than their grammarians, more supple than their singers, more certain than their Koran readers, more expert than their physicians, more competent than their calligraphers, more clear than their

---

[84] Lyons, Jonathan, 2009, p. 55.

logicians, more zealous than their ascetics, better jurists
than their magistrates, more eloquent than their preachers
…".[85]

Education: Mosques, Schools and Libraries

By the mid-8th century, the bookshops had developed the first
discussion circles for various sciences. Debates and discussions
were also held in royal courts and in the libraries. The use of
libraries for study and research was common. On rare occasions,
space in library was also used as a classroom.[86] According to
historical sources the mosques of the early period were bustling
with crowds and activities. By the 9th century, the *Jami Masjid*
(Central Mosque) of al-Mansur held about 50 *halaqah* classes.[87]
This led to a literary society diffusing from the mosques to the
streets and reaching the palaces during the Abbasid period.[88]

Towards the end of the 10th century, Badr ibn Hasanwayh al-
Kurdi, a governor of the Shi'ah Buwayhid sultan, established 3,000
masjid-khans—mosques with an adjunct inn. The mosques
provided higher study and the inns were for impoverished
students who did not have lodgings or means to stay in the city.
Nizam al-Mulk, the prime minister of Seljuk Sultan Alp Arsalan,
founded the famous Nizamiyyah university-madrasah in Baghdad
and affiliated institutes in Nishapur, Balkh, Herat and Isfahan.
The Spanish Muslim traveller from Valencia, Ibn Jubayr (d. 1217)
mentioned that there were 30 madrasahs in eastern Baghdad, each
as marvellous as a palace.[89] The madrasahs consisted of multiple
faculties and the students were provided scholarships, free

---

[85] Wiet, Gaston, 1937, p. 10.
[86] Hossain, M. Amjad, 2013, p. 124-125.
[87] *Ibid.*, p. 94.
[88] *Ibid.*, p. 64.
[89] *Ibid.*, p. 105.

boarding and lodgings.[90] The madrasah archetype served as the model for scholarship of impoverished students and the residential colleges in Bologna, Paris, Oxford and Cambridge.[91]

There were scholars and students who would study in private circles. The most famous among them were Jabir ibn Hayyan, the father of chemistry; Omar Khayyam, the famous mathematician and poet; and al-Ghazali, who left the Nizamiyyah Madrasah and continued his research and writing while visiting various private circles of scholars. Scholars and students are also known to have taken residence in mosques and study in the libraries. The most famous of such scholars are al-Ghazali, again, who resided in the Damascus *jami* mosque for a period of time, Ibn al-Haytham, who resided is al-Azhar mosque and carried out research in its library, and Ibn Khaldun, who studied at the Zaytuna mosque and the Abdaliyyah library.[92]

The Umayyad chancery had consisted of state departments such as the Secretariat of Land Tax, Secretariat of the Army, Secretariat of the Police, and other branches. The Abbasid expanded the chancery to include more departments like the postal department, the water department and the intelligence department.[93] All these departments employed a vast number of professionals. The chancery provided its own schools or educational institutions to educate and groom such professionals.[94]

Except for philosophy and logic, the natural sciences were taught mainly outside the madrasah in scientific institutions and private circle.[95] Science scholars found support in institutes built

---

90 *Ibid.*, p. 107-108.
91 Stanton, Charles Michael, 1990, p. 38.
92 Hossain, M. Amjad, 2013, p. 127.
93 Young and Serjeant, 1990, p. 155-167.
94 Hossain, M. Amjad, 2013, p. 128-129.
95 Nasr, Seyyed Hossein, 1987, p. 187.

by the royalty providing all that was needed to study the sciences. Every caliph or sultan sponsored scientists in their courts.

Bayt al-Hikmah established by Caliph Harun al-Rashid and developed by al-Ma'mun was a remarkable research and study institute for the sciences. It was the biggest such institute in the world of its time and nothing like it had ever been seen before. It had a huge library which had space for study, administrative support, financial support for scholars and various amenities. It was so well endowed that extensive and complex outdoor geodetic experiments could be planned and commenced from there. Great scholars like al-Khwarizmi and the Banu Musa brothers were attached to the *Bayt al-Hikmah*.

In the 10th century CE, the scholar Abu al-Faraj Muhammad ibn Ishaq al-Nadim, a scholar and book dealer, wrote an index of the curricula of Islamic institutions called the *Fihrist (Index of the Sciences)*. It contained sixty thousand topics on all the subjects found across the bookshops and libraries of the caliphate.[96] At about the same time a Sufi fraternity known as 'the Brethren' also compiled a similar encyclopaedia.[97] Al-Farabi produced the following summary classifying various disciplines available in his work *Ihsa al-Ulum (The Enumeration of the Disciplines)*[98]:

- Propaedeutic (introductory) sciences and their branches: arithmetic, geometry, optics, astronomy, music (sound), the science of weights and mechanical devices

- Natural Sciences: principles of natural philosophy, study of simple bodies, generation and corruptions, minerals, plants and animals, accidents pertaining to elements

- Metaphysical sciences: science of qua being, principles of

[96] Hossain, M. Amjad, 2013, p. 127.
[97] Stanton, 1990, p. 45.
[98] Hossain, M. Amjad, 2013, p. 115.

the sciences and discussion of non-material bodies

- the discipline of society and its branches: jurisprudence and theology

- the discipline of the language and its branches: elements such as grammar, dictation, recitation and prosody

- logic and its branches: the categories, on interpretation (*peri hermenias*), prior analytics, posterior analytics, topics, sophistic rhetoric and poetics.

All the disciplines itemised by al-Farabi were taught at their appropriate designated centres.

The First Modern Hospitals

Al-Mansur appointed Persian Nestorian Christian Jurjis Ibn Bukhtishu, the dean of the Jundi-Shapur hospital, as the court physician in Baghdad. During the reign of the son of al-Mansur, Caliph al-Mahdi, the first proper hospital (*Barmaki*) was built in Baghdad. Its director was the Indian scholar Ibn Dahn al-Hindi, who along with another Indian scholar, Mankah al-Hindi, translated the Indian medical opus *Susruta*.

Soon, hospitals spread all over the Muslim world. Most hospitals had medical schools with lecture halls and grants for libraries. In the 10th century, a decree was passed by Caliph al-Muqtadir that no one could practise medicine in Baghdad without being examined and qualified by the chief physician Sihan ibn Thabit. Eight hundred and sixty physicians underwent this qualifying examination under a board. In the same century, Muhammad ibn Zakariyyah al-Razi, dean of the Baghdad hospital, initiated a character test for all physicians. Every student of medicine had to obtain a good character certificate from the police chief.[99]

A few madrasah-hospitals also emerged during the 13th century. The first such combination of hospital and medical school-madrasah was the one built in Keysari by Seljuk of Rum Sultan Ghi'yath al-Din ibn Qilij Arsalan and his sister Gevher Nesibe.[100]

International Quest for Ancient Knowledge

By the time of al-Mansur, the Muslims had become the best intellectuals in the world. They had started to come in contact with the works of ancient civilisations. Al-Mansur decided it was time to harness the great classical intellectual heritage of the rest of the world. Starting from al-Mansur, the Abbasids launched history's greatest effort to harness the knowledge of the entire world becoming the worthy heir to the classical traditions of Persia, India, Greece, Mesopotamia,[101] China and Egypt. The translation movement brought multifarious and marvellous ideas to the Muslims. Al-Mansur's court took succour from the once great centres of learning of the world and then outshone them all.

Persia had long ago fallen to the Muslims and its existing knowledge, including astrology and medicine, had been incorporated by Muslim scholars. Astrology was not the 'magical' subject of a shaman predicting one's future love-life by gazing at the stars. 'Astrologers' was the term that Persians had used for their philosophers. What was philosophy to the classical Greeks was astrology to the ancient Persians. It was one massive discipline which also included the study of nature. It obviously contained non-scientific and speculative content but over time those would be rejected and removed by the Muslim scholars.

---

[99] Hossain, M. Amjad, 2013, p. 116-117.
[100] Hossain, M. Amjad, 2013, p. 122.
[101] Lyons, Jonathan, 2009, p. 22.

The Muslim 'astrologers', thus, studied the nature of things; they studied animals, plants and minerals and their changing states according to the seasons. They mastered the basics from the ancient knowledge and then brought about specialisation in all the different disciplines like complex trigonometric functions, utmost precision in instrumentation and timekeeping, preparing star tables accurate not just to minutes of degrees but to finer than seconds.[102]

In 771, according to Ibn Sa'id's *Tabaqat al-Umam*, Caliph al-Mansur received in audience a native of India who had a thorough knowledge of the calculation of the stars known as the *Sindhind* (*Siddhanta*). Ibrahim ibn Habib al-Fazari extracted the elements and methods of calculation of the astronomical tables and named those *zij* (plural:*azyaj*). Ya'qub ibn Tariq composed a similar book based on the *Siddhanta* and other resources brought in by another mission from India.[103] The Hindu sages also introduced the trigonometric function of sine. Muslim scholars studied this knowledge and improved on it. By the 9th century, all the six trigonometric functions—Sine, Cosine, Tangent, Cotangent, Secant and Cosecant—had been worked out. The last five being discovered by Muslim scholars which laid the foundation of modern mathematical astronomy and trigonometry.[104]

The Hindu works on natural philosophy were difficult to translate and understand. They were present as concepts within 'difficult' to understand religious texts. There was not much offered as explanation, procedure and proof. This led the Muslims, at times, to grapple with scientific fundamentals and resolve it rather than just copy some readily discernible

[102] Thorndike, Lynn, 1955, p. 277.
[103] Holt, P. M. et al., 1970, p. 758.
[104] Gingerich, Owen, 1986.

theorem.[105] At instances, the Muslim scholars had to work out some problems first and later realise what the classical writings meant.

Alexandria came under Muslim rule during the Rashidun Caliphate, thus Hellenic works, including Ptolemy's Almagest was available to them. Ptolemy of Alexandria in Egypt had prepared a remarkable work on astronomy which was named *Megale Syntaxis* (*The Great Composition*). It used information from a number of Greek sources. It gave the movements of the fixed stars, sun, moon and the five known planets. Like the Persian and Indian texts this book also provided Muslim scientists another impetus for further research. It was translated and studied a number of times. The final product was given an Arabic name— *Al Magest*.

The Muslim scholars also inherited the classical Greek philosophy, which included some theoretical concepts of natural sciences as well. They sent delegations to Byzantium to secure texts and manuscripts. How successful were those efforts is a matter of imagination as, quite long ago, most of the persecuted scholars of Byzantine had escaped to Persia. Probably, more successful was the contact with Nestorian monks, in and around Central Asia, who still held on to the works of the Greeks even though they had lost the ability to understand those in any details. The abstruse Greek works were studied, corrected and improved, and applied in further research.[106]

Muslim scholars ferreted out the mistakes of Greek philosophy and Persian astrology. Al-Ghazali, in the 11th century, would make two lists of subjects—praiseworthy and blameworthy. For instance, he upheld astronomy as praiseworthy but described astrology as blameworthy. In philosophy, he rigorously critiqued

---

[105] Goldstein, Bernard R., 1967, p. 4.
[106] Lyons, Jonathan, 2009, p. 65.

certain concepts of the philosophers which were fallacious but he endorsed logic.

The classical information that the Muslim scientist acquired were just the starting point for their endeavours. They continued to improve on such academic works. And much later scientists like Danish astronomer Tycho Brahe would use information originating from Muslim sources to progress their research.

For nearly a century after al-Mansur, this search for knowledge continued. The ancient information that was gathered was used to bolster and cross-check with local researches. This quest and research became an obsession and soon the Muslims were producing very advanced books. As the ancient knowledge was overtaken by the progress of local knowledge, the need for international search declined. As local resources developed the quest transformed into an internal one. Soon scholars and students from other regions came to Muslim domains in search for knowledge.

The Muslim scholars continued the *rihlah* method in their quests internally. The 9th century scholar Hunayn ibn Ishaq narrates about the search for a missing medical manuscript,

> "I myself searched with great zeal in quest of this book over Mesopotamia, all of Syria, Palestine and Egypt, until I came to Alexandria. I found nothing except about half of it in Damascus".[107]

Arab biographer Yaqut in his *Dictionary of Learned Men* states that he wandered for seventeen years from Spain to Cairo, Makkah, Madinah, Baghdad, Aleppo, Damascus and Mosul in a scholarly quest which yielded a large number of books.[108] In that age, those were the cities to search for knowledge in.

---

[107] Meyerhof, Max, 1926, p. 690.
[108] Pedersen, Johannes, 1984, p. 21-22.

Scientific Progress: Experimentation, Investigation and Innovation

By the early 9th century, as higher education became organised, major Muslim cities developed universities.[109] The passion for knowledge continued uninterrupted leading to rapid intellectual development. Sa'id al-Andalusi, a Muslim historian of Spain, stated, 'There was a surge in spirit and an awakening in intelligence. The first of this dynasty to cultivate science was the second caliph, Abu Ja'far al-Mansur. He was, may Allah have mercy on him, in addition to his profound knowledge of logic and law, very interested in philosophy and observational astronomy; he was fond of both and of the people who worked in these fields'.[110]

Al-Mansur had directed all the classical works to be translated to Arabic. The aim was to facilitate research work for future scholars. By then the general public had become significantly educated and all the academic activities attracted a lot of public interest. 'Once in possession of these books, the public read and studied them avidly'.[111] Arabic became the *lingua franca* for all scientific endeavours.

Al-Mansur, in his vision, had also planned the intellectual dimension of the capital city he built as well. He did not only utilise skilled craftsman and engineers but a diverse range of people were included. People like Imam Abu Hanifah, the greatest jurist in the world of his time, was also consulted and involved. One of the academic institutions al-Mansur built was *Khizanah al-Hikmah* (*Treasury of Wisdom*). It contained libraries, working space and materials, and administrative support for the large number of scholars working there. They were also provided

---

[109] Lyons, Jonathan, 2009, p. 64.

[110] Salem, Semaan I. and Kumar, Alok, 1991, p. 44.

[111] Paul Lunde and Caroline Stone 1989, p. 388.

financial support and sponsorship. This was a precursor to the House of Wisdom, *Bayt al-Hikmah*, to be developed by the latter Caliph al-Ma'mun. Here, al-Mansur would gather many famous scholars and carry out scholarly works including scientific ones.

All the early Muslim rulers were lovers and sponsors of knowledge. All spent sufficiently to make Muslims the most advanced scholars in the world. But al-Mansur and al-Ma'mun have carved out a special place in history of world knowledge. Al-Mansur was the visionary. He visualised the future and knew exactly what needed to be done. His work was put to remarkable fruition at the time of al-Ma'mun. The entire world owes a great debt of gratitude to such Muslim rulers. There are very few such examples in the entire history of mankind—the ruler, epitome of the scholar-emperor.

Education was highly and systematically sought after in all levels of the society—by social and political elites, merchants, bankers, military officials and the wives and slave-wives of the caliphs. The caliphs ensured proper education for their children. According to al-Mas'udi, the legendary Caliph Harun al-Rashid, mentioned in *Thousand and One Nights*, told the tutor of his son al-Ma'mun, 'Let no hour pass without giving him the benefit of some new knowledge, but don't let him be bored or overwhelmed. Don't go too easy on him, and don't allow him to enjoy being idle'.[112] Ibn al-Nadim, the famous scholar and book dealer, states that the qualities of al-Ma'mun were too many to enumerate.[113] Al-Ma'mun used to arbitrate in theological debates between Christian and Muslim scholars. One bishop who debated Muslim scholars said, 'When the renowned philosopher converses with al-Ma'mun, incapacity of speech dries up the tongue'.[114]

---

[112] Cooperson, Michael, 2005, p. 22.
[113] Dodge, Bayard, 1970, p. 254.
[114] Swanson, Mark N., 2003, p. 67.

Al-Ma'mun launched a systematic program of astronomical studies in specialised observatories established in Baghdad and Damascus as well as the first large scale expedition devoted to scientific investigation.[115] In a geodetic experiment, he used two groups of astronomers, surveyors and engineers (instrument makers) to traverse a 'degree' length in the desert to calculate with remarkable accuracy the circumference of the earth. Such scientific projects had never been carried out before. Later, the brilliant al-Biruni found a better and much easier method to measure the circumference by using basic observations and simple trigonometry.[116]

Al-Ma'mun's observatory experiments produced a star map that was more accurate than the *Sindbind* and the Almagest. Apparently, Ptolemy had used data from previous sources that were inaccurate.[117] The new tables provided the exact position of sun, moon and the five visible planets—Mercury, Venus, Mars, Jupiter and Saturn. It could also be used to tell the time of day or night based on observing the sun and the stars, in determining the lunar month, and also facilitated measuring spherical geometry.[118] Ptolemy's book was originally named *Megale Syntaxis*, but the fact that it came universally to be known by its Arabic name, *Almagest*, speaks something about the authority and contribution of the Muslim scientists on the subject.

The Muslim scholars' drive to refine astronomy would assist to transform the very concept of the centre of the universe. The Maragha astronomers' theorems, Nasir al-Din Tusi's discovery of the 'Tusi Couple' and Ibn al-Shatir's planetary models were instrumental in Copernicus' heliocentric theory which uses the

---

[115] Sayili, Aydin, 1960, p. 53.
[116] Ali, Jamil, 1967, p. 191.
[117] Lyons, Jonathan, 2009, p. 76.
[118] *Ibid.*, p. 72-73.

above theorems. Copernicus had studied in Italy from 1496 to 1503 where the works of Muslim scholars were known[119] and taught.

Muslim scientists' works were diverse and influential. Jabir al-Hayyan, using his pioneering scientific approach, had founded the practical science of chemistry.[120] Thabit ibn Qurrah had produced original works on calculus, number theory and mechanics.[121] Euclid's thirteen-book collection of geometry, *The Elements*, was studied by Muslim scholars with obsession and its most serious shortcoming about parallel line behaviour in infinity was identified and resolved in a creative manner.[122] Such commentaries, in due course, introduced Euclidian geometry to Europe.

Geography and Maps

Early Muslim scholars have also been inspired to investigate both physical and cultural geography due to various verses of the Qur'an like:

> *Have We not made the earth like a wide expanse,*
> *and the mountains as pegs?*

—Qur'an, Al-Naba' 78:6-7

> *Travel through the earth and see what the end*
> *of those who rejected Truth was.*

—Qur'an, Al-An'ām 6:11

---

[119] *Ibid.*, p. 200.
[120] Lyons, Jonathan, 2009, p. 109.
[121] *Ibid.*, p. 106.
[122] *Ibid.*, p. 112.

One of the very early geographical investigations was ordered by the second Rashidun Caliph Umar. After the conquest of Egypt, Syria and Iraq, he had written to one of his aides, 'Describe therefore to us the towns, their air (climate), their position and how people are affected by the land and the air.' Over time, such endeavours would lead to the production of maps and books.

The book *Geography* by Ptolemy was translated to Arabic. It had some basic information but also had many inaccuracies. The length of the Mediterranean was wrong and was corrected from 62 degrees to 42 degrees. The Indian Ocean was considered to be landlocked by Ptolemy, which was corrected and that led for the first time to realise that the global land mass (the continents) was surrounded by a huge body of water (the oceans). Two more *climata* zones were added to the global map.[123] The Muslim scholars of later times would investigate and correct these mistakes in their works and these corrected maps would go to Europe. Meanwhile, Ptolemy *Geography* appears to have been lost.

One of the great achievements of al-Ma'mun was a world map and its associated geography. Such detailed information had never been produced before. The map contained 530 important cities and towns, 5 seas, 290 rivers and 200 mountains. The estimated reserves of the deposits of metals and precious stones in the mountains were also mentioned. It also detailed famous and marvellous things to be found in different parts of the world. It was the first world map that showed the Great Wall of China.

Al-Ma'mun's map opened up the eyes of humanity to the entire world. It also advanced the corroborative empirical and investigative methods needed to carry out such geographical endeavours. Thus, the Muslims discovered the world about six hundred years before Europe's 'Age of Discovery'. One person who would try to emulate the great al-Ma'mun in map making

---

[123] Lyons, Jonathan, 2009, p. 89.

was Roger II king of Sicily who engaged al-Idrisi to make a map of the world.

These maps of al-Ma'mun and Roger became instrumental not only in opening the Europeans' eyes to the world's people, culture and lands but also became important in Western cartography and navigation. European copies of these maps would start appearing in the 13th century.

Enlightened Cities

Such a scholarly environment and intellectual aptitude had a huge impact on the Muslim cities. The Muslim cities were not only aesthetically spectacular but were stunning marvels in spirit and mind. Baghdad became an accomplishment of pure architectural marvels. For miles stretched exquisite suburbs with gardens and parks, bazaars and bookstores, superb mosques and beautiful promenades by the clear shining riverside. The greatest minds and scholars of the time gathered in Baghdad harnessing the knowledge of the entire world needed to run the all-encompassing empire. Besides the local greats, philosophers and scientist from India, Persia, Byzantium and other regions of the world debated in the House of Wisdom in Baghdad. The best Christian and Jewish minds would go to Baghdad to become part of this enlightenment.

The Umayyads of Spain and their successors produced some of the greatest philosophers, scientists and thinkers whose ideas would change Europe forever. The regions of Spain and Sicily were among the most important staging grounds of ideas and technology that began to trickle to western Europe as early as the 10th century CE.[124]

Cordoba, a city that could rival Baghdad, was described by a

---

[124] Lyons, Jonathan, 2009, p. 22.

visiting German Saxon nun named Hrotsvitha as 'the ornament of
the world'. In 950 Cordoba had 600,000 people, 50 hospitals and
one university with 300 colleges. The university alone had 20,000
students. The city had 300 public baths and 72 public libraries.
One average house would have more books than all of Europe in
that time.[125] It was a vast mesmerising symphony of high learning
and sophisticated culture, an interweaving of perfume and poetry,
mathematics and philosophy, theology and science, delicacies on
porcelain, glorious palaces lush with gardens and flowing water,
an architectural orchestration with paved streets having street
lights and houses with running water with faucets—a way of life
that was to influence and change Europe forever.

Important intellectual centres thrived all over Muslim
domains from Edessa near the Mediterranean to Jundishapur in
Persia, and further to the Central Asian oasis of Marv.[126] This
enlightenment spread to other cities all over the known world—
Basra, Kufa, Cairo, Cordoba, Bukhara, Samarqand, Ghazna,
Shiraz and Konya. It had already reached Europe through Spain
and Sicily; next it would go to Italy and France.

Such intellectual centres would continue to spread further
east into Asia and west into Africa with scholars travelling from
one intellectual centre to another. West Africa, Saharan and Sub-
Saharan Africa and North Africa were centres of learning for
liberal arts. Timbuktu was an extraordinary centre of learning
with a famous university and library.[127] Learning would continue
to thrive there producing the golden age of Timbuktu in the 15th-
16th centuries.

The greatest intellectual innovations emerged from such
cities. Algebra, trigonometry, chemistry, engineering, astronomy

[125] WR21.
[126] Lyons, Jonathan, 2009, p. 57.
[127] WR16.

and medicine became definite and discrete sciences. The knowledge of the great masters of the past—Greek, Indian, Chinese and others—were amassed, translated, challenged and corrected. Hundreds of scribes were continuously recording the innovative works in numerous books. There were roads in the cities with their sides lined up with hundreds of bookshops.

Shortly before the First Crusade, a Muslim traveller from his native Spain had found Jerusalem to be an intellectual melting pot 'teeming with scholars'. It was an ideal meeting place for experts in all three of the great monotheistic faiths. His narrative gives details about the competing schools of Islamic Law and the famous intellectuals who gathered to debate around the central mosque. "We entered the Holy Lands and reached the al-Aqsa mosque. The full moon of knowledge shone for me and I was illuminated by it for more than three years".[128]

Age of Books

When books and libraries are mentioned with regards to ancient civilisations they mostly refer to things like papyrus scrolls, or very few book-like codices made of parchment. Ancient China had seen some use of paper but that was restricted to scholars or to the official use in the royal palace. In the contemporary world, paper books are one of the most common items. It was not so before the Muslims who learned the art of paper-making from the Chinese and put it to commercial use. In the 8th century, the Muslim world had set up a paper book-publishing industry. This was many centuries before Europe would establish its book industry.

The first mention of a paper factory dates to 795 in Baghdad. The capital boasted of hundreds of bookshops and stalls[129] when

---

[128] Hillenbrand, Carole, 1999, p. 258.
[129] Lyons, Jonathan, 2009, p. 59.

Europe had no knowledge of paper-making. The few books, mostly containing outdated ideas, available in Europe were scattered in cathedrals, monasteries or royal libraries[130] and were made of parchment (animal skin dried and stretched), papyri or velum. The production of such materials was difficult and writing on them was painstaking and slow.

During the same period, Baghdad had different grades of papers like the *Ja'fari* paper and the *Tahiri* paper. With the availability of paper this made the writing of books much easier. Scholars could write in large volumes and students had notebooks where they could take down notes.[131] The book publishers employed a troupe of copyists to produce books. These books found their way to palaces, mosques, *madrasahs*, libraries, private collections, students and shops of the book dealers.[132]

The availability of books on a mass scale led to the development of numerous libraries. The library became integral to Muslim education. The library of Sultan Adud al-Dawlah in 10th century Shiraz, Persia, consisted of a complex of buildings surrounded by gardens containing waterways and lakes. It contained 360 rooms furnished with carpets. The rooms were divided into departments with each department having catalogues on the shelves.[133] The Fatimid Sultan al-'Aziz of Egypt maintained forty rooms filled with eighteen thousand volumes.[134] When, in 1234, the Mustansiriyyah Madrasah was opened in Baghdad, it received an initial bequest of eighty thousand books from the caliph.[135]

All kinds of books were written as the Muslim scholars did

---

[130] Hossain, M. Amjad, 2013, p. 124.
[131] Hossain, M. Amjad, 2013, p. 84-85.
[132] *Ibid.*, p. 124.
[133] *Ibid.*, p. 15-16.
[134] Atiya, Aziz S., 1962, p. 209.
[135] *Ibid.*, p. 115-116.

not shy away from any subject. Scholars while writing great works also wrote 'popular' books such as on the 'talisman' of the Sabians and the 'magic' of Persian astronomy. Though these works were not much thought of among the learned circles, such books were popular to the average readers among the general masses, as books on astrology, aphrodisiacs and zodiac remain popular even today.

This was the period which started the 'Age of Books' and that age continues even today. This was also the start of the 'Age of Mass Education'. An academic network developed consisting of a variety of schools, libraries and higher education institutes supported by the elite and royalty. Besides scholars getting engaged in what was cutting-edge research of their time, people from all levels of society acquired literacy.

CHAPTER 4

Influence of Muslim Scientists and Scholars

Copious volumes would be needed to list the names and works of the great masters of the centuries when the Muslims ushered in the golden era of the world. And for each one of these names a thousand names have been lost in the erosion of time. But an introduction to some of the masters would give an understanding to the quality of work done, width of the fields engaged in and the dedication behind it.

A significant portion of this chapter is summarised from the book *Medieval Muslim Thinkers and Scientist*.[136] See Note 2, following the appendices, for details of the book.

Jabir ibn Hayyan (died 803)[137]

Jabir (latinised as Geber) was one of the first prominent Muslim scientists. His date of birth is not known but he was a student of the famous Imam Ja'far al-Sadiq who was the great grandson of the Prophet. Even before him the Umayyad Prince Khalid ibn

---

[136] Said, H. M., 1991.

[137] *Ibid.*, p. 37-38.

Yazid is known to have studied alchemy. It was during this time that alchemy developed a scientific base and metamorphosed to chemistry. Jabir was the son of a druggist (*attar*) and practised medicine and alchemy in Kufa around 776 CE. In the early days he also earned patronage from the Barmakid *vizier* (prime minister) of the Abbasid Caliph Harun al-Rashid.

Before him alchemy was a vague non-scientific discipline, the practitioner of which would try to find ways to convert metals into gold, make poison used for assassinations, make flaming liquids that could be thrown at enemies at times of battle or engage in similar endeavours. Jabir introduced experimental investigation and scientific method into alchemy, which rapidly changed its character to modern chemistry. He is the Father of Chemistry.

He built a proper chemical laboratory where he built laboratory instruments and carried out his chemical experiments. His contributions, of fundamental importance to chemistry, include the perfection of scientific techniques such as crystallisation, distillation, calcinations, sublimation and evaporation and the development of several instruments to carry out experiments for the same. Jabir discovered minerals and acids which he prepared for the first time in a laboratory using the alembic (*anbique*). The alembic is his invention, which systematised and made easy the process of distillation. He discovered *aqua regia* that is used to dissolve gold.

Besides the preparation of new compounds and the development of chemical methods, he also developed a number of applied chemical processes. His achievements in the applied side include preparing various metals, developing steel, dyeing cloth, tanning of leather, varnishing water-proof cloth, using manganese dioxide in glass-manufacturing, preventing rusting, lettering in gold and identifying paints, greases, *etc.* During the course of these practical endeavours, Jabir laid great stress on experimentation and accuracy in his work.

He divided substances into three distinct types: metals (iron, gold, silver, *etc.*), compounds (that could be converted to powder) and spirits (that vaporise on heating). This classification still exists in modern chemistry in the form of metals, non-metals and volatile substances. Several technical terms devised by Jabir, such as *alkali*, are still found in various European languages and have become part of scientific vocabulary.

His fame rests on over 100 monumental treatises, of which 22 relate to chemistry while the others are on medicine and astronomy. His books on chemistry, including his *Kitab al-Kimiya* and *Kitab al-Sabin* were translated into Latin and various European languages. These translations were popular in Europe for several centuries and have influenced the evolution of modern chemistry there. According to Max Mayerhof, a distinguished early 20th century German scientist, the development of chemistry in Europe can be traced directly to the works of Jabir ibn Hayyan.[138] Commenting on Jabir's works, George Sarton, founder of the discipline *History of Science*, says, 'We find in them remarkably sound views on method of chemical research, a theory on geological formation of metals.'

The pioneering scientific spirit of the Muslim scholars is ingrained in the superlative statement that was made by Jabir:

> "The first essential in chemistry is that you should perform practical work and conduct experiments, for he who performs not practical work nor makes experiments will never attain to the least degree of mastery. But you, O my son, do experiments so that you may acquire knowledge.

---

[138] Ahmad, K. Jamil, 1984, p. 146.

Scientists delight not in abundance of material, they rejoice only in the excellence of their experimental method."[139]

This statement founded what we know as 'scientific theory and methodology' in the world of science.

Muhammad ibn Musa al-Khwarizmi (died c. 840)[140]

Al-Khwarizmi was born in Kheva, Khwarizm (Central Asia). He thrived during the time of al-Ma'mun in Baghdad. He was a mathematician, astronomer and geographer. He was another early Muslim scholar and carried out his works before any significant philosophy had developed in Muslim academe.

He was the founder of new concepts in mathematics. For his remarkable contributions to mathematics he remained the most influential mathematician in the world for centuries. He founded algebra and systematically developed it to the extent of giving analytical solutions of linear and quadratic equations. The term 'algebra' is derived from the name of his book on the subject, *Al-Maqalah fi Hisab al-Jabr wa al-Muqabalah*. He also showed how simple algebraic equations can be used to solve complex practical problems of land estates and *zakat* 'tax'. He developed the art of analysis by using applied algebra and placed it on an equal footing with the then more famous geometry.[141] The discovery of algebra changed the world of mathematics which was mainly based on geometry before him.

He developed several arithmetic procedures including operations on fractions. He developed detailed trigonometric tables containing the sine functions. This was probably extrapolated to tangent functions by Maslamah al-Majriti. Al-

---

[139] Al Hassani, 2007, p. 75.
[140] Said, H. M., 1991, p. 39-40.
[141] Lyons, Jonathan, 2009, p. 74.

Khwarizmi also perfected the geometric representation of conic sections and developed the calculus of two errors, which practically led him to the concept of differentiation. This would lead to the development of calculus and higher mathematics.

He, in *Kitab al-Jam wa al-Tafriq bi al-Hisab al-Hindi* (*Book of Addition and Subtraction According to the Hindu Calculation*), enumerated and standardised the ten-digit numeric system now in use the world over. He used nine digits and the placement of '0' in tens, hundreds, thousands, *etc.* The '0', a philosophical deduction of the Hindu sages, used only for addition and subtraction at previous times, was put into practical scientific utility by Muslim scientists the world over. Within a century, decimal fractions and roots of numbers were discovered. The value of pi was found to an amazingly correct sixteen decimal places.[142]

In geography, he collaborated in the geodesic measurements organised by Caliph al-Ma'mun which aimed at measuring the volume and circumference of the earth. His work on geography corrected and revised the inconsistencies of Ptolemy. He also put forth original contributions in works related to clocks, sundials and astrolabes.

Several of his books were translated to Latin in the 12th century. These include *Kitab al-Jam wa al-Tafriq bi al-Hisab al-Hindi* on arithmetic, *Al-Maqalah fi Hisab al-Jabr wa al-Muqabalah* on algebra and *Kitab Surah al-Ard* on geography together with maps. His astronomical tables were also translated into European languages and, later, into Chinese. In addition, he wrote a book on the Jewish calendar *Istikhraj Tarikh al-Yahud* and two books on the astrolabe. He also wrote *Kitab al-Tarikh*, and his book on sundials was captioned *Kitab al-Rukhmah*, but both of these books have been lost. His translated books were used

---

[142] J. J. Berggren, 2003, p. 7.

as university texts up to the 16th century.

Banu Musa Brothers (9th century)

Musa ibn Shakir, an astronomer, educated his three sons to become great mathematicians and experts in mechanics. Muhammad, Ahmad and Hasan, the three Banu Musa brothers were born in the first decade of the 9th century and are renowned for their work on automatic and mechanical devices, astronomy and mathematics.

They are famous for their *Book of Ingenious Devices* and the *Book on the Measurement of Plane and Spherical Figures*.[143] It included theorems that were not known previously. In the 12th century, Gerard of Cremona translated the books to Latin naming them *Liber Trium Fratrum de Geometria* and *Verba filiorum Moysi Filii Sekir*.

The Banu Musa brothers researched and worked in the House of Wisdom and in the astronomical observatory of Baghdad. They were also included by al-Ma'mun to work with the team of scientists making geodesic measurements in the extensive desert expedition to determine the length of a degree.[144]

Thabit ibn Qurrah (836-901)[145]

Thabit ibn Qurrah ibn Marwan al-Sabi al-Harrani was born in the year 836 CE in Harran (present-day Turkey). Thabit ibn Qurrah, a Sabian, was hand-picked by Muhammad ibn Musa ibn Shakir and taught by the three Banu Musa brothers and became a famous scholar. Thabit contributed to several branches of science, notably mathematics, astronomy and mechanics in addition to translating

---

[143] Casulleras, Josep, 2007, p. 92-94.
[144] *Ibid.*, p. 92-94.
[145] Said, H. M., 1991, p. 55-56.

ancient works from Greek to Arabic. Later, he was patronised by the Abbasid caliph al-Mu'tadid. After a long career of scholarship, Thabit died in Baghdad in 901 AD.

Ali ibn Rabban (838-870)[146]

Ali ibn Rabban's family came from Marv, Tabaristan (present-day Turkmenistan / Mazanderan). He was a Muslim of Jewish background. He received his education in the disciplines of medical science and calligraphy from his scholarly father Sahl Rabban. His main contribution is the *Firdaws al-Hikmah*, the first proper medical encyclopaedia. Following are some contents of its seven parts:

> **Part one:** The contemporary ideology of medical science; the principles that form the basis of medical science (*kulliyyat tibb*)

> **Part two:** An explanation of the organs of the human body, instructions for keeping good health and a comprehensive account of certain muscular diseases

> **Part three:** A description of diets to be taken in different conditions of health and disease

> **Part four:** A list of diseases from head to toe. This part, consisting of twelve papers, is central to the book. It is the largest section constituting almost half of the book. The title of the twelve detailed sections are:

> > i.   General causes relating to the eruption of diseases.

> > ii. Diseases of the head and brain.

---

[146] Said, H. M., 1991, p. 53-54.

iii. Diseases relating to the eye, nose, ear, mouth and teeth.

iv. Muscular diseases (paralysis and spasm).

v. Diseases of the regions of the chest, throat and lungs.

vi. Diseases of the abdomen.

vii. Diseases of the liver.

viii. Diseases of the gallbladder and spleen.

ix. Intestinal diseases.

x. Different kinds of fever.

xi. Miscellaneous diseases with brief explanations of organs of the body.

xii. Examination of pulse and urine.

Part five: A description of flavour, taste and colour

Part six: Drugs and poisons

Part seven: Diverse topics including a brief mention of Indian medicine.

He wrote *Firdaws al-Hikmah* in Arabic and simultaneously translated it into Syriac. He has two more compilations to his credit, namely *al-Din wa al-Dawlah* and *Hifz al-Sihhah*. These works are still extant.

Abu Abdullah al-Battani (858-929 CE)[147]

Abu Abdullah al-Battani was born in Harran (present-day

---

[147] Said, H. M., 1991, p. 9-10.

Turkey), and was initially educated by his father, Jabir ibn Sinan al-Battani, who was also a well-known scientist. He received higher education in the city of al-Raqqa, situated on the banks of Euphrates (in present-day Syria). At the beginning of the 9th century he moved to Samarra', a city on the Tigris (present-day Iraq), where he did most of his scientific work. His discoveries in astronomy and trigonometry made him a famous astronomer and mathematician.

He determined with remarkable accuracy the angle of tilt of the equator relative to the orbiting plane of the earth (obliquity of the ecliptic), length of the seasons, true and mean orbit of the sun, and the change in the sun's apogee. His determination of the solar year—365 days, 5 hours, 46 minutes and 24 seconds—comes very close to the current estimate.

He proved the variation of the apparent angular diameter of the sun and possibility of annular eclipses. He rectified several orbits of the moon and the planets and propounded a new and very ingenious theory to determine the conditions of visibility of the new moon. His excellent observations of lunar and solar eclipses were used by Richard Dunthorne, English astronomer and surveyor, in 1749 to determine the secular acceleration of motion of the moon. He also provided very neat solutions by means of orthographic projection for some problems of spherical trigonometry. He was the first to replace the use of Greek chords by the superior sines and developed the cotangent and furnished their tables in degrees.

He wrote a number of books on astronomy and trigonometry. His most famous book was his astronomical treatise *Zij* with tables. Astronomical tables were designed to facilitate the calculation of lunar phases, eclipses, position of the planets and other calendar information. The tables sometimes included supplementary information explaining astronomical instruments. His astronomical tables were more accurate than all previous ones. They were translated into Latin in the 12th century and became renowned as the *De Scienta Stellerum—De Numeris Stellerum et Motibus*. It was retranslated into several languages and directly influenced Europe up to the renaissance. One of the translations is still available in the Vatican.

Al-Razi (864-930)[148]

Abu Bakr Muhammad ibn Zakariyya al-Razi was born in Rayy, Iran. By his time, Muslim civilisation had advanced far.

Al-Razi studied medicine, mathematics, astronomy, chemistry, music and philosophy. His greatest contribution was in medicine with major contributions in chemistry and philosophy. He studied under renowned teachers including a student of Hunayn ibn Ishaq (who had, among his studies, examined all the past medical systems of the Persians, Greeks and Indians) and also Ali ibn Rabban (who had the Jewish understanding of past medical systems). He initially worked in the Royal Hospital in Rayy and then moved to Muqtadari Hospital in Baghdad. He gained much experience while working there. His renown spread such that students and patients came to him from distant parts of Asia. For a long time he was the head of the hospital. He visited various cities from time to time on academic missions.

In medicine, his contribution is comparable to that of Ibn Sina. His work in medicine, *Kitab al-Mansuri*, comprised ten volumes and dealt exhaustively with all medical knowledge of his time. His *al-Judari wa al-Hasbah* provided the first treatise on smallpox and chicken-pox and is largely al-Razi's original contribution. It was translated into various European languages. *Al-Hawi* became the largest medical encyclopaedia composed. It contained information from his own research as well as important

---

[148] Said, H. M., 1991, p. 49-50.

information on all medical subjects that was available from Arabic and Greek sources. He laid stress on the effect of both dietary and psychological factors on health. He experimented remedies first on animals in order to evaluate effects and side effects. He was an expert surgeon and was the first to use opium for anaesthesia. The above works and *Kitab al-Muluki* earned him everlasting fame.

In addition to being a physician, he compounded medicines. This gave him insight into chemistry and, in his later years, he indulged in experimentation. He discovered several chemical reactions and also provided designs and descriptions of twenty instruments used in chemical investigations. *Kitab al-Asrar* deals with the preparation and utilisation of chemical substances. He classified 'source substances' into plants, animals and minerals, and this classification of the three kingdoms still holds. He was the first to produce sulphuric acid and also prepared alcohol by fermenting sweet products.

His contribution as a philosopher is also well known. The basic elements of his philosophical system are the creator, spirit, matter, space and time. He discussed their characteristics in detail. His concepts of space and time as constituting a continuum are outstanding. His philosophical views were, however, criticised by a number of Muslim scholars of the era.

He was a prolific author, who has left monumental treatises on numerous subjects. He has more than 200 outstanding scientific contributions to his credit, out of which about half deal with medicine and 21 with chemistry. He also wrote on physics, mathematics, astronomy and optics, but these writings are no longer extant. A number of his books, including *al-Jami fi al-Tibb, Kitab al-Mansuri, al-Hawi, Kitab al-Judari wa al-Hasbah, al-Muluki, Maqalah fi al-Hasa fi al-Kulli wa al-Mathanah, Kitab al-Qalb, Kitab al-Mafasil, Kitab al-Ilaj al-Ghuraba, Bur al-Sa'ah,* and *al-Taqsim wa al-Takhsir*, were published in various European languages.

His works were translated to Latin in the 13th century in Sicily by the Jewish physician Faraj ibn Salim under the orders of Charles I, king of Sicily, and was named the *Continens*. Its influence on European medicine was very significant. His works were again translated into other European languages and printed in various places—in Venice in 1489, in Brussels in 1549, in London in 1747 and in Gottingen in 1781—being published more than forty times. About 40 of his manuscripts are still extant in the museums and libraries of Iran, Britain, France (Paris) and India (Rampur and Bankipur). His contribution has greatly influenced the development of science, in general, and medicine, in particular.

"Indeed, Pharmacy can trace much of its historical foundations to the singular achievements of this ninth-century Persian scholar" was stated by Michael E. Flannery, Executive Vice President and Chief Financial Officer of the Duchossois Group—a multibillion dollar investment company. Al-Razi and Ibn Sina remained up to the 17th century the indisputable authorities on medicine in the world.

Abu al-Nasr al-Farabi (870-950)[149]

Al-Farabi, son of a General, was born in a small village named Wasij, near Farab in Turkistan. In Europe his Latinised name is Al Pharabius. His early education took place in Farab and Bukhara (now a city of Uzbekistan) after which he undertook higher studies in Baghdad where he attained remarkable heights in his scholarship. He worked as a *qadi* (judge) and later as a teacher. Based in Baghdad he travelled to different lands and also studied in Damascus and Egypt for some time. He faced much hardship and even worked as a caretaker in a garden. Later he became a

---

[149] Said, H. M., 1991, p. 15-16.

courtier and companion of King Sayf al-Dawlah in Halab (Aleppo, Syria).

Al-Farabi, a multi-lingual encyclopaedist, dedicated his entire life to an academic pursuit and never married. His major contributions are in philosophy, logic and sociology with notable contributions in music, medicine and mathematics. He was a Neoplatonic philosopher and synthesised Platonism and Aristotelism with theology. He wrote rich commentaries on Aristotle's 'Physics', Meteorology, Logic, *etc*. In philosophy, he came to be known as the 'Second Teacher' (*al-Mu'allim al-Thani*) with Aristotle being the First. One of the important contributions of al-Farabi was the division of logic into two categories: *takhayyul* (idea) and *thubut* (proof). It put logic in a better perspective and made its study easier to understand.

In addition, he produced a large number of books on several other subjects embodying his original contribution. Although many of his books have been lost, 117 are known, out of which 43 are on logic, 11 on metaphysics, 7 on ethics, 7 on political science and 17 on music, medicine and sociology, while 11 are commentaries. Some of his more famous books include the book *Fusus al-Hikam*, which remained a text book of philosophy for several centuries in various centres of learning. His books on psychology and metaphysics were largely based on his own work. In physics he demonstrated the existence of void.

The book *Ara Ahl al-Madinah al- Fadilah* (*Opinions of the People of the Virtuous City*) is a significant early contribution to sociology and political science. This was the most famous of several such books written by him. The book *Kitab lhsa al-Ulum* discusses classification and fundamental principles of science in a unique and useful manner. He also wrote a book on music, captioned *Kitab al-Musiqa*. He was a great expert in the art and science of music and invented several musical instruments, besides contributing to the knowledge of musical notes. It has been reported that he could play his instrument so well as to make people laugh or weep at will.

Al-Farabi exercised great influence on philosophy, science and social science for several centuries both in the East and West.

Abu al-Abbas Ahmad al-Farghani (c. 860)[150]

Al-Farghani was born in Farghana (a region in Central Asia running through Uzbekistan, Kyrgyzstan and Tajikistan). He was a renowned astronomer and scientist serving the *Bayt al-Hikmah* at the time of Caliph Ma'mun. He was known as Alfraganus in Europe and a lunar crater is named after him.

His famous work was the *Kitab fi al-Harakat al-Samawiyyah wa Jawami Ilm al-Nujum* (*The Book on Celestial Motion and Thorough Science of the Stars*), which came to be known as the 'Elements of Astronomy'. He worked with the diameter of the earth, the distances and diameter of other planets. He believed that axial precession affected the planets and stars. This indicates that al-Farghani knew that the planets were not just spherical but were rotating bodies whose axis changed. Ptolemy had believed that precession affected the stars only.

Two Latin translations of his book were done in the 12th century. It influenced *The Sphere* by Sacrobosco (13th century teacher in University of Paris). A Hebrew translation was completed by Jacob Anatoli (Jacob was a 13th century translator of Arabic works to Hebrew sponsored by Emperor Frederic II) from which a third Latin translation was done in 1590. Jacob Golius (Dutch orientalist and mathematician, who also translated the *Sihah* of al-Jawhari) produced another translation along with the Arabic original in 1669.

The *Fihrist* of Ibn Nadim ascribes two more books to al-

---

[150] Said, H. M., 1991, p. 17-18.

Farghani, *Kitab al-Fusul Ikhtiyar al-Majisti* (*The Book of Chapters: A Summary of Almagest*) and *Kitab Amal al-Rukhamat* (*Book for Construction of Sundials*).

Abu al-Qasim Khalaf al-Zahrawi (936-1013)[151]

Abu al-Qasim Khalaf ibn al-Abbas al-Zahrawi (Abulcasis) was born in Zahra in the neighbourhood of Cordoba in Spain. He was one of the most renowned physician, surgeon and dentist of his time with remarkable contributions in surgery including dental surgery.

His amazing medical breakthroughs are embodied in his famous encyclopaedia called *al-Tasrif*. It comprises different aspects of medical science in thirty volumes. Three of these volumes or books are on surgery. In these books he describes in details various aspects of surgical treatment including cauterisation, styptics, removal of stones from the bladder, dissection of animals, midwifery and surgery of the eye, ear and throat. He perfected several delicate operations, including removal of a dead foetus and amputation. He gave a comprehensive account of surgical treatment in specialised branches, whose modern equivalents are E.N.T., ophthalmology, *etc*. He perfected cauterisation and applied it on a variety of surgical operations.

In his book, al-Zahrawi also discussed the preparation of various medicines and the application of such techniques as sublimation and decantation. He was the first to describe haemophilia (impaired blood clotting) in detail. Al-Zahrawi was also an expert in dentistry, and his book contains sketches of various instruments used and developed by him. In his books he gives details of various important dental operations and the

---

[151] Said, H. M., 1991, p. 59-60.

instruments used in those operations. He discussed the problem of non-aligned or deformed teeth and how to rectify these defects (orthodontics). He developed the technique of preparing artificial teeth and of replacement of defective teeth by the artificial ones.

Among the instruments he invented are those for internal examination of the ear and urethra and another one for removing foreign bodies from the throat. His book contains numerous diagrams and illustrations of surgical instruments used or developed by him.

Al-Tasrif was first translated by Gerard of Cremona into Latin in the Middle Ages. Several other editions followed and it became a part of the medical curriculum in European countries for many centuries. Al-Zahrawi influenced the field of medicine, surgery and dentistry profoundly.

Al-Mas'udi (died 957)[152]

Abu al-Hasan Ali al-Mas'udi was a descendent of Ibn Mas'ud, a famous Companion of the Prophet. He was a pioneering geographer, historian and earth scientist. He travelled extensively and acquired first-hand knowledge of geography, cultures, *etc.* He visited Istikhar, Fars, Baghdad, India (Multan, Mansurah—capital of Sindh, Gujarat, Deccan), Sri Lanka, Indo-China and China. On the western side of the Indian Ocean, he is known to have visited Madagascar and proceeded to Zanzibar, Oman and then to Basra.

In Basra, he wrote the *Muruj al-Dhahab wa al-Ma'adin al-Jawahir* (*Meadows of Gold and Mines of Precious Stones*) in which he narrates in captivating detail his experiences in various countries, climates and his contacts with various people—Jewish, Persian, Indian and Christian societies. He recorded his experiences with true scientific inquisitiveness and neglected no

---

[152] Said, H. M., 1991, p. 45-46.

source of information. He also provided important information about music of the early Arabs and other countries. In this book of world history, al-Mas'udi was one of the first to combine history and 'scientific' geography in a large-scale work.

From Basra he went to Cairo via Syria. He wrote his second comprehensive book *Muruj al-Zaman* in thirty volumes. In it he described in details the geography and history of the countries that he had visited. The book was completed in 947 CE. He also prepared a supplement, called *Kitab al-Awsat*, in which he has compiled historical events chronologically. In 957 CE, the year of his death, he completed his last book *Kitab al-Tanbih wa al-Ishraf*, in which his systematic study of history takes into account the perspectives of geography, anthropology, sociology and ecology. He also included a summary of his earlier book as well as an erratum. He mentions having written 34 books in addition to *al-Tanbih* itself, but, unfortunately, only two others have survived.

Using a scientific and analytical approach he gave an account of the causes of the earthquake of 955 CE, and discussed various topics of earth sciences including the water of the Red Sea. He is the first author to mention windmills, which were invented by the Muslims of Sijistan. It is interesting to note that he was one of the early scientists who propounded a theory of evolution, namely from minerals to plant, plant to animal and animal to man.

His researches, books, records and views were based on a scientific approach and provided important contributions to social and earth sciences which influenced the understanding and development of these subjects. Al-Mas'udi also had insight into the causes of rise and fall of nations. By introducing the elements of analysis, reflection and criticism, he initiated a change in the art of historical writing, which was later on improved and established by Ibn Khaldun.

Abu al-Wafa Muhammad al-Buzjani (940-997)[153]

Al-Buzjani was born in Buzjan, Nishapur, in north-eastern Persia. He was a great applied mathematician and astronomer. He carried out his major work in Baghdad, Iraq.

In mathematics, he made immense contributions, especially, in geometry and trigonometry. In geometry, he gave solutions of geometrical problems using one opening of the compass and developed the method of constructing equivalent squares, regular polyhedras, regular hectagons, taking for its side half the side of the equilateral triangle inscribed in the same circle, and parabola by points and geometrical solution of the equations:

$$x^4 = a \quad \text{and} \quad x^4 + ax^3 = b.$$

His contribution to trigonometry was extensive. He was the first to show the generality of the sine theorem relative to spherical triangles. He developed a new method of constructing sine tables with the value of sine 30 being correct to the eighth decimal place. He developed the relations for sine (a+b) and the formula:

$$2\sin^2 - a/2 = 1 - \cos a$$

$$\sin a = 2\sin - a/2 \cos - a/2$$

He introduced the secant and cosecant for the first time and advanced the study of the tangent and calculated a table of tangents. A significant part of today's trigonometry can be credited to him. In astronomy, his works were of about the same level as those of Tycho Brahe who studied trigonometry six centuries later.

Sometime between 961 and 976 he wrote *Kitab fi Ma Yahtaj*

---

[153] Said, H. M., 1991, p. 13-14.

ilayh al-Kuttab wa al-Ummal min Ilm al-Hisab (Applied Mathematics for Scribes and Businessmen). This was an applied mathematics book, the first of its kind, for people of other professions. Abu al-Wafa did not use the numerals in this book. All the numbers were written in words and all calculations had already been worked out to make it easy for professionals who did not have a mathematical background. In the preface to this book Abu al-Wafa wrote that it 'comprises all that an experienced or novice, subordinate or supervisor in arithmetic needs to know,' and was for 'the art of civil servants, the employment of land taxes and all kinds of business needed in administrations, proportions, multiplication, division, measurements, land taxes, distribution, exchange and all other practices used by various categories of men for doing business and which are useful to them in their daily life.'

He wrote a large number of books on mathematics and other subjects. Most of these books are no longer extant or exist in modified form. His extant books include *Kitab Ilm al-Hisab*, a practical book on mathematics, *Al-Kitab al-Kamil (The Complete Book)*, *Kitab al-Handasah (Book on Applied Geometry)*.

Abu al-Hasan al-Mawardi (c. 972-1055)[154]

Abu al-Hasan Ali ibn Muhammad al-Mawardi was born in Basra. After completing his general education, he studied *fiqh* (Islamic jurisprudence) from the jurist Abu al-Wahid al-Simari. He then went to Baghdad for advanced studies under Sheikh Abd al-Hamid and Abdullah al-Baqi.

His expertise in *fiqh* and political science gave him the opportunity to avail high positions. He initially served as a judge and then as the chief justice. After that he was appointed as the ambassador of the Abbasid Caliph al-Qa'im bi Amr Allah. He was

---

[154] Said, H. M., 1991, p. 47-48.

sent to a number of countries as the head of special missions. He established harmonious relations between the declining Abbasid Caliphate and the rising powers of the Seljuks and Buwayhids. For his professionalism he was favoured with rich gifts and tributes by most of the rulers. Al-Mawardi was a great diplomat, jurist and the most able political scientist in the Middle Ages.

His contribution in political science comprises a number of monumental books, the most famous of which are *Kitab al-Ahkam al-Sultaniyyah, Qanun al-Wazarah* and *Kitab Nasihah al-Mulk*. The books discuss the principles of political science, with special reference to the functions and duties of the caliphs, the chief minister, ministers and relationships between various elements of public and government and measures needed to strengthen the government and ensure victory in war. Two of these books, *Al-Ahkam al-Sultaniyyah* and *Qanun al-Wazarah*, have been translated and published into various languages.

His 'Doctrine of Necessity' favoured a strong caliphate and was against the delegation of unlimited powers to the governors which tended to create chaos. On the other hand, he also laid down clear principles for the election of the caliph and qualities of the voters. He asserted that chief among those characteristics was attainment of a high degree of intellectual level and high morality.

He was an eminent jurist and his book *al-Hawi* on the principles of jurisprudence is held in high repute. He was also known as a *muhaddith* or expert on hadith traditions of the Prophet and wrote a book on ethics called *Kitab Adab al-Dunya wa al-Din*. This book became very popular and can still be found in some Muslim countries.

Al-Mawardi is the most famous and original thinkers in political science in the Middle Ages. His work was further developed later on by Ibn Khaldun. There is also similarity between the life and works of Niccolo Machiavelli to that of al-Mawardi. Machiavelli also worked as a diplomat and wrote *The*

Prince, a political book on the rule of conduct for the princes about 500 years after al-Mawardi.

Abu Ali Hasan ibn al-Haytham (965-1040)[155]

Ibn al-Haytham (Alhazen) was one of the most eminent physicists of the past with outstanding contribution in optics. He was born in Basra and after initial education there he moved to Baghdad for further studies. He was employed by Caliph al-Hakim to find means to stop the floods of the River Nile in Egypt. Not inclined towards engineering he did not comply and instead feigned madness till the caliph died. He travelled to Spain and pursued subjects of his interest—optics, mathematics, physics and medicine. He produced remarkable books on each of the subjects and was another pioneer in the development of the scientific method.

He laid the foundation of modern optics with exactly the same understanding and principles as is recognised today. He was the first to write a book on the subject. He studied the transmission of light through various mediums and discovered the laws of refraction. He was the first to carry out experiments on the dispersion of light. He investigated into the theories of various physical phenomena related to light like eclipses, shadows, rainbows and the physical nature of light. For his extensive researches and contributions in optics, he is considered the father of modern optics.

He is the first to describe the process of vision with an accurate description of the various parts of the eye and the earliest use of the camera obscura. The word 'camera' is derived from the dark room, '*qamarah*'[156] where he carried out his experiments. He also investigated the magnifying power of a lens. Al-Haytham, in

---

[155] Said, H. M., 1991, p. 25-26.
[156] Al Hossaini, 2007, p. 29.

Mizan al-Hikmah, described atmospheric refraction and the density of the atmosphere developing a relation between atmospheric height and density.

Ancient Greek philosophers maintained two types of idea about vision. They thought either something went out of the eyes so that people could see things or something entered the eyes to make vision possible. The second speculation was nearer to the truth.[157] Ibn Haytham contradicted Ptolemy and Euclid's theory that eyes emit rays with which objects are seen. He showed, scientifically, that the rays originate not from the eye or from any object but were light reflected in the objects of vision. He researched in catoptrics (reflections) with spherical and parabolic mirrors and discovered an important problem known as Alhazen's problem. He also worked with the ratio between the angle of incidence and refraction which has now developed into Snell's Law.

His contributions in physics and mathematics were far-reaching. He discussed the theories of attraction between masses, and apparently was aware of the magnitude of acceleration due to gravity. In mechanics, regarding the motion of a body, he was the first to say that a body moves in a straight line perpetually unless an external force changes its direction or stops it. This is equivalent to the first law of motion by Newton. The *Historian's History* states that Newton owed the law of gravity more to the Muslims than to the fall of an apple in his garden.[158] In mathematics, he established links between geometry and algebra, thus developing analytical geometry.

The scientific method, developed and applied by the Muslims, comprising a systematic empirical observation of physical phenomena and linking together into a scientific theory,

---

[157] Al Hassani, 2007, p. 26-27.
[158] Hasan, M., 2004, p. 598.

is apparent in his writing. This was a major breakthrough in scientific methodology, as opposed to guesswork and gestures of the past, and placed scientific pursuits on a sound foundation comprising a systematic relationship between observation, hypothesis and verification. He wrote about 200 books but very few have survived. He had written a book on the subject of evolution and his work on cosmology was translated into Latin, Hebrew and other languages. The Latin translation of his main work, *Kitab al-Manazir*, influenced Western science.

George Sarton said,

> "He, Ibn Al-Haytham, was the greatest Muslim physicist and student of optics of all times. Whether it be in England or far away Persia, all drank from the same fountain. He exerted a great influence on European thought from Bacon to Kepler".[159]

Leonardo da Vinci was also among those whom he influenced.[160] Max Meyerhof admits that Roger Bacon and all early European scholars, notably Pol Witelo, base their optical works largely on the Latin translation of Ibn Haytham's *Book of Optics*.[161]

The Alhazen crater in the moon was named after al-Haytham.

Abu Rayhan al-Biruni (973-1048)[162]

Al-Biruni was one of the greatest scientists of all time. Works such as his and those of others like Jabir and al-Haytham laid down the foundation of modern science. A contemporary of the famous Ibn

---

[159] Al Hassani, 2007, p. 27.
[160] Ahmad, 1984, p. 169.
[161] *Ibid.*, p. 169.
[162] Said, H. M., 1991, p. 11-12

Sina (Avicenna) he was born in Kheva, former capital of Khwarizm and now located in Uzbekistan. His fame as a scholar grew from his youth and later he became part of the court of Sultan Mahmud of Ghazni who ruled an empire consisting approximately the area of Afghanistan, eastern Iran and Pakistan.

On a number of occasions, he travelled with Sultan Mahmud on expeditions to India. There he studied Indian philosophy, religion, and mathematics. He developed the geography of India and recorded all the historical and social observations of India in a book named *Kitab Tarikh al-Hind*. His details were so graphic and complete that it was still being referenced 600 years later in *Ain-e Akbari* written by Abu al-Fadl during the Moghul times. He translated two books from Sanskrit to Arabic: the *Sakaya* (*Samkhya*) on philosophy, which deals with cosmogony, the creation of things and their types, and *Patanjal*, a metaphysical book on what happens after the soul leaves the body according to Indian religious philosophy.

His book *Al-Athar al-Baqiyah* is about geography and history. He provided the latitudes and longitudes of various places in the book along with several aspects of physical and economic geography of those regions. He observed that the Indus valley of India must be considered as an ancient sea basin filled with alluvial sediments. Such geological deduction was remarkable and so advanced for his time as it was centuries later that concepts of sedimentation and orogeny developed in Europe.

After completing his study of India, he returned to Ghazni where he worked on his most famous book *al-Qanun al-Mas'udi*. The book discusses several theorems of astronomy, trigonometry, solar, lunar and planetary motions and related topics. His *Kitab al-Jamahir al-Jawahir* is a book on minerology that deals with the properties of various precious stones. He accurately determined the densities of 18 different stones. In the *Kitab al-Saydanah*, an extensive medical encyclopaedia, he incorporated the Indian medical information into the vast Arabic medical knowledge.

He discussed the rotation of earth on its axis, centuries before anyone else, in his book *Miftah Ilm al-Hay'ah* (*Key to Astronomy*). This book is no longer extant but the book and its purpose is mentioned in his *Tarikh al-Hind*. He determined that the speed of light was immense compared to the speed of sound. He investigated into phenomena like Siamese twins and also observed that flowers contained 3, 4, 5, 6 or 18 petals but never 7 or 9.

Al-Biruni is considered the first anthropologist and a pioneer of experimental psychology and comparative religion. Arthur Jeffery, Australian professor of Semitic languages, states,

> "It is rare until modern times to find so fair and unprejudiced a statement of the views of other religions, so earnest an attempt to study them in the best sources, and such care to find a method which for this branch of study would be both rigorous and just".[163]

Ibn Sina (980-1037)[164]

Abu Ali al-Husayn ibn Abdullah ibn Sina was born in Afshana near Bukhara and was educated there. He was another great versatile genius the world has seen and his contribution in a variety of disciplines is remarkable.

He started general studies as a child and became a *hafiz* of the Qur'an by the age of 10. He then studied medicine and became famous for his expertise. By the age of 17 he had cured the king of Bukhara from an ailment after many established physicians had failed. When the king wanted to reward him, he only asked for permission to study in the king's uniquely stocked library. After further enriching his knowledge, he moved to Jurjan where the

---

[163] WR5.
[164] Said, H. M., 1991, p. 33-34.

Khwarizm shah welcomed him. It was here that the historic meeting between the two great minds of the world, Ibn Sina and al-Biruni, took place. Later, he moved to Rayy and then to Hamadan where he also treated King Shams al-Dawlah of Hamadan successfully for colic. From there he went to Isfahan where he wrote many of his monumental works. Finally, he returned to Hamadan where he died.

His major contribution in medicine was the phenomenal book *al-Qanun* known as the *Canon* in Latin. It was an immense medical encyclopaedia of over a million words. The book included all his knowledge and discoveries. It also contained researches from all the previous Muslim and ancient sources. Its systematic approach, formal perfection and intrinsic value made it a milestone in medical knowledge. It dealt with such subjects as the distribution of diseases by water and soil, the interaction between psychology and health, and made an immense advancement from previous works like the *Hawi* of the al-Razi and the work on contagious nature of phthisis and tuberculosis by Ali ibn Abbas. He was the first to describe meningitis and made a rich contribution to anatomy, gynaecology and child health. The book described 760 drugs for different diseases.

He had studied philosophy and logic, of both Muslims and ancient Greeks, in Bukhara under Abu Abdullah al-Natili, a famous philosopher of the time. In philosophy he synthesised Muslim theology with Aristotelian and Neoplatonic traditions. His greatest encyclopaedic work was the *Kitab al-Shifa*, an incredibly long compendium which covers every kind of knowledge—medicine, philosophy, astronomy, history, ethics, psychology, *etc.* He divided the sciences into two broad categories:

i. Theoretical knowledge: physics, geosciences, mathematics and metaphysics.

ii. Practical knowledge: ethics, economics and politics.

The *Shifa* was also a source of inspiration to the founders of geological thought in Europe, such as Leonardo Da Vinci and Steno in the 17th century and James Hutton in the 18th century.[165] His treatise on minerals was one of the main sources of geology of the Christian encyclopaedists of the 13th century. Besides the *Shifa* his well-known treatises in philosophy are *al-Najah* and *al-Isharat*.

In physics his contribution included the study of different forms of energy (heat, light and mechanical), concepts of force, vacuum and infinity, the finite speed of light, specific gravity and the use of an open-air thermometer. In mathematics he explained the 'casting out nines' test for verification of squares and cubes.

In the field of sound and music, he improved al-Farabi's work. His work led towards the harmonic system, the limit of consonances above which human's ear is unable to distinguish. In chemistry, he did not believe in chemical transmutation and opined that metals differed fundamentally.

Nizam al-Mulk (1018-1092)

Nizam al-Mulk was the title of the Seljuk *wazir* (prime minister) Abu Ali al-Hasan al-Tusi. He was the chief administrator of Khorasan under the Ghaznavids before becoming the *wazir* for the Seljuk sultans Alp Arsalan and Malik Shah.

Historian Gibbon regarded him as 'one of the most illustrious ministers of the East.' Besides being an administrator extraordinaire, he also was a great scholar and social scientist. He wrote the extensive treaties *Siyasat Nama* (*Book of Governance*) which is concerned, among other topics, with guiding the ruler with regard to the facts, structure and ideals of the government and how it should be run. 'The work is devoted to explicating the

---

[165] Al Hassani, 2007, p. 244.

proper role of soldiers, police, spies and finance officials'[166] and provides ethical advice emphasising the need for justice and religious piety in the ruler. Nizam al-Mulk defines in detail what he views as justice— that all people be 'given their due' and that the weak be protected. He also wrote a book titled *Dastur al-Wuzara*, written for his son Abu al-Fath Fakhr al-Mulk, which outlines princely education, manners and conduct.

Nizam al-Mulk established a large number of colleges of higher education and libraries throughout the country. The most famous were the schools of Nizamiyyah University which gained world renown. These schools, in many aspects, were to be the models of universities that were established in Europe.

After administering the affairs of Malik Shah for some thirty years Nizam al-Mulk was overthrown by his enemy the Chamberlain Taj al-Mulk due to the instigation of the sultanah (queen) Turkhan Khatun. He was impeached after he had impetuously declared that his cap and ink-horn, the badges of his office, were connected by divine decree with the throne and diadem of the sultan.

There are legends about him, Omar Khayyam and Hasan ibn Sabah, leader of the Assassins of Alamut. In 1092 he is said to have been assassinated at an old age, near Nahavand of Persia, by a member of the Assassin sect who had approached him disguised as a dervish. Nizam al-Mulk was buried in Isfahan in the grounds of a theological school, in the north of Ahmad Abad, which he had built. The mausoleum contains a number of other graves which include those of Malik Shah and Turkhan Khatun.

Omar Khayyam (c. 1044-1123)[167]

Ghiyath al-Din Abu al-Fatih Umar Ibn Ibrahim al-Khayyam was

---

[166] Lapidus, Ira, 2002, p. 151.
[167] Said, H. M., 1991, p. 41-42.

born in Nishapur, provincial capital of Khorasan. His contributions are in mathematics, astronomy, poetry and metaphysics. He was a dedicated scholar and refused employment in the sultan's court preferring to stay away from politics even though he was acquainted with Nizam al-Mulk. He dedicated himself to the seeking of knowledge and travelled to great centres of learning in Samarqand, Bukhara, Balkh and Isfahan.

In algebra, he classified most algebraic equations including third degree equations. He offered solutions for a number of them including geometric solutions of cubic equations and partial geometric solutions of most other equations. He also developed the binomial expansion when the exponent is a positive integer. His contributions in other fields of science include the development of a method to measure specific gravity and a study of generalities of Euclid.

Assigned by Sultan Malik Shah, he developed a solar calendar in the observatory in Rayy. It was remarkably accurate with the error of 1 day in 3770 years and was superior to the Georgian calendar which had an error of 1 day in 3330 years. He was also an eminent poet. His book *Rubai'yyat-e Khayyam* (*The Quatrains of Khayyam*) was translated by Edward Fitzgerald in 1839 and is recognised as a world classic.

He wrote a number of books and monographs, of which ten books and thirty monographs have been identified of which four are about mathematics, one algebra, one geometry, three physics and three metaphysics. His masterpieces include *Maqalat fi al-Jabr wa al-Muqabalah* in algebra, *Risalah dar Wujud* and *Nawruz Namah* in metaphysics.

His influence on geometry in general and analytical geometry, in particular, is remarkable. Five hundred years later, Descartes applied the same geometrical approach in resolving cubes.

Abu Hamid al-Ghazali (1058-1128)[168]

Abu Hamid al-Ghazali was born in Khorasan. He studied in renowned academic centres of Nishapur and Baghdad. Due to his remarkable intellect and scholarship he was awarded professorship in the Nizamiyyah University of Baghdad, the most famous university in the world of that time. Soon, he would become the head teacher in the university at a significantly young age. As his fame grew, many scholars enrolled in his classes. Royalties and nobilities from all over competed to send their scions to his classes. He became significantly wealthy.

A few years later, he went through a, seemingly, epistemological crisis. He gave up his position, severed all worldly interests and relationships and became a wandering scholar visiting other scholars and living an isolated frugal life. But the volume of books that he produced during this phase of his life and remarkable outpouring of intellect in it does not show any sign of crisis. If anything, the crisis was an intense abnegation of self pride that he had developed with so much worldly success, and also a self doubt that he was not engaged in the right way of seeking knowledge.

After the initial period of self purging, for what others see as a crisis, for him it appears to be an epistemological challenge. He endeavoured on learning and cleansing the whole gamut of knowledge of the world that had accumulated up to his time period. It was too intense a work to be done with any worldly distractions or commitments. He must have known that to make such an immense contribution in all the fields of knowledge, earthly ties and wants would only fetter him. So, he left everything and went on a journey to 'experience' knowledge himself rather than being satisfied with theoretical assessments. He also took recourse to solitary contemplation and live in mosques.

---

[168] Said, H. M., 1991, p. 19-20.

Al-Ghazali lived in an era when philosophy, science, theology and Sufism were all in confused flux. Multiplicity of thoughts, both correct and incorrect, abounded. With his vast intellect he summed up all the knowledge that existed during his time and cleansed it all of fallacies.

In philosophy, he discovered a lot of speculations in the works of both the Greek and Muslim philosophers. With great intellectual discernment and logic, he refuted such Incoherencies in his book *Tahafat al-Falasifah* (*Incoherence of the Philosophers*). He cleansed Sufism of superstitions that contradicted religion. He did not agree with their 'union' with God concept but accommodated 'nearness' to God.[169]

He made a list of subjects and classified these either as praiseworthy or as blameworthy. For example, he said that astronomy or mathematics were praiseworthy while astrology was blameworthy. In short, he declared which subjects were real sciences and which were fallacies. Al-Ghazali, thus, changed the overall trend of knowledge.

He wrote a large number of books, one of the masterpiece of which Is *Ihya Ulum al-Din* (*The Revival of the Religious Sciences*) in which he discussed all aspects of Islam as a religion. Some of his books were translated to European languages during the medieval ages. He influenced many European thinkers and scholars.

Abu Marwan ibn Zuhr (1091-1161)[170]

Ibn Zuhr was born in Seville, of Muslim Spain, and studied medicine. After specialisation he became the physician of the last al-Moravid and the first al-Mohad rulers. He was very systematic in his research and work. He laid stress on observation and experimented on animals before applying the drugs to human

[169] Sharif, M. M., 2016, p. 623.
[170] Said, H. M., 1991, p. 35-36.

beings. His systematic approach allowed him to make several remarkable breakthroughs and discoveries. His methodology is, more or less, still being followed in the world.

He was the first parasitologist describing correctly contagious scabies and itch mites. He prescribed tracheotomy and direct feeding through the gullet and rectum (rectal alimentation) in cases where normal feeding was not possible. He also gave proper clinical descriptions of intestinal phthisis, mediastinal tumours, inflammation of the middle ear, pericarditis, *etc.*

He wrote a number of books out of which only three are extant. *Kitab al-Taysir fi al-Mudawah wa al-Tadbir* (*Book of Simplification Concerning Therapeutics and Diet*) was written at the request of the Spanish jurist and philosopher Ibn Rushd (Averroes). It is the most important work of Ibn Zuhr and describes several of Ibn Zuhr's original contributions. The book systematically first gives the pathological conditions in details followed by the therapy. His *Kitab al-Iqtisad fi Islah al-Anfus wa al-Ajsad* (*Book of the Middle Course Concerning the Reformation of Souls and the Bodies*) gives a summary of diseases, therapeutics and hygiene written specially for the benefit of the layman. Its initial part is a valuable discourse on psychology. *Kitab al-Aghdhiyah* (*Book on Foodstuffs*) describes different types of food and drugs and their effects on health.

His contributions greatly influenced medical science for several centuries both in the East and the West. His books were translated into Hebrew and Latin. He influenced the philosopher-physician Maimonides. In Europe, his works remained popular as late as the advent of the 18th century.

Abu Abdullah Muhammad al-Idrisi (1099-1166)[171]

Al-Idrisi was born in Ceuta and educated in Cordoba of Muslim Spain. He travelled considerably and upon the invitation of King Roger II ended up in Palermo, Sicily. His contribution was in two areas: botany and geography.

In botanical studies he researched medical plants for use as medicines and drugs. He studied all the medical literature regarding plants from various sources and realised that only some progress has been accomplished since the time of the Greeks which, in itself, was limited. He went on to rectify that by launching an investigative field work and research. He collected plants and data not known previously into a botanical catalogue and made special references to those with medicinal properties. He wrote several books on this subject but his major contribution was *Kitab al-Jami li Sifat Ashtat al-Nabatat*. Due to his work a large number of plants and their medicinal properties came to be known to all the medical practitioners. He also wrote about zoology specifically fauna of certain regions.

His other major contribution was in the field of geography. Apparently, in his widespread travels (*rihlah*), he had picked up significant geographic knowledge. In Palermo, al-Idrisi led a team of geographers and cartographers and used a range of sources that primarily included the Muslim classical works. He produced a silver planisphere map of the earth. He also wrote a book which he named *al-Kitab al-Rujuri* (*The Book of Roger*)[172] with geographical descriptions of different regions of the world—Asia, Africa and Europe—and included various information, for example, the complex geography of Upper Nile, the caste system in India, the gold trade of Ghana, the Buddhist belief of Chinese

---

[171] Said, H. M., 1991, p. 21.
[172] Lyons, Jonathan, 2009, p. 94.

kings, the cannibals of Borneo, *etc.*[173] His work developed into a geographical encyclopaedia of the world of his time.

His books were translated to Latin and for several centuries remained popular in both the East and the West.

Ibn al-Baytar (d. 1248)[174]

Abu Muhammad Abdullah ibn Ahmad ibn al-Baytar was one of the best scientists of Muslim Spain and the greatest botanist and pharmacist of his age. He was born in Malaga (Malaqah). He learned botany from a learned botanist named Abu al-Abbas al-Nabati. Initially he, along with al-Nabati, collected and studied plants from in and around Spain. In 1219, he left Spain on an academic field work which took him along the northern coast of Africa and well into Asia Minor (Turkey). He carried out major studies in regions that includes Bugia (Eastern Algeria), Tunis, Tripoli, Barqa (Cyrnaica of eastern Libya), Adalia (Antalya, Turkey) and Constantinople (Istanbul, Turkey). After 1224, he was appointed the chief herbalist by al-Kamil, the ruler of Egypt. After that he studied the plants of Damascus, Arabia and Palestine.

Ibn Baytar's major contribution is his book *Kitab al-Jami fi al-Adwiyah al-Mufradah* (*Compendium on Simple Medicaments and Foods*). It became one of the greatest compilations dealing with medicinal plants. It contains 1,400 different studies mainly about medicinal plants and vegetables. It includes 200 plants not known earlier. He referred to 150 authors mostly Arabic and also 20 Greek medicinal writers. His full work was published in Latin in 1758 but parts of it came to be known in the West much earlier. His other major contribution is *Kitab al-Mughni fi al-Adwiyah al-*

---

[173] Lyons, Jonathan, 2009, p. 94.
[174] Said, H. M., 1991, p. 23-24.

Mufradah, an encyclopaedic work on plants that are used in the treatment of various diseases related to the head, ear, eye *etc.*

Ibn Rushd (1128-1198)[175]

Abu al-Walid Muhammad ibn Ahmad ibn Muhammad ibn Rushd (Averroes) was born in Cordoba, Spain. His father and grandfather were both judges and well versed in jurisprudence (*fiqh*) of the Maliki school in Shari'ah. Ibn Rushd studied philosophy and law from Ja'far Harun and Ibn Bajjah. He also studied medicine making remarkable contributions in jurisprudence, medicine, logic and philosophy.

His book on jurisprudence, *Bidayah al-Mujtahid wa Nihayah al-Muqtasid*, is considered one of the best in the Maliki school. In medicine, his famous book *Kitab al-Kuliyyat fi al-Tibb* was written around 1160. Its Latin translation is called the *Colliget*. In it Ibn Rushd throws new light on various aspects of medicine, including diagnosis, cure and prevention of diseases. This medical encyclopaedia dwells on specialised areas rather than approach the vaster scope of Ibn Sina's *al-Qanun*. He has written 20 books on medicine.

In response to al-Ghazali's *Tahafat al-Falasifah (Incoherence of the Philosophers)* he wrote the *Tahafut al-Tahafut (Incoherence of the Incoherence)*. Al-Ghazali believed that any individual act of a natural phenomenon occurred only because God willed it to happen. On the other hand, Ibn Rushd believed that phenomena followed natural laws that God had created.[176] He also wrote three commentaries on the works of Aristotle which became very popular in Europe.

Ibn Rushd had also written commentaries on al-Farabi's

---

[175] Said, H. M., 1991, p. 31-32.
[176] Kadri, Sadakat, 2012, p. 118-119.

logic, Plato's *Republic*, Galen's treatise on fevers, *etc.* In astronomy, he wrote a treatise on the motions of the sphere and named it *Kitab fi Harakat al-Falak*. He also wrote a summary based on the *Almagest* dividing it into two parts: a description of spheres and the movement of spheres. This was translated into Hebrew by Jacob Anatoli in 1231. Ibn Rushd wrote a zoological commentary on Aristotle's *De Anima*. It was translated into Latin by Michael Scot.

Eighty-seven of his books are extant. He was one of the greatest thinkers of all time and influenced the West from the 12th to 16th century. Aquinas' interest in Islamic studies could be attributed to the infiltration of 'Latin Averroism' in the 13th century, especially in the University of Paris. The treatises of Saint Thomas Aquinas show being profoundly influenced by and, in fact, are based on the works of Ibn Sina, al-Ghazali and Ibn Rushd.[177] Maimonides, the medieval Sephardic Jewish philosopher who became one of the most influential Torah scholars of the Middle Ages, was a student of Ibn Rushd.[178]

Fakhr al-Din al-Razi (1149-1209)

Fakhr al-Din al-Razi, often confused with al-Razi, was born in 1149 in Rayy (today a district of Tehran). Fakhr al-Din, theologian, philosopher and scientist, wrote many books of which *Sharh Uyun al-Hikmah* (*Commentary on Uyun al-Hikmah*) became very famous. It is divided into three parts: logic, physics and metaphysics. The ancient term physics, as defined by Aristotle, meant 'nature'. Muslim scholars took a scientific view of it. The 'physics' (*tabi'iyyat*) section of al-Razi includes topics like space, bodies, time, motion and meteorology. Another book, *Al-*

---

[177] Lyons, Jonathan, 2009, p. 190-192.
[178] WR21.

Mabahith al-Mashriqiyyah fi Ilm al-Ilahiyyah wa al-Tabi'iyyat (*Eastern Studies in Metaphysics and Physics*), also deals with similar topics.

He criticised the geo-centric model of the universe. Eight hundred years ago, he had proposed the notion of multiple universes beyond the known universe based on his *tafsīr* (interpretation) of the Qur'an. This theory has been reiterated by prominent theoretical physicists only in recent times.[179]

Nasir al-Din al-Tusi (1201-1274)[180]

Abu Ja'far Muhammad ibn Muhammad ibn al-Hasan Nasir al-Din al-Tusi was born in Tus, Khorasan (in present-day Iran). He was one of the greatest scientists and prolific writers of his era. He was the student of Kamal al-Din ibn Yunus who was in turn the student of Sharaf al-Din al-Tusi, a famous scholar in mathematics and astronomy in the late 12th century.

Nasir is said to have been among those who were kidnapped by the agents of the radical Hasan ibn Sabah (the Assassins) and sent to their impregnable mountainous stronghold of Alamut. But in 1256, Alamut was conquered by the Mongols. Halagu Khan, the Mongol leader, was deeply impressed by Nasir's knowledge and appointed him as one of his ministers, and, later on, as administrator of the *awqaf* (endowment department).

He was the chief scientist and astronomer of the Maraghah observatory. It was equipped with the best instruments like astrolabes and representations of constellations, epicycle, *etc.* gathered from the Islamic academic centres captured by the Mongols. He invented the turquet, an instrument with two planes.

After 12 years of devoted work with the assistance of his group of scholars, he produced a book of astronomical tables

---

[179] WR18.
[180] Said, H. M., 1991, p. 57-58.

called *Zij-e Ilkhani* dedicated to *Ilkhan* (Halagu Khan). The initial plan was to complete the tables in 30 years, the time required for the completion of planetary cycles. But Halagu Khan ordered it to be completed in 12 years. The tables were largely based on original observations, but also drew upon the then existing knowledge on the subject. The *Zij-e Ilkhani* became the most popular tables among astronomers and remained so till the 15th century and influenced the Copernican reforms.

Nasir al-Din was a remarkable scholar with a variety of major contributions. He established and compiled trigonometry into a new subject of its own. He developed spherical trigonometry including six fundamental formulas for the solutions of spherical right-angled triangles.

He also contributed in ethics, logic and metaphysics. His book on ethics entitled *Akhlaq-e-Nasiri* became the most important book on the subject and remained popular for centuries. His book *Tajrid al-Aqaid* was a major work on *kalam* (Islamic scholastic theology) and enjoyed widespread popularity. Several commentaries were written on this book including super commentaries on the major commentaries, such as *Sharh-e Qadim* and *Sharh-e Jadid*.

Carl Brockelmann lists 56 and George Sarton 64 books and commentaries by him. About one-fourth of these are about mathematics, one-fourth astronomy, another fourth religion and philosophy, with the remainder on other subjects. The books, originally written in Arabic and Persian, were translated and printed in Latin and other European languages during the Middle Ages. His books were widely consulted for centuries and held in high repute for their rich contributions.

Ibn al-Nafis (1213-1288)[181]

Ala al-Din Abu al-Hasan Ali Abu al-Hazm, known as, Ibn al-Nafis was born in Damascus. His expertise was in medicine and jurisprudence. He studied medicine in the hospital-college established by Nur al-Din Zangi, the ruler of Aleppo and Damascus (Syria).

After acquiring experience, he moved to the famed Nasri Hospital in Cairo, Egypt, where he became the principal. He trained a large number of medical specialists including a famous surgeon named Ibn al-Quff al-Masihi. He also served in the Mansuriyyah School in Cairo. He died in Cairo having bequeathed his house, library and clinic to Mansuriyyah Hospital.

He significantly improved medical science. He discovered the blood circulatory system in the human body and described the interactive system of the human body's vessels for air and blood. He also described the function of the coronary arteries as feeding the cardiac muscles. He was the first to correctly describe the constitution of the lungs and gave a description of the bronchi.

Muslim scholars like al-Nafis understood health holistically—healthy social body, healthy physical body and healthy mental body—comprehending psychology and mental health by the 15th century. Sidi Ahmad Zarruk (d. 1492) discussed aspects like obsessive compulsive behaviour in that period.[182]

Mujaz al-Qanun was Ibn Nafis' most famous book. A number of commentaries were written on this book by later scholars. Kitab al-Mukhtar fi al-Aghdhiyah is another of his famous book which included original contribution on the effects of diet on health. He wrote several volumes on Ibn Sina's Qanun, which are still extant. His other commentaries include one on Hunayn ibn Ishaq's and Hippocrates' books. His most

---

[181] Said, H. M., 1991, p. 7.
[182] WR16.

voluminous book is *Al-Shamil fi al-Tibb*, which was designed to be an encyclopaedia comprising 300 volumes. But he died before completing it.

Ibn Khaldun (1332-1395)[183]

Abd al-Rahman ibn Muhammad is known as Ibn Khaldun after a remote ancestor. His ancestors were of Yemeni Arab origin and had settled in Spain in the 8th century. In the 13th century, after the fall of Seville to the Christian rulers during the Reconquista, his family migrated to Tunis where Ibn Khaldun was born. He finished his education locally and displayed a great thirst for knowledge. As he lived during a politically turbulent time, he moved from one place to another working as an academic and holder of various political positions under different rulers. He finally settled in Egypt for the last 24 years of his life where he worked as the chief judge and lectured at al-Azhar University.

He has made the most remarkable pioneering contributions in the social sciences—sociology, histography, demography, economics and political science. He introduced the scientific methods to these sciences.

He introduced sociology (*umraniyyat*) as a new discipline. He discussed the concept of the rise and fall of civilisation, to which the main contributing factor, he ascribed, was a group feeling (*asabiyyah*) that unified people. He is universally accepted as the Father of Sociology. In history, unlike previous historians, he emphasised the environmental, sociological, psychological and economic factors in the interpretations of historical events, thus founding histography and demography.

He developed the foundation of economics introducing the theories of economic growth and supply and demand.[184] 'He was

---

[183] Said, H. M., 1991, p. 29-30.
[184] Weiss, Dieter, 1995.

the first to systematically analyse the functioning of an economy, the importance of tools, specialisation and foreign trade in economic surplus, and the role of government and its stabilisation policies to increase output and employment. Moreover, he dealt with the problem of optimum taxation, minimum government services, incentives, institutional framework, law and order, expectations, production, and the theory of value'.[185] Thus, he is also considered the founder of modern economics.

His most famous work is *Kitab al-Ibar* (*Book of World History*) which comprises a number of books. It consists of the history of ancient civilisations—Persian, Greek, Roman, Arab, Jewish, *etc.*—and the Muslim and European history of his contemporary world with emphasis on Egypt and North Africa. The chief aim of the book was to identify psychological, economic, environmental and social factors that contribute to the advancement of human civilisation. The first book of this work is known as *Al-Muqaddimah*, which is known as the *Prolegomena* in Greek, meaning 'Introduction'. This book contains fascinating new insights into sociology, histography, demography, economics and political science. It became famous during his lifetime. His works were translated to French and German in the 19th century as shown below.[186]

- 1806 and 1816 translated by Sylvester De Sacy—French Orientalist.

- 1812 and 1822 translated by Von Hammer-Purgstall—Austrain orientalist.

- 1858 translated by Quatermere de Quincy—French archaeologist and writer.

Not surprisingly, France and Germany saw the evolution of

---

[185] Cosma, Sorinel, 2009, p. 52.
[186] Enan, Mohammad Abdullah, 2007, p. 118-119.

the first European sociologists soon after these translations. His influence in the development of social sciences in Europe is paramount, specifically on system builders like Vico, Comte and Marx.

CHAPTER 5

Influence of Muslim Philosophers

Muslim philosophy is a monotheistic continuation of ancient philosophies, mainly Aristotelian and Neoplatonic. The main difference between the Muslim and the Greek philosophers is that the Muslims were monotheists and the Greeks were pagans. But Greek philosophy also has a monotheistic tendency, a concept of a singular god-like being, which fits in with the Muslim monotheism.

To the Greek philosophers the beautiful design of the universe suggested that there must be a designer. For Aristotle the world was not created, nor cared about or known by God. His philosophically derived deity led a blissful life of eternal contemplation while the world organised itself into a cosmos out of love and admiration of Him and trying to become like Him. This notion contradicted the Muslim concept of creation but the Muslim philosopher found a solution from this contradiction in the Neoplatonic emanation theory.[187]

The philosophers explained the origination of the world through an emanative scheme that was suggested by Plotinus, founder of Neoplatonism. He considered that the world came to

---

[187] Sharif, M. M. 2016, p. 501.

be as an emanation from god like light emanates from the sun. The philosophers consider a step-by-step emanation (creation) of ten spheres of intelligence and beings, the last being the world of humanity. This suggested that the universe comes from God in stages. Thus, the ancient philosophical system was not difficult for the Muslim philosophers to remodel and concur with. Whatever they found in Greek philosophy they explained within the terms of their monotheistic ideal.

Muslim philosophers sought to study, improve and complete the Greek philosophical systems. They took their guiding inspiration from the Qur'an—a book of religion and guidance with notional history and science among other subjects in it—which provides a complete and unique supra-system of reality, existence and knowledge that philosophers try to arrive at.

It is important to know about the works of the Muslim philosophers because it gives a clear idea of the great influence they had on Europe. Over time, there were many Muslim philosophers. The following list includes the names of the main ones from the 9th to the 13th centuries: al-Kindi, Muhammad ibn Zakariyya al-Razi, al-Farabi, Abu Ya'qub al-Sijistani, Abu al-Hassan al-Amiri, Ibn Miskawayh, al-Ma'arri, Ibn Sina (Avicenna), Hamid al-Din al-Kirmani, Nasir Khusraw, Ibn Bajjah, Afdal al-Din Kashani, al-Ghazali, Ibn Rushd (Averroes), Ibn Tufayl, Fakhr al-Din al-Razi, Ibn Arabi, Nasir al-Din al-Tusi, Ibn al-Nafis, and Ibn Sabin. Most of them were not just philosophers but polymaths. The most notable of these philosopher-polymaths were al-Kindi, al-Farabi, Ibn Sina, al-Ghazali and Ibn Rushd. They are discussed below briefly.

Al-Kindi

Al-Kindi (9th century) was the first great Muslim philosopher. He translated many Greek philosophical books, clarified their difficulties and summarised their deep theories, conciliating the Hellenistic heritage with Islam.[188] He did not simply translate Greek philosophy; he further developed and improved it as well. Al-Kindi stated,

> "It is fitting then to remain faithful to the principle which we have followed in all our works, which is first to record in complete quotations all that the Ancients have said on the subject, secondly to complete what the Ancients have not fully expressed, and this according the usage of our Arabic language, the customs of our age, and own ability."[189]

He was the first to form an accord between Islam and Greek philosophy thus paving the way for al-Farabi, Ibn Sina and Ibn Rushd to further develop philosophical insight. To him Aristotle's 'Unmovable Mover',[190] the primary cause of all motion in the universe, is 'God the Creator'. In Aristotelian system the world is finite in space but infinite in time. Al-Kindi disagreed with this notion and maintained that the world is not infinite in time.[191] His theories were not at conflict with traditional Islam and he was, in fact, considered one of the ulema.

Al-Kindi was also a scholar of the sciences which were of no less significance than his philosophical works. He had carried out major work on optics. Two of his treatises were used in the 13th century by Roger Bacon and German physicist Witelo in their *Perspectiva* (Optics). According to Sebastian Vogal, 20thcentury Danish scholar, 'Roger Bacon not merely counted al-Kindi as one of the masters of perspectiva but in his own *Perspectiva*, he and

---

[188] Sharif, M. M., 2016, p. 422-423.
[189] Walzer, Richard, 1945-1946, p. 175-176.
[190] WR1.
[191] Sharif, M. M., 2016, p. 431.

others in his field, referred repeatedly to al-Kindi's optics'.[192] Al-Haytham further developed optics into a science of its own.

Gerolamo Cardano, 16th century Italian polymath and the most renowned mathematician of the Renaissance, said that Al-kindi was 'one of the twelve giant minds of history'. Ibn Nadim and al-Qifti (13th century biographer of famous scholars) listed 270 of his works in 17 different categories such as logic, philosophy, geometry, arithmetic and astronomy.[193] Most of these are now lost.

Al-Farabi

Abu al-Nasr al-Farabi was born in about 870 and was of Turk origin. He was born near the town of Farab, in Central Asia, where Islam had been introduced at the beginning of the 9th century. After completing his early studies in his hometown, he went to Baghdad, the outstanding intellectual center of the world. He studied under Bishr Matta ibn Yunus, the most renowned among the distinguished circle of logicians residing there. In due course of time, he surpassed his teachers, attained an eminent position and came to be known as the 'Second Teacher', with Aristotle being the first. After 20 years in Baghdad he went to the court of Sayf al-Dawlah in Aleppo (in current Syria)—another enlightened and scholarly centre. He also visited Damascus and Egypt on academic purposes.[194]

Al-Farabi emerged as a great philosopher. He adopted certain doctrines of previous philosophers, reconstructed those in a form fit for his own cultural environment, and made them harmonious and systematic.[195] His main work was on logic and included

---

[192] D. M., Dunlop, 1971, p. 223.

[193] Sharif, M. M., 2016, p. 422.

[194] *Ibid.*, p. 451-452.

[195] *Ibid.*, p. 454.

commentaries and paraphrases of Aristotle's *Organon*. Al-Farabi agreed with the laws of causality, that there is a connection between causes and effects,[196] and that causes act directly or indirectly in producing an effect. His other works were on ethics and metaphysics, the rest being on music, physics, mathematics and politics.[197]

Al-Farabi gave a new shape to the neoplatonic philosophy and proposed the formation of the universe through an emanative scheme (see appendix 4 for a brief description). According to al-Farabi, God has always possessed absolute perfection with eternal attributes. The universe is a 'necessary' emanation of his attributes of perfection which overflowed due to its super abundance giving it a sort of 'pre-eternal' existence. Al-Farabi, thus, reconciled Aristotle's eternal universe with the Islamic tradition. If God is eternally merciful then how could he be merciful if there was nothing to be merciful to! So, there must always have been a universe to which God could be merciful.[198]

But on the other hand, it introduced problematic thoughts into Muslim discourse as the Qur'an says that the universe was created, which means before a point in time the universe did not exist. That creation was not a necessary consequence, like an automated system, of God's perfection or attributes. But God *chose* to create the universe and it was all under His superlative control. He could have chosen not to create the universe.

Al-Farabi's work set the ground for a great time-transgressing battle between Ibn Sina and al-Ghazali in the following two centuries. There are also hints of a rebuttal to these Farabian concepts in the *Aqidah* of Imam al-Tahawi who was roughly contemporary with al-Farabi. The Imam spent

---

[196] Sharif, M. M., 2016, p. 461.
[197] *Ibid.*, p. 453.
[198] WR20.

considerable time establishing that God was forever the Creator before He created anything. He was forever merciful even when there was nothing to be merciful to.

Al-Farabi's theory on prophecy holds that the basis of every revealed religion is revelation and inspiration of a prophet. The prophet is a man who has the gift of communion with God and the ability to express God's will.

He stresses the importance of the study of 'society and its needs'. His most famous treatise on politics is the *Al-Madinah al-Fadilah* or *'The Virtuous City'*. He states that a city is like an organism, if one part becomes ill all the other parts react to take care of it.[199] The 'Republic' by Plato was written about a similar topic at around 380 BC on the character of a just city-state and the just man.

Al-Farabi's works, seventy according to biographers, became famous among the philosophers and he developed followers in different places including Muslim Spain.[200] Some of his writing were translated to Hebrew and Latin and influenced Jewish and Christian scholasticism.[201]

Ibn Sina (Avicenna)

Ibn Sina's (980-1037) worldview looms large in the history of philosophy as in other epistemologies and, thus, he was called *al-Shaykh al-Ra'is* or *'Prince of the Learned'*. He built a complete and elaborate system of philosophy. His elements were Greek, Aristotelian and Neoplatonic, certain reformulations Farabian, but the method of arriving at definitions and the system itself was his own.[202] He uplifted philosophical thinking to a new level.

---

[199] Sharif, M. M., 2016, p. 463.

[200] *Ibid.*, p. 452.

[201] Menasce, P. J. de, 1948, p. 27-28.

[202] Sharif, M. M., 2016, p. 480.

His context, obviously, was monotheistic. Ibn Sina's philosophy states that in all of universe God is the only thing without cause, being the *necessity* on which all others are contingent. God is unique and does not have any separate essence because that would cause multiplicity in His being. He exists and exists necessarily and so His essence is identical with His necessary existence. The above discernment is quite close to the interpretation of Surah al-Ikhlas of the Qur'an.

Ibn Sina produced a brilliant and elegant synthesis of Aristotelian and Neoplatonic philosophy[203] and modified and completed the Farabian emanative scheme.[204] The scheme states that a series of cosmic emanation from God ultimately led to the formation of the world and the human and prophetic souls. In his model, from God flows the First Intellect which forms the First Sphere and from which emanates the Second Intellect which forms the Second Sphere, and the emanations continue to further intellects and spheres. This emanatory process continues to subsequent levels till it reaches the Tenth Intellect level that comprises the sublunary world of humanity.[205] God's connection to creation is via this emanative series. His awareness of particular elements of the world is not via sense perception but in a universal way since everything has emanated from him[206].

According to Ibn Sina the only way to conceive creation rationally is to conceive it being created outside of time. Thus, the world is both created and infinite (being created before time makes it infinite). His system argues in favour of a 'world', being contingent on God, but existing eternally with God[207] which fits in

---

[203] WR20.

[204] Marmura, p. xix.

[205] Sharif, M. M., 2016, p. 481.

[206] *Ibid.*, p. 501-502.

[207] *Ibid.*, p. 503.

with Aristotle's model of an eternal world.[208]

Ibn Sina regarded himself as a perfectly orthodox Muslim. If he could not work something out he would go to the mosque and pray to Allah for guidance and illumination. But the basic method he used to define 'truth' was not revelation but by reason. He considered the Prophet to be the 'philosopher king' of Plato and all the other prophets to be philosophers. Their knowledge of God, according to him, came via the absolutely correct philosophical understanding of reality—how things really are. So, they are to be followed not because they were carrying a message but because they had wisdom. According to him, revelations were guidance and explanation of esoteric truths for the layman and thus people with understanding of deep and perfect philosophy could interpret revelation philosophically.[209]

According to his eschatology heaven and hell are all purely spiritual existences for the righteous and damned souls. Heaven is the manifestation of God's mercy and hell is the manifestation of God's wrath and majesty. But Ibn Sina negated the 'physical' aspects of hereafter. Ibn Sina further postulates that the soul is non-material and rejected that the resurrection of man will be in the flesh.[210] He provides arguments in favour of the notion that the mind can exist independent of the body.[211] Ibn Sina's further elaborated the Farabian model of prophethood (see Appendix 4). Many of his postulations would later be criticised by al-Ghazali.

Unlike him, the orthodox theologians did not negate the physical aspects of the hereafter but accepted the fact that it is not possible to understand existence in the hereafter from the experience of this world. Even Ibn 'Abbas, the famous

---

[208] WR2.

[209] WR20.

[210] Sharif, M. M., 2016, p. 504; Marmura, p. xxi.

[211] *Ibid.*, p. 487.

Companion of the Prophet and interpreter of the Qur'an, had said that 'in the hereafter nothing remains but names'.[212] Thus, there are gardens in paradise and there is fire in hell, but its nature is very different from what is experienced in this world. That is the difference between the philosophical approach and orthodox theological approach. The orthodox concept being that the Qur'an is not just guidance for layman but for all the believers including people of intellect.

Ibn Sina's philosophy not only influenced the Muslim world but Europe as well. His works were first translated to Latin in 1166 in Toledo of Spain. By 1250 over a hundred of his philosophical writings, including those on the soul and psychology, were translated. In the 13th century he was the leading authority for the Western philosophers.[213] His popularity among the European philosophers and theologians would last for centuries.

His works fundamentally influenced the reformulations of Roman Catholic theology via the works of Albert the Great, and especially that of Thomas Aquinas.[214] Ibn Sina's influence is evident on Aquinas' *Summa Theologica* and *Summa Contra Gentiles* and is mentioned in many pages of *De Ente et Essentia* (the word *summa* itself comes from a Maliki Muslim (Arabic) term[215]). Whether being referenced or critiqued by Aquinas and others, it only provides evidence of the widespread influence and esteem for his work. Aquinas' metaphysics would be unintelligible without understanding the debt it owns to Ibn Sina.[216]

The *De Anima* translated by the 12th century Spanish philosopher Dominicus Gundisalvus is largely a transportation of

---

[212] WR20.

[213] Lyons, Jonathan, 2009, p.190.

[214] Sharif, M. M., 2016, p. 480.

[215] WR21.

[216] Sharif, M. M., 2016, p. 505.

Ibn Sina's doctrines. Duns Scotus and Count Zabarella, the finest of the late medieval European commentators on Aristotle, also bear testimony to Ibn Sina's influence on philosophy. Dr. S. Van Den Bergh, in his *Averroes' Tahafut al-Tahafut,* finds that the influence of *Shaykh al-Ra'is* Ibn Sina continues down to modern philosophy.[217]

Al-Ghazali

Al-Ghazali (1058-1128) was a multidimensional intellect and, in turn, a canon lawyer and a scholastic, a philosopher and a sceptic, a mystic and a theologian, a traditionalist and a moralist. He spent his life in search of knowledge and finally became an arbiter of the known knowledge of his time—identifying what was true knowledge and what was superstition and speculation in the guise of knowledge.

According to him all knowledge should be investigated and nothing should be considered dangerous or hostile, as he states,

> "I poked into every abyss. I scrutinised the creed of every sect and I fathomed the mysteries of each doctrines. All this I did so that I might distinguish between the true and the false. There was not a philosopher whose system I did not acquaint myself with, nor a theologian whose doctrines I did not examine. If ever I met a Sufi, I coveted to probe into his secrets, if an ascetic, I investigated into the basis of his austerities; if one of the atheistic *zindiqs*, I groped into the causes of his bold atheism".[218]

He came to the conclusion that the greatest hindrance in the search for truth was the acceptance of beliefs on the authority of

---

[217] Sharif, M. M., 2016, p. 505.
[218] *Ibid.*, p. 588.

others and blind adherence to past heritage. So, he decided to reconstruct all his knowledge from its very foundations and was led to make the following reflections:

> "The search after truth being the aim which I propose to myself, I ought to, in the first place, ascertain what are the bases of certitude. In the second place I ought to recognise that certitude is the clear and complete knowledge of things, such knowledge as leaves no room for doubt nor any possibility of error"[219].

This proposed test led him to doubts; doubts even of sense perceptions, such as hearing and seeing: 'We cannot hope to find truth except in matters which carry their evidence in themselves, *i.e.*, in sense perception and necessary principles of thought. We must, therefore, first of all establish these two on a firm basis.' But he doubted the evidence of sense perception, as did Rene Descartes long after him, because they so deceive people. No eye can perceive the movement of an object's shadow under the sun yet the shadow moves. A finger held up against the night sky would cover a star, but the stars are vastly larger than the earth.[220] His doubt or skepticism was a basic aspect in his search for truth.

He divided the various 'seekers' after truth of his time into the four distinct groups: theologians, mystics, authoritarians (*Ta'limis*) and philosophers. He was able to find faults in all of them and critiqued those faults. Though he considered the doctrines of the theologians correct he was dissatisfied with their scholastic approach. For it did not bring any intellectual certainty. He criticised the extravagantly pantheistic utterances or antinomian tendencies of the intoxicated Sufis. He also thought they could be delusional. He had a poor opinion of Ta'limior

---

[219] Field, Claud, 1909, p. 13.
[220] Sharif, M. M., 2016, p. 589.

authoritative instructions known among the Isma'iliyyah and Batiniyyah—a kind of Muslim popery or Montanist movement—for they renounced reason and believed the hidden truth can only be attained by submission to an infallible Imam. But it was the philosophers and their concepts that troubled him the most and thus forced him to critique them particularly.[221]

A few hundred books have been attributed to al-Ghazali. According to Abdur Rahman Badawi, professor of philosophy, 72 of those books are by al-Ghazali, the others commentaries or works on his works.

Al-Ghazali on Scientific Knowledge

The natural sciences, at least the theoretical concepts, had been part of philosopher's discourse till the Muslim scholars treated the sciences as empirical and independent disciplines separate from philosophy. True to the original philosophical discourses al-Ghazali divided the philosopher's discipline into metaphysics, logic, ethics, politics, mathematics and physics. Then he approached all of these in a scientific manner ready to accept any postulation on the basis of reason. He accepted what the philosophers had to offer about mathematics, physics and logic without hesitation. He conformed with much of their politics and ethics. But it was in their metaphysics that he found serious faults for these were not grounded on reason or inquiry, rather on fanciful conjecture and speculations. Even the philosophers themselves did not agree with one another with regards to their metaphysics. Had metaphysics been grounded on reason then all the philosophers would have agreed on it as they agreed on their mathematical sciences.[222]

He accepted astronomy as science but considered astrology

---

[221] Sharif, M. M., 2016, p. 591.
[222] *Ibid.*, p. 594.

as blameworthy. Logic was philosophically neutral and was, thus, acceptable to him.[223] It is abundantly clear that al-Ghazali's battle was with the theological space that metaphysics violated speculatively, not the sciences that philosophy advocated rationally.

Al-Ghazali on Philosophy

Al-Ghazali was completely versed in philosophy and critiqued the fallacies of the philosophers rather than actively construct a system of his own. He approached the works of others with a keen acumen and penetration and gave clear expositions and remarkable criticisms. Nothing frightened or fascinated him, he was in supreme control. After he had removed the hubris what was left in philosophy was clean and pristine. So, in effect, he did leave a modified system but never claimed it as his own. In his *Mishkat al-Anwar* he also did introduce a cosmological structure of the universe based on the 'Verse of Light' of the Qur'an (Al-Nūr 24:35), an alternate to the Neoplatonic emanation scheme.

After studying the entire sweep of philosophy of his time he wrote his first major work on philosophy named *Maqasid al-Falasifah* (*The Intention of Philosophers*). This compendium was faithful to the Aristotelian-Ibn Sinan model and was meant to be a preliminary understanding of the existing philosophy prior to his future critique. But due to its quality it alone became very influential. A Latin translation was done in 1145 by the Spanish philosopher Dominicus Gundisalvus. Albert the Great, Thomas Aquinas and Roger Bacon all have repeatedly mentioned the name of the author of *Intention of Philosophers* along with Ibn Sina and Ibn Rushd as the true representation of Aristotelianism.[224]

---

[223] Marmura, 2000, p. xviii.
[224] Sharif, M. M., 2016, p. 593.

But al-Ghazali turned out to be more than a corroborator of philosophy, he not only comprehended philosophy, he cleansed it as well. He countered Ibn Sina's *Shifa'*, as he knew the strength and power of the philosophical movement and its divergences and digressions. That produced his critique of philosophy *Tahafut al-Falasifah* (*The Incoherence of the Philosophers*). Only after that he laid down the correct 'path to truth' and that was the *Ihya Ulum al Din* (*The Revival of Religious Sciences*).

Al-Ghazali, in his scheme, divided the philosophers into three main groups: the materialists (*dahriyyun*), the deists or naturalists (*tabi'iyyun*) and the theists (*ilahiyyun*).[225]

The materialists were the total atheists, completely dispensing with the idea of God, who believed that the universe existed eternally only as a natural phenomenon with no creator. The deists seeing design, wisdom and beauty in nature and in the universe were convinced that there had to be a wise Designer or Creator behind it all. But they rejected the idea of spiritualism or hereafter or immortality of the soul. The theist were the philosophers who believed in a Creator and soul. They held a more final position having comprehended and critiqued the other two groups. Al-Ghazali placed Socrates, Plato and Aristotle in the theist group. He concentrated on Aristotle because Aristotle had critiqued all the past philosophers including his own teacher Plato: 'Plato is dear to us. And truth is dear to us too. But truth is dearer than Plato.'

The world at the time of al-Ghazali was a running battleground between orthodox-rational Ash'ari-Maturidi theologians and the philosophers. Among the Muslim philosophers he concentrated on al-Farabi and, especially, Ibn Sina as these two were the most 'evolved' of the philosophers of his time. Thus al-Ghazali took it upon himself to counter and

---

[225] Sharif, M. M., 2016, p. 593.

correct the best of the philosophers.

He found that al-Farabi and Ibn Sina, in an attempt to reconcile philosophy with religion, had made some of the metaphysical conjectures acceptable, thus falling into inconsistencies and heresies.[226] Al-Ghazali cleansed these speculative inconsistencies in his master philosophical work *Tahafut al-Falasifah*. His attack was limited to a number of metaphysical points which were simply incompatible with in-depth rational discourse and with Muslim belief. He used rational tools to show the inherent faults of these metaphysical contradictions of the Ibn Sinan Neoplatonic world view. The *Tahafut* criticises the philosophers on twenty points (see Appendix 5), claiming they were based on inconsistent and confused thoughts. From the theological sense he considers all of these heretical but the following three of the twenty points to be outright infidel:

1. the concept of the eternity of the world,

2. denial of God's knowledge of particular things and

3. denial of bodily resurrection in the hereafter.

Al-Ghazali deals with the first point, the concept of eternity, most rigorously. The Aristotelian philosophers maintain that there is a 'prime' material existing co-eternal with God and God merely brings forth different things in the universe from the prime material. Since the 'prime' material is eternal thus the universe and time are also eternal. Al-Ghazali, on the other hand, does not believe in the existence of any eternal material but provides his arguments in favour of God creating *ex nihilo*, out of nothing. Thus, the universe is not pre-eternal but finite in time. One way of explaining it would be that God had willed that

---

[226] Sharif, M. M., 2016, p. 595.

certain objects come into being at certain times. God's will is eternal but the object comes to 'exist' at a certain time.[227]

The difficulty that arises among the philosophers is that they try to understand the 'will' of God in terms of man's will. But as God's eternal knowledge is not like man's transient knowledge, God's will is also not like man's will. Further, he criticises the dissimilar constructions of time and space by the philosophers faulty as they consider time to be infinite but space to be finite. Within Aristotelian concept time, space and movement are interrelated. Thus, it causes an inconsistency if space is finite and time is infinite, as over infinite time infinite things would be formed filling up all the finite space.

Furthermore, as space and time are co-implicant of movement, if philosophers consider space to be finite then they should also consider time to be finite. If the philosophers cannot contemplate empty space (or movement) without time, then they should also not postulate empty time without space.[228] (These two hypotheses of creation can be considered as precursive examples to the thesis and antithesis of Kant's First Antinomy). To al-Ghazali's credit, with the big bang theory being accepted, the pre-eternity of the universe in no longer tenable.

Al-Ghazali considers the emanation scheme of creation simply wild guesswork, arbitrary reasoning and idle speculation— 'darkness piled upon darkness'. Al-Ghazali's criticism shows that emanation fails, among other things, to account for multiplicity and composition of the universe and also fails to maintain the unity of God.[229] Al-Ghazali's rational is outstanding and he defeats the emanation scheme on its own logic. He does not go about just quoting the Qur'an at the philosophers but shows how

---

[227] Sharif, M. M., 2016, p. 559.
[228] *Ibid.*, p. 600.
[229] *Ibid.*, p. 603-604.

their own system does not add up. Recent intellectuals like F. R. Tennant, scientist and theologian, hold the emanation theory in a similar estimation.[230]

Al-Ghazali points out that Ibn Sina's philosophy suggests that God seems to be unaware of the particulars or individual things[231] as He does not perceive via senses. The Aristotelean conception is that God has only self-knowledge. Ibn Sina subscribed to that conception but adds that God's self-knowledge implies knowledge of all existent things in the universe, in so far, as He is the ultimate source of all of it.

He further states that perception of things causes changes in the discernment of the perceiver. But God does not change and so sense perception does not apply to God. Besides, to sense and distinguish between two different things in space, the perceiver has to be near or far from those two things, *i.e.*, in a definite position related to those two things. That is not possible as far as God, omnipotent and omnipresent, is concerned. So God does not perceive particulars but in a universal way. (Philospher Fazlur Rahman considers that Ibn Sina ultimately means that God knows particulars in a different way rather than through sense perception[232]).

But al-Ghazali states that this theory fails to take into consideration the eternality of God's knowledge and the transiency of human knowledge. The point that Ibn Sina made that God's self-knowledge also means the knowledge of the universe cannot be logically validated. Self-knowledge and knowledge of others can exist separately. Al-Ghazali raises many more points of criticism similar in nature which fully brings out

---

[230] Sharif, M. M., 2016, p. 603.
[231] Lyons, Jonathan, 2009, p.178.
[232] Sharif, M. M., 2016, p. 502.

the modern 'positivistic' and 'analytic' thrusts of his thought.[233] Thus, his works and thought can be considered the originator of modern philosophical concepts.

The philosophical concept of 'causality'—that 'causes' leads to 'effects'—was also challenged by al-Ghazali. Generally, causality connects two events like drinking quenches thirst, not-eating causes hunger, fire burns things. He stated that there may not be a connection between what is perceived as cause and effect. Cause and effect are both inert events to which 'will' and 'action' cannot be attributed. Causes themselves do not have a 'will' to do anything and a cause cannot take an 'action' on its own. It is only God's will that these two events are connected. One appears to follow the other, drinking is followed by quenching of thirst, only because God has willed it so. But fire may not burn something if God so wishes which would then appear as a miracle. This concept is known as occasionalism by philosophers. This same concept is also found much later in thoughts of philosophers Hume, Malabanche and others. Hume's analysis on occasionalism is so strikingly close to al-Ghazali's that it appears to have been influenced by him.

It may be easier to conceptualise this phenomenon of occasionalism by conceiving that at every instant there is some change in all things. For example, as a tree grows there is change in it at every moment of time. As reality is composed of matter which is composed of atomic particles every change manifested is occurring at the microscopic atomic particle level.

Al-Ghazali propounded that 'reality' was a series of new realities, each created by God in every moment of time. Thus, for change to happen, atoms are created every instant, they vanish every instant and are recreated every instant by God in a changed form, which brings forth the continuous changes in the world. So,

---

[233] *Ibid.*, p. 610-611.

atoms do not have duration and their motions (or changes) are not causally related but are a result of constant recreation. It is only because God is being consistent that 'effects' seems to follow 'causes' constantly, and that gives the appearance of a causal relationship. But the same cause, if God so wishes, may not give rise to the anticipated effect and then that is viewed as a miracle or a defect. For example, fire may not burn, and not eating may not cause hunger.

In short, what al-Ghazali means is that everything is under God's control and that there is no power and no change except with God. When cause and effect succeed one another it only proves succession not causation, a conjunction not a connection. The connection in causality is not logical but illusory or psychological as people see the one particular event always follow another and infer these to be cause and effect. In the *Tahafut* al-Ghazali deals with causality in his seventeenth out of twenty critiques. He brings forth very highly sophisticated arguments in all his twenty critiques.

In the mechanistic 19th century, as atoms became to be understood and, in fact, could be measured, occasionalism came to be considered absurd. But modern quantum mechanics now indicates that the duration or existence of subatomic particles cannot be spoken of as was thought previously. They can be seen as particles, waves or instances of a universal component.

In 1993, Karen Harding's paper 'Causality Then and Now: Al-Ghazali and Quantum Theory' describes several 'remarkable' similarities between al-Ghazali's concept of occasionalism and the widely accepted Copenhagen interpretation of quantum mechanics. She states, 'In both cases, and contrary to common sense, objects are viewed as having no inherent properties and no independent existence. In order for an object to exist, it must be brought into being either by God (al-Ghazali) or by an observer (the Copenhagen Interpretation).'

Al-Ghazali's attack was not on philosophy *per se* but on the centuries of fanciful conjectures and speculative accruements in philosophy. Al-Ghazali systematically refuted all those errors. Even though, there were others who critiqued his work, Ibn Rushd being the most outstanding, much of what al-Ghazali had proposed was silently and implicitly accepted by philosophers and theologians of later ages. The arguments and general motif of the *Tahafut* is clearly reflected in the works of modern philosophers like Hume, Scheiermacher, Ritschl and even the current logical positivists.[234] Al-Ghazali actually reconstructed philosophy and not destroy it as some scholars claim.

The width of al-Ghazali's intellectual endeavour was all consuming. He studied and wrote about all kinds of epistemologies. Thus, his critics were also a variety of scholars. Not only people like Thomas Aquinas critiqued his theology, but Ibn al-Jawzi also criticised, saying, 'How cheaply has al-Ghazali traded theology for Sufism.' Ibn Taymiyyah, on the other hand, accused him of trading theology for philosophy. Ibn Rushd blamed him of despoiling philosophy.[235] These were all remarkable scholars, giants in their own fields. But everyone saw him from a different perspective—their own.

Al-Ghazali influenced both Muslim and European philosophers. Margaret Smith writes, 'There can be no doubt that al-Ghazali's works would be among the first to attract the attention of these European scholars'.[236] She further states, 'The greatest of these Christian writers who were influenced by al-Ghazali was St. Thomas Aquinas (1225-1274), who made a study of the Arabic writers and admitted his indebtedness to them, having studied at the University of Naples where the influence of

---

[234] Sharif, M. M., 2016, p. 595.

[235] *Ibid.*, p. 638.

[236] Smith, Margaret, 1944, p. 220.

Arab literature and culture was predominant at the time.'

Al-Ghazali has also achieved another feat. Long ago, during the times of Saint Paul and Saint Constantine the Great, some of the fundamental concepts of Christianity were influenced by Greek philosophy causing changes in Christianity. The theology of al-Ghazali and literal interpretation of religious scriptures by Imam Hanbal stopped the same from happening to Islam.

Ibn Rushd

Muhammad Ibn Rushd or Averroes (1126-1198) was basically a legal scholar from the Maliki school of jurisprudence. He was appointed as the judge in the court of Seville and wrote a number of books on Islamic law (*Sharia*). Besides Islamic law he also studied philosophy, medicine and theology.[237] While still working as a full time jurist he was commissioned to explain and illuminate Aristotle's works by Sultan Abu Ya'qub Yusuf.

Aristotle's *Metaphysics* is quite hermetic and difficult to understand. Ibn Rushd wrote three rationalised commentaries on Aristotle's metaphysics that changed its vague or shallow understanding. Some interpreted his commentary or treatises to implicitly mean that God created the universe and let it follow its universal laws and left it to man to make his own way.[238] His work, in fact, was much more involved and made clear Aritotle's work for the following generations of scholars.

The treatises were of three different sizes and with differing degree of details. Apparently, these were intended for three different levels of scholars: *jami*, a summary for beginners; *talkhis*, for intermediate students; and *tafsīr* for advanced students. The lesser commentary is about the same size of the original work. The middle commentary was more serious and elaborated the smaller

---

[237] Lyons, Jonathan, 2009, p. 173.
[238] *Ibid.*, p. 174.

one. The longest one included original contributions based on Ibn Rushd's own analysis and had interpretation of Qur'anic concepts. His commentaries became very famous and he came to be known as the 'Commentator' in medieval Europe.

While Ibn Sina and al-Farabi were more Neoplatonist, Ibn Rushd was influenced more by Aristotelian thought. When the works of Ibn Rushd were translated to Latin it started a philosophical movement in Europe called Averroism. It consisted of Aristotelian philosophy as interpreted by Ibn Rushd, his distinction between philosophy and theology, his empirical rationalism and his theory about intellect.[239] One of the important works of Ibn Rushd is his theory of intellect in which he mentions two types of intellect, practical and theoretical, and discusses the operations of intellection.

In his works, Ibn Rushd brings an accord between science, religion and philosophy, by rationally harmonising philosophy with the Qur'an. According to Ibn Rushd the main subject matters of religion are the existence of God, prophesy and resurrection. These are the three principals that every Muslim should believe.[240] About predestination Ibn Rushd states that man is predisposed neither to fatalism nor to free will but is determined. Determinism is the production of acts owing to both internal (human will) and external (furnished by God) causes. This determined interaction or concurrence between external and internal results in what is called predestination.[241]

Al-Ghazali had categorised philosophers into three groups. In turn, Ibn Rushd categorised the theologians into five principal kinds: Ash'aris, Mu'tazilis, Batinis, Hashawis and Sufis. In his book *Al-Kashf 'an Manahij al-Adillah*, the Mu'tazilis were briefly

---

[239] Sharif, M. M., 2016, p. 555.
[240] *Ibid.*, p. 546.
[241] *Ibid.*, p. 550.

mentioned and the Batinis not at all. The Hashawis believed that faith is attained by listening to oral transmission as was in the time of the Prophet, and reason had nothing to do with it. The Ash'aris, to which group belonged al-Ghazali, were mentioned in greater detail.

Ibn Rushd maintained that the Ash'aris held that the way to God is by reason but they did not adhere to the way that the Qur'an directs. They start from a dialectical premise, such as 'the world is temporal', 'bodies are composed of atoms', 'atoms are created' or 'the agents of the world are neither temporal nor eternal'. Ibn Rushd complains that the premise of the theologians is not understood by common people and are unconvincing and inconsistent. The Sufis on the other hand believe that knowledge of God comes from high above and can be accessed when people rid themselves of earthly desires. But, again, this is not attained by all people and negates the 'thinking' that is encouraged in the Qur'an.[242] It is interesting to note that Ibn Rushd considered the Sufis a theological group.

In the 12th century, some philosophers were accused of heresy. Ibn Rushd came to their defence. In his treatise *Fasl al-Maqal fi Ma bayn al-Hikmah wa al-Shari'ah min al-Ittisal*, he begins by asking the question whether philosophy is permitted, prohibited, recommended or ordained in *Shariah* (Islamic law). He puts forward the point that philosophy, so far as it is rational in consideration, is ordained or, at least, recommended, as the Qur'an exhorts people to such rational considerations.[243] Ibn Rushd believed that revelation and philosophy were different approaches to the same truth, a notion that had been more profoundly expounded by al-Kindi.

In his *Tahafut al-Tahafut (Incoherence of the Incoherence)* he

---

[242] Sharif, M. M., 2016, p. 457-458.
[243] *Ibid.*, p. 545.

responded to al-Ghazali's *Tahafut al-Falasifah* (*Incoherence of the Philosophers*). But on many cases the difference between the two views was not subjective but rather perspective. Ibn Rushd states that everything in the world happens with a perfect regularity which can be understood in terms of cause and effect. He also explains Aristotle's doctrine of four causes, stating, 'Denial of cause implies denial of knowledge, and denial of knowledge implies nothing in this world can be really known.' Scientific knowledge is the knowledge of things along with their 'causes' that produce them.[244] Ibn Rushd meant that causes and effects and the processes that binds them together have all been put in place by God that thus the changes that occur appear 'automatic'.

While Ibn Rushd's explanation was in the 'process' level, al-Ghazali had gone into a more granular level. He defined the process at the very atomic level. A cause and its effect is brought about by not just changes on the superficial level, but by the changes in atomic level. In every instance God is directly recreating and changing the atoms that leads to consequent changes on the superficial level which is perceived by human beings. Thus, Ibn Rushd is not against al-Ghazali's notion that God controls everything; he differs on how God controls everything. According to Ibn Rushd, there are processes set up by God according to which changes happen. Both offer equivalent interpretations but from differing perspectives.

Hume's philosophy agrees with al-Ghazali's separation of cause from effect. On the other hand, similar to Ibn Rushd, Kant tries to find a rational ground on which causality can stand. Bertrand Russel opines, 'Whether from pure prejudice, or from the influence of tradition or for some other reason, it is easier to believe that there is a law of nature to the effect that causes are always followed by their effects than to effect that this usually

---

[244] Sharif, M. M., 2016, p. 559.

happens'.[245] Over time, philosophers have moved away from metaphysical conjectures and moved towards rational concepts due to the objections raised by al-Ghazali and the critique by Ibn Rushd. It is all part of the same dialectical process not one in spite of the other.

The conflict between Ibn Sina, al-Ghazali and Ibn Rushd was not about the place of God in philosophy but how God has set up the universe to work. It is fascinating that such a debate took place spanning over two centuries and over a wide geographical area nearly a thousand years ago. Ibn Sina writes in the beginning of the 11th century in Central Asia and Persia, which is critiqued nearly a century later by al-Ghazali in the Middle East, then the critique is critiqued in another century in Spain by Ibn Rushd. This was the time when there were no mechanical vehicles, no electronic mediums and no automated printing. How such ideas had travelled to and fro only proves the remarkable scholarly passion of the period!

Ibn Rushd's major works were translated by Michael Scot,[246] after which Emperor Frederick ensured that those were sent to the Italian universities.[247] The initial translations left out some of the Islamic context of the commentaries,[248] but their remnant monotheistic container along with rationalism appealed to Europe. Soon, these new ideas coming in from the Muslim lands caused a titanic struggle between the new intellectuals and the old theologians of Europe that opened up the doors for investigation into the laws of existence, *i.e.*, natural sciences.[249]

Initially there were attempts to ban these new ideas. During the 13th and 14th centuries Paris University issued over a dozen

---

[245] Russel, Bertrand, 1984, p. 472.
[246] Lyons, Jonathan, 2009, p. 173.
[247] *Ibid.*, p. 184.
[248] *Ibid.*, p. 183.
[249] *Ibid.*, p. 174.

lists of ideas that were banned from being studied. But it was a losing battle and over time the Dominican order, to which Saint Aquinas belonged, started to study those works and Pope Gregory XI modified the ban on natural philosophy. Soon, such studies started to increase rapidly in Paris University.[250]

Heir of Greek Philosophy

It is time to accept the inaccuracy of one fundamental notion. The orientalist scholars deliberate that modern Europe to be the heir of Greek philosophy. That is unfortunately not accurate. First of all, ancient Greece and Rome were not European entities but Mediterranean civilisations along with Egypt, Persia, Mesopotamia and Babylon. They were made part of 'European' civilisation much later after the medieval period. Secondly, after the Greco-Hellenic period the practice of philosophy came to an end for a long time and was only revived by the Muslims.

After the classical Greeks, the Hellenistic philosophers (approximately in the 4th to 1st centuries BCE) continued the Greek philosophical trend in Athens. The Hellenistic schools were the Epicureans, Stoics and the Skeptics. None of these schools developed a full system of their own. Neoplatonism arose in the 3rd century CE. But the philosophical schools were closed by the edicts of the Roman Emperor Theodosius in the 4th century CE and that of Emperor Justinian in the 6th century CE. As a consequence, philosophy and rational intellectualism was no longer practised over the Christian Greco-Roman world. Much of the philosophical works were lost during this period; in fact, in a large part of Europe philosophy had never prevailed.

Whatever philosophy survived found a home in the Muslim lands. It was the Muslim scholars who rediscovered philosophy,

---

[250] Lyons, Jonathan, 2009, p. 187-188.

worked with it, debated it, accepted it and rejected parts of it, but they progressed it. For centuries it was the Muslim scholars who worked with Greek philosophy. Europe inherited philosophy, in turn, from the Muslims. Philosopher Roger Bacon said, 'Philosophy is drawn from the Muslims'.[251]

The Muslim philosophers and theologians did not see eye to eye. The theologians believed that the philosophers placed too much authority on Greek notions, while philosophers, based on reason, saw the theologians as too literalist with the scriptures. Despite that there was significant correlation, such as, the philosophy of Ibn Sina draws inspiration from the Ash'ari theology and the mystical traditions of Islam on which Neoplatonism could stand on. Both these disciplines, Muslim philosophy and theology, would influence European philosophy.[252]

Saint Anselm of Canterbury (1033-1109), a Benedictine monk, was the first great Catholic theologian with access to some Greek texts in Latin translation. He was an original thinker and his theology was based on his own independent intellectual pondering of biblical scripture. But neither he nor his successor Peter Abelard were able to create any philosophical model. They simply used some elementary tools of Greek dialectics to illuminate already established truths. But by doing so they set the stage for the introduction of Muslim philosophy to form the foundation of the subsequent Western Christian philosophical system.[253]

Adelard of Bath had proposed that the rulers should be philosopher-kings who speak the truth and are guided by natural justice and reason. He has been unwittingly paraphrasing Plato

---

[251] Aziz, S. Atiya, 1962, p. 220.
[252] WR12, 2016.
[253] *Ibid.*

who had said the same thing in his *Republic*. Adelard most likely had picked up the idea from his visit to the Muslim domains as Plato was not much known to Europe at that time. The translations of Muslim philosophy to Latin had not yet started in earnest.

Thus, by the beginning of the 12th century there was no overarching sophisticated Christian philosophy which could express or defend the Christian faith. When the Arabic texts started to be translated, the existing academic curricula in Europe consisted of seven disciplines in two categories known as the *Trivium* and the *Quadrivium*. *Trivium* included grammar, rhetoric and logic, and the *Quadrivium* included arithmetic, geometry, music and astronomy for the more advanced students. There were no philosophy or philosophical theology, ethics or similar abstract disciplines.[254]

This situation changed after the arrival and translations of Muslim philosophy and theology. The most important of these translations were made by Dominicus Gundisalvus, the Archdeacon of Segovia in Spain, and Gerard of Cremona who worked in Toledo in Spain. Gundisalvus not only translated these texts but also popularised them and made them comprehensible to people whose education was restricted by the meagreness of the *Trivium* and *Quadrivium* syllabus. He wrote small books like the 'Immortality of the Soul' entirely derived from Ibn Sina, which became immensely popular. He was one of the early sources of the Ibn Sinan neoplatonic worldview in Europe. The *De Anima* of Gundisalvus is largely a transportation of Ibn Sina's doctrines. The *Shifa'* was also translated to Latin and was named *Sufficientia*.[255]

Even more influential on the long term was the translation of

---

[254] WR12.
[255] *Ibid.*

al-Ghazali's book *Maqasid al-Falasifah* (*Intentions of the Philosophers*). It summed up the Ibn Sinan neoplatonic view with great brilliance. The medieval Europeans, on reading the *Maqasid*, considered al-Ghazali to be an Ibn Sinan neoplatonic philosopher. Thus, his work was considered not a rejection but rather an affirmation of Ibn Sina's work.[256] This book of about three hundred pages became the classic short manual of philosophy. When Aquinas quoted in his works from 'al-Gazal' he was actually quoting from this book. This was one of the most frequently studied philosophical texts in medieval Europe.[257]

The three commentaries of Ibn Rushd on Aristotle also had a major effect on Europe. These were translated to Latin even before he died. Ibn Rushd's works were taken up by the Dominican order of priests who were the torch bearer of Christian intellectualism before the emergence of the Jesuits. He came to be known as 'the Commentator' in Europe for his commentaries on Aristotelian metaphysics. Albertus Magnus and Aquinas were quite influenced by these commentaries.[258]

Thomas Aquinas, in the 13th century, in his brilliant summation of scholastic learning, drew from Ibn Sina's *Suficientia*, al-Ghazali's *Maqasid* and Ibn Rushd's Aristotelian commentaries. He produced from them, in essence, a synthetic theology. As Ibn Sina had fused Aritotelian and Neoplatonic worldviews with the Islamic view, Thomas Aquinas took Greek philosophy inherited mainly via Ibn Sina, al-Ghazali and Ibn Rushd and superimposed Christian beliefs on it, critiqued the part that did not agree with Christianity and intellectually fused the rest together. He had his detractors in Europe but his adroit intellect overcame it all. The influence of this great Thomist theo-

---

[256] Marenbon, John, 1987, p. 60-62.
[257] WR12.
[258] *Ibid.*

philosophical system continues even today.[259]

Another group among those influenced by Ibn Rushd were the Latin Averroists. Unlike al-Ghazali or Aquinas, who were more intent on showing the symbiosis between revelation and reason, the Latin Averroists erred more on the side of rationality. They picked on the idea of Ibn Rushd's theory of Double Truth. This theory was used to reconcile the apparent conflict between the conclusions of logic and the clear requirement of belief as set forth by revelation. They interpreted the double truth as two contradictory propositions that can both be true. They discerned that the epistemological register of revelation is completely different than that of reason. So, it can be simultaneously said that the world has always existed *in Godhead* and it can also be said that the world came into existence *in time*. The greatest Latin Averroist was the 13th century Siger of Brabant.[260]

During the early medieval times only small bits of Aristotelian logic the *Organon* was known in Europe by the agency of Byzantine scholars. But the majority of Aristotle's work on logic was made available in its complete form and understanding from the Arabic translations. Of 'Ethics', Hunayn ibn Ishaq's translation of the Aristotelian 'Nicomachean Ethics' is considered as good as the modern English translation. Another person who earlier had much influence on Europe is al-Farabi, the Neoplatonic philosopher whose system was the most important one up to the time of Ibn Sina. He was known as the 'Second Teacher' with Aristotle being the first.[261]

These were the main sources from which flowered modern European philosophy. Europe owes a great debt to the Muslims not just for the transmission of Greek philosophy but also for the

---

[259] *Ibid..*
[260] WR12, 2016.
[261] *Ibid.*

original philosophical and theological works of the Muslims and their commentaries on ancient philosophy. Before that, some bits and pieces of ancient philosophy had survived in Europe but it is evident that the initial European philosophical systems were mainly influenced by Muslim philosophy and theology.

Medieval Europe translated the Muslim works to European languages, worked with it, debated it, implicitly accepted it, rejected parts of it, ascertained whatever original Greek works they could find and progressed from it to develop modern European philosophy. Whatever they did, though, they did after inheriting the major works from the Muslims. Modern Europe is the heir of not Greek philosophy, but the philosophy of the early Muslims.

CHAPTER 6

Influence of Muslim
Literature and Culture

Literature, languages and cultures have developed extensively in the Islamic empires and influenced other civilisations. Abu al-Hasan, commonly known as Ziryab, was a genius poet, musician, connoisseur of food and celebrity trendsetter from Baghdad. In the early 9th century he migrated to Spain and introduced chess during the reign of Abd al-Rahman II. (*Chaturanga*, the precursor to chess, originated in India. From there it went to Persia where the name was change to *shatranj* and became popular among the Muslims[262]).

From Spain chess went across the Pyrenees into Europe. There was some religious resistance to chess in Europe, especially because it came from the Muslim lands. Cardinal Petrus Damiani (1007-1072) of Ostia wrote a letter to Pope-elect Alexander II and the Archdeacon Hildebrand (later Pope Gregory VII) complaining about chess. In 1061, Alexander II forbad the clergy in his domain from playing chess, though it was resumed after his

---

[262] Al-Hassani, 2007, p. 18.

death.[263]

It was Muslims who first wrote books on chess with its history and game strategies that included openings, endings and game moves that made the game interesting and popular. Chess was a favourite of the Abbasids and produced great masters like al-Suli, al-Razi and al-Adani. Written around 1370 the *Book of the Examples of Warfare in the Game of Chess* first introduced the 'Blind Abbess and Her Nuns' game plan which is still practised by grandmasters.[264] The moves and strategies devised a thousand years ago by the likes of al-Suli are at times considered innovative in the current period.

Baghdad was the centre of fashion and Ziryab came to Spain with more than just chess. He brought all the fashions of Baghdad like formalised multi-course fine dining and luxurious dresses that included 'winter and summer wear' along with the dates for the seasonal change of the dresses. Ziryab became a fashion icon or 'brand' in Spain. Hair fashion, toothpaste, deodorant and leather shoes with light cork soles supported by him were in vogue. The highly cultured Spanish Muslims were neighbours to the Franks. They influenced the Franks who would gradually become highly cultural by the time of 'Sun King' Louis XIV of the 17th century.

Ziryab also started a consortium of music in Spain. It became very popular. Spanish music then moved into Europe through the troubadours—the travelling musician singing love songs. They moved far into provincial France and Britain and Celtic lands.[265]

In the field of literature Muslims works like *Arabian Nights*, *Sinbad the Sailor* and *Ali Baba* are quite well-known classics. But there are other more profound literature that have influenced the

---

[263] Murray, H. J. R., 1985, p. 408.
[264] Al-Hassani, 2007, p. 18-19.
[265] WR21.

West. One such work is *Hayy ibn Yaqzan* a mystico-philosophical tale by Ibn Tufayl of a solitary man on an Island. This work has influenced many other works including Daniel Defoe's *Robinson Crusoe* as established by A. R. Pastor.[266]

In the musical arena, al-Kindi provided a detailed fretting of the *ud,* which was the ancestor of instruments like the lute. Al-Farabi wrote five books on music theory, the masterpiece being *The Great Book of Music* which was translated to Hebrew and then to Latin. He invented the *rababah*, the older version of rebec of the violin family, and the *qanun*, a table zither. The guitar comes from the Muslim *quitara* and the naker drum from the *naqqara.*[267] Even the quintessential traditions like the English 'Morris' folk dance is really a corruption of the 'Moorish' dancing, harkening back to a time when Arab minstrels entertained the nobility of Muslim Spain.[268]

The European minstrel class of the Middle Ages adopted the instruments and devices from the Arabs. Research and clues in the Medieval Latin treatises on music leads to the conclusion that the teaching and writing of Arabian and Mozarabian theories of music also had influenced the theory of music of western Europe.[269]

Europe even learned manners and etiquette from the Muslims. *The Book of Contemplation*, a book on the Muslim genre of behaviour and etiquette, chastised the Crusaders for their loose morals, poor diet and general bad habits. Those who lived for some time among the Muslims, generally, improved their manners.[270] The book also recounts a Muslim doctor's amazement

---

[266] Sharif, M. M., 2016, p. 539.

[267] Al-Hassani, 2007, p. 34-35.

[268] Lyons, Johnathan, 2009, p.2.

[269] Farmer, Henry George, 1932, p. 561.

[270] Lyons, Johnathan, 2009, p. 20-21.

at the primitiveness of the European medical techniques which led to the death of patients.

The importance of the progressive Muslim talents and culture was recognised quite early. During the First Crusade, when Edessa fell to the Crusaders, Baldwin of Boulogne, one of the leaders of the crusade, declared himself Count of Edessa. Frankish princes and their vassals were appointed to the top politically sensitive positions but he retained sufficient positions for locals due to their talents.[271] When Antioch fell to the crusaders its residents enjoyed water supplies and other civic amenities like the public water clock (clepsydra) which were unknown to the West.[272] By the time the scholar Adelard of Bath arrived in Antioch in 1114, Arab culture held sway over much of the life in the so-called Latin East.[273]

Antioch also became an important centre of translation of Muslim texts to Latin. The texts seized by conquering Crusaders were available in the bazaars of this city.[274]Centuries of translation not only vastly improved the knowledge of Europe but also gave it a brand-new lexicon. The invaluable bequest of the Muslims includes terms of modern technical lexicon from azimuth to zenith and from algebra to zero. Words like *alchemy, alcohol, amulet, cipher, cheque, elixir* and *tariff* have direct Muslim origin.

The Muslim influence can be found in everything from the more mundane foods—apricots, oranges and artichokes, to name a few—to such common nautical terms as *admiral, sloop* and *monsoon*. Fulbert (d .1028), bishop of Chatres, who developed the Cathedral School of Chatres into Europe's chief centre of learning, was among the first to introduce Arabic words into Latin—the

---

[271] Lyons, Johnathan, 2009, p. 17.

[272] *Ibid.*, p. 18.

[273] *Ibid.*, p. 27.

[274] *Ibid.*, p. 104.

names of stars in the constellations. Many of the stars and constellations which bear Latin name are actually of Arabic provenance, such as, Batanalhaut (Batan al-Hut)[275], Aldebaran, Menke and Rigel.

Muslims developed not just Arabic but other languages and linguistics as well. Persian, an ancient language, was brought to its modern form by the ink of Muslim poets like Firdawsi and Hafiz. Another good example of such linguistic development is India. Languages like Urdu and Bengali developed locally by the sponsorship of Muslim sultans in India who reigned before the Moghul emperors.

Islam also gave India its greatest empire, the Moghuls, and a unique political identity. Before the Muslims, India used to be a region with a large number of independent kingdoms or nations divided on the basis of languages, cultures and ethno-religious identities—Dravidians, Aryans, Buddhist, Jains and others. Despite that, Muslims like al-Biruni promoted the concept of these different people within the region extending from the Himalayas to Cape Comorin as one civilisation. Amir Khosrow, 14th century scholar, poet and musician, lovingly articulated about India as a nation where people spoke Sindhi, Bengali, Punjabi, Telegu, Tamil and Kannada.[276] It was, of course, the Moghuls starting from Akbar who cemented India into one political entity or nation concept. The British followed with the Moghul's 'one entity' political India concept.

There has always been a vast versatility in the cultural and literary world of the Muslims. Discussion on some unique contribution in poetry, humour and romantic literature follows.

---

[275] Lyons, Johnathan, 2009, p. 40.
[276] Wood, 2007.

The Verses from Spain

Poetry found succour in all Muslims domains. The Rashidun Caliphs Abu Bakr and Ali were poets of very high calibre. Umar ibn Abi Rabiʿah and the female poet al-Khansaʾ spun their verses in the earliest Muslim era. As the Umayyads established their empire, Arabic became the international language and soon Arabic poetry was being written from Spain to the borders of India in sweeping verses of great emotions and beauty about the rulers and warriors as well as about nature and landscape.

Various types of poetry were written and new genres, like the ghazal, were introduced. In the early Abbasid period, poetry further diversified under the influence of the Sufis. Many poets like al-Mutanabbi and Abu al-Ala al-Maʿarri flourished in this period.

Muslim poets wrote poetry in different languages and forms. Persian poetry was being written in the later Abbasid period. Historical stalwarts like Firdawsi, Omar Khayyam, Rumi, Hafiz and Nizami penned their emotions during this era. A few centuries later, Muslims having introduced the Urdu language were writing Urdu poems. Bengali poems were also sponsored and written by Muslims.

The variety of poetry that was originated by the Muslim poets had not been encountered before and would influence the poetic brilliance of the European Romantic age. This influence would initiate from Andalusia (Muslim Spain). As early as the 10th century, Muslim Spain was a poetic seat of variegated verdant verses. Following are representative verses from poets of that era.[277]

> *I have never seen nor heard of such a thing.*
> *Her modesty turns pearl into carnelian.*

---

[277] WR3.

Her face is so clear that when you gaze on its perfections
You see your own face reflected.

—*White Skin*, Ibn Abd Rabbih
10th century, Cordoba

The garden of green hillocks dresses up
for visitors in the most beautiful colours.
As if a young woman's dowry was spread out
glittering with gold necklaces.
Or as if someone had poured out censers of mush powder
mixed with the purest aromatic oils.
Birds trill on the branches like singing girls
bending over their lutes.
And water falls continuously like
neck-chains of silver and pearls.
These are splendours of such perfection.
They call to mind the beauty of absolute certainty,
the radiance of faith.

—*The Garden*, Abdullah ibn al-Simak
12th century, Granada

My eye frees what the page imprisons:
the white the white and the black the black.

—*Reading*, Ibn Ammar,
11th century, Silves

Look at the ripe wheat bending before the wind
like squadrons of horsemen fleeing in defeat,
bleeding from the wounds of the poppies.

—*Grainfield*, Ibn Iyad
12th century, Central Andalusia

The river of diaphanous waters
murmuring between its banks
would have you believe
it is a stream of pearls.

At midday tall trees
cover it with shadows
turning it the colour of metal.

So now you see it, blue,
wrapped in brocade,
like a warrior in armour
resting in the shade of his banner.

—*Blue River*, Muhammad ibn Ghalib al-Rusafi
12th century, Ruzafa, Valencia

Don't cross me off as fickle
because a singing voice
has captured my heart.

One must be serious sometimes
and light-hearted at other times:

like wood from which come
both the singer's lute
and the warrior's bow.

—*Apology*, Ibrahim ibn Uthman
12th century, Cordoba

When the West Wind ripped the river's tunic
the river overflowed its banks
to pursue and take revenge;

but the doves laughed, and made fun
from a sheltering thicket,
and the river, shame-faced, crawled back
into his bed to hide under its veil.

—*Tide in the Guadalquivir,* Ibn Safr al-Marini
12th century, Almera

From al-Zahra I remember you with passion.
The horizon is clear, the earth's face serene.
The breeze grows faint with the coming of dawn.
It seems to pity me and lingers, full of tenderness.

The meandering waterway with its silvery waters
shows a sparkling smile.
It resembles a necklace unclasped and thrown aside.

A day like those delicious ones now gone by
when seizing the dream of destiny we were thieves of
pleasure.

...

Today, alone, I distract myself with flowers
that attract my eyes like magnets.
The wind roughhouses with them bending them over.

The blossoms are eyes.
They see my sleeplessness and weep for me;
their iridescent tears overflow staining the calyx.

In the bright sun, red buds light up the rose bushes
making the morning brighter still.

Fragrant breaths come from the pome of the waterlilies,

Sleepyheads with eyes half-opened by dawn.
Everything stirs up the memory of my passion for you
Still intact in my chest
Although my chest might seem too narrow to contain it.

Would God grant calm to my heart
if it could cease to remember you
And refrain from flying to your side
on wings trembling with desire

If this passing breeze would consent to carry me along,
It would put down at your feet a man worn out by grief.

Oh, my most precious jewel, the most sublime,
The one preferred by my soul, as if lovers dealt in jewels!

In times gone by we demanded of each other
payments of pure love
And were happy as colts running free in a pasture.

But now I am the only one who can boast of being loyal.
You left me
and I stay here,
still sad, still loving you.

—Written from *al-Zahra*, Ibn Zaydun
11th century, Cordoba

The couplets of *zajals* (*ghazals*) and *jarchas* (*kharjah*) of *muwashshah*s poetic form written during Muslim Spain would directly influence the formation of later Spanish genres. One of earliest example is the *Cantigas de Santa Maria* which were religious songs depicting Virgin Mary composed upon the order of Alfonso X, King of Castile and Aragon.[278] It was followed by the *Cantigas De Amigos* and *Villancicos* and would lead to the emergence of amazing dramatic plays of the 16th century.

The Epic of Romance

It is impossible to conceive of men and women without thinking of romance. Writers of all the ages have written stories of love and passion. But pure romance—the all annihilating human love—took its form in the hands of the Sufis. They invoked a love so ardently human that it pushed animal lust to the sidelines and pure human feelings burned more brightly like an unquenchable flame. Thus was born the epic of pure romance. One of the greatest of such writers was Nizam al-Din Abu Muhammad Ilyas known as Nizami (1141-1209) of Azerbaijan.

Johann Wolfgang von Goethe, the 18th century German poet, novelist and playwright, stated that Nizami was 'A gentle, highly gifted spirit who, after Firdawsi, had collected the heroic traditions, chose for the material of his poems the sweetest encounters of the deepest love. He presented lovers, Majnun and Layla, Khusraw and Shirin, who were meant for one another by premonition, fate, nature, habit, inclination and passion and staunchly devoted to each other, but become divided by mad ideas, stubbornness, chance, necessity and force, then miraculously reunited, yet in the end again in one way or another torn apart and separated from each other.'

One of the most famous of Nizami's works is the story of *Layla and Majnun.* This story is based on the love of an 8th century Bedouin poet, Qays ibn al-Mulawwah, known as Majnun, for a girl of his tribe, Layla al-Amiriyyah. His love was reciprocated by her, but it only led them to a great tragedy. Their

---

[278] Al Hassani, 2007, p. 35.

houses did not approve of their union. A star-crossed fortune separated them and, finally, both died unable to bear the separation.

Nizami's love epic was to endure through the changing world. Over centuries, from the original Persian hundreds of versions were written in various languages including Arabic, Latin, Turkish, Urdu, Hindi, English and Bengali. Different versions of the story still continue to be written. Many songs in different languages have been sung crowning the love of Layla and Majnun mesmerising millions. The story was adapted for opera while dozens of movies had been made. It became the inspiration of a new genre of creative arts.

There are many parallels between *Romeo and Juliet* and *Layla and Majnun*. To start with, the names of both the stories are the names of the two lovers. There is a quarrel between the two houses of the lovers. Both the lovers die in the end. The story mentions both Majnun and Romeo as a 'madman' in love. The heroine is loved by a second person, the husband of Layla and the fiancé of Juliet. Both are victims of circumstances and both die as well towards the end. There is a benevolent prince in both stories who sadly is unable to save the lovers.

Character of Humour

The great Seljuk empire disintegrated at the end of the 12th century. One of its direct offshoots was the Seljuk Sultanate of Rum. This dynasty (1077-1307) ruled over what is now Anatolian Turkey with its capital in Iznik and later in Konya (Iconium). In the 13th century, during the rule of this prosperous dynasty a man by the name of Nasruddin Hodja is believed to have been born in the village of Hortu in Sivrihisa, Eskisehir. He lived most of his mature life in Aksehir and then in Konya. This man, who was a Sufi-philosopher and would become a judge, possessed a tremendous sense of humour for which he was very famous. His witty and satirical sayings came to be celebrated far and wide.

Based on this character, Muslim literature presented the first international comedian to the world. There developed a large number of popular tales and anecdotes about him. The anecdotes present Nasruddin as a simpleton but in many cases, there is a wisdom, philosophy and morale behind the light humour. Some contain amusing ingredients against despotic rulers or dull judges while others are purely humorous and silly:

A man asked, 'How old are you?'

Nasruddin replied, 'I am forty.'

The man said, 'But you said the same two years ago.'

'I am a man of my word. I still stand by what I said,' replied Nasruddin.

ೕ•ೞ

Returning from the desert, Nasruddin said, 'In the desert I caused a whole tribe of dangerous bloodthirsty Bedouins to run.'

'Wow!' said one of the listeners. 'How did you manage that?'

'Easy. When I saw them I just ran and they ran after me.'

ೕ•ೞ

A neighbour who was always borrowing things came over and wanted to borrow Nasruddin's donkey. Nasruddin didn't particularly like the man and said, 'Sorry, but the donkey is not here.'

Just then the donkey let out a bray. The man turned and said, 'I just heard your donkey.'

'Well, are you going to believe me or a donkey!' said Nasruddin.

❧

Nasruddin started a consultancy. His sign read: 'All questions answered. 100 dirhams for two questions'. A trickster trying to upset Nasruddin went to him and said, 'Isn't 100 dirhams too much for just two questions?'

'Yes,' replied Nasruddin. 'What is the second question?'

❧

One day, in the market place, Nasruddin declared that he was a fool. To prove the point, he stood by the market place and said if anyone offered him two coins he would take the lesser one no matter how much the bigger one was worth. Some people offered him two coins and he took the smaller coin. Soon, people were laughing at him for taking coins of very small denominations in place of gold dinars. When he was alone, a man asked him, 'Why are you making a fool of yourself?'

Nasruddin smiled and said, 'This way they give me a lot of money for nothing just to prove that it's not them but I who am the fool.'

❧

His wife asked, 'Nasruddin, why do you always answer a question with another question?'

Nasruddin said, 'Do I?'

During the Ottoman era, his fame and anecdotal tales spread to distant lands of Asia and Europe. Over time, thousands of such tales were attributed or added to his repertoire. His tales are known to have circulated in a large number of languages— Albanian, Arabic, Armenian, Azeri, Bengali, Bosnian, Bulgarian, Greek, Chinese, Hindi, Italian, Pashto, Persian, Romanian, Russian, Serbian, Turkish and Urdu. As the tales about Nasruddin spread, he came to be called by slightly different names in different cultures—Nasruddin Hoca in Turkey, Hoja Nasreddin in Greece, Juha in North Africa, Molla Nasruddin or Nasruddin Hodja in Azebaijan, Aghanistan, Iran, India, Pakistan and Bangladesh, Nasir ad-Din in Arabic countries, and other such variations.

Besides the variation in name due to linguistic differences, different cultures fashioned local characters in line with Nasruddin. Sly Peter of Bulgaria and Macedonia, Birbal and Gopal Bhar of India, Giufa of Sicily, Djoha of the later Sephardi Jews and many such characters are based on Nasruddin or were associated with him in tales.

In later periods, numerous books and whole novels were written about Nasruddin. In 1943, Yakov Protazanov of the Soviet Union made the film 'Nasreddin in Bukhara'. In Bukhara of Uzbekistan there is a bronze statue of the smiling Hodja riding on his famous donkey. In Aksehir of Turkey the 'International Nasreddin Hoca Festival' is held every year between July 5-10. UNESCO proclaimed the year 1996 as the 'Nasreddin Hoca Year'.

Firdawsi

Firdawsi's full name is Hakim Abu al-Qasim Firdawsi Tusi (935-1020). He was a great Persian poet and the author of the *Shahnama* (*Epic of the Kings*), which is the greatest and longest epic poem ever written and is the national epic of Iran. He devoted 35 years of his life to this masterpiece.

The Shahnama narrates the mythical and historical past of Persia (*Aeran Veage* of the Gathas) from the creation of the world up to the Islamic conquest of Persia in the 7th century. The final edition of the Shahnama contained some sixty thousand distiches (couplets of verses). The work is divided into three successive parts or ages: the mythical, heroic, and historical ages. The mythical part is the shortest, with about 2100 verses. It gives an account of formation of the world and creation of the first man as portrayed in the Sassanians mythology. The age of the heroes consists of about two third of the Shahnama. The rest comprises the historical age in which Firdawsi mentions the Achaemenids, Sekander (Alexander) and the Sassanids in resplendent poetry—rich, lavish and moving.

Firdawsi revived and regenerated the Persian language and cultural traditions. Though written a thousand years ago, Firdawsi produced such a profound language that there has not been any significant change in the language over this period. Many modern Iranians see him as the father of the modern Persian language.

He started his work under the patronage of the Samanid Dynasty. But before he finished the epic the Samanid Dynasty fell to the Ghaznavids. He continued to work under the new patrons. Wrapped in seven massive volumes he took the finished work to the court of Sultan Mahmud of Ghazni. But, it is said, the sultan not finding himself included as a protagonist in the book's acknowledgement, was irate. Instead of giving Firdawsi the agreed 60,000 gold dinar, he offered 20,000 silver dirhams.

The poet, angry and sad, rejected the offer and returned to Tus. Finally, the sultan coming to understand the greatness of the work sent the money to Firdawsi. But Firdawsi died just before the money reached him. His daughter, in respect to her esteemed father, refused to accept the money. The money was used to build a beautiful stone caravanserai nearby, on the road from Merv to Tus, for travellers to rest, trade and tell stories. Firdawsi was buried at the yard of his own home, where his mausoleum now stands. Firdawsi was aware of the greatness of his work and thus wrote:

> *I've journeyed to the end of this great epic*
> *All the lands will talk of me.*
> *I shall not die, for the seeds I've sown*
> *Will keep my name from the grave,*
> *All men of sense and wisdom will acclaim*
> *When I am gone, my praise and my fame.*

Charles Augustin Saint-Beuve, French literary critic of the 19th century, said, 'If we could realise that great works such as the Shahnama exists in the world, we would not become so much proud of our own works in such a silly manner.'

Several copies of the great work are extant. Though two of the most famous, the *Houghton Shahnama* and the *Great Mongol Shahnama*, were split up into sheets to be sold separately in the 20th century. A single sheet of the *Houghton Shahnama* was bought by the Aga Khan Museum for Euros 904,000 in 2006. The *Bayasanghori Shahnama* is included in UNESCO's *Memory of the World Register* of cultural heritage items.

Jalal al-Din al-Rumi (1207-1273)

Jalal al-Din Muhammad al-Rumi was born in Balkh (present-day Afghanistan). His father Baha al-Din was a renowned religious scholar who arranged Rumi's education under local scholars. This was an unsettling time with the Mongol onslaughts on Muslims regions. The invasion caused his family to migrate from place to place. Eventually, they settled in Konya when he was about 18 years old. After the death of his father, Rumi was appointed as a professor of a famous madrasah in Konya at the age of 24. When he was 25, for some time, Rumi went to Aleppo and then to Damascus on academic purposes.[279]

He continued his studies up to the age of 40. He was influenced by the poetry of Attar and Sana'i.[280] He learned Sufi mysticism, an ascetic meditative life, from Burhan al-Din and later from Shams al-Din Tabriz. His fame as a poet, religious scholar and Sufi spread wide. He remained a teacher in the madrasah where he taught a large number of pupils. After his death the famous Maulvi Order of *tasawwuf* considered him their founder.

His major contribution lies in Muslim culture, poetry and poetic mysticism. His poetry encompassed many aspects of knowledge and life. In the *Mathnawi*, the main subject is the relationship between man and God on the one hand, and between man and man on the other. Rumi draws on a variety of subjects and derives numerous examples from everyday life. He portrayed the various stages of man's evolution in his journey towards the Ultimate.

Soon after the completion of the *Mathnawi*, other scholars started writing detailed commentaries on it, in order to interpret its rich propositions on *tasawwuf*, metaphysics and ethics. Several commentaries in different languages have been written since then. Apart from the *Mathnawi*, he also wrote his *Diwan* (collection of poems) and *Fihi Ma Fih* (a collection of mystical sayings).

His writing has profoundly influenced the literature, mysticism, culture and philosophy throughout Central Asia. Many religious scholars, mystics, philosophers, sociologists, script writers, *etc.* have referred to his verses during all these centuries since his death. Currently, he is the most-read poet (English

---

[279] Said, H. M., 1991, p. 51-52.
[280] Jafri, Maqsood, 2003, p. 238.

translation particularly by A. J. Arberry and Coleman Barks) in the USA and probably in the world. The year 2007 was declared as 'Rumi's Year' by UNESCO. A medal was also issued by UNESCO to commemorate his eight hundredth birthday in the same year.

Muslims were the best poets and writers in those periods gone by. They had developed a Muslim culture that influenced the rest of the world. Such influence is still discernible in the contemporary world like the popularity of Rumi and Khayyam's poems the worldover and the influence of the works of poets like Mir Taki Mir, Ghalib, *etc.*, in the lyrics and development of Indian Hindi cinema.

CHAPTER 7

Age of Total Knowledge

The passion for knowledge in the early Islamic period led to the Age of Total Knowledge in which there was no conflict between religion and and other disciplines like science. Muslims studied all known disciplines of knowledge—religious disciplines, natural sciences, theology, philosophy, Sufism, cultural and literary disciplines—and became the best in all of these disciplines in the world. Each scholar specialised in certain disciplines but understood and respected the relevance of other disciplines as well.

The source of inspiration for all these disciplines, though, was the Qur'an and the *Sunnah* from where Muslims inherited a very wide epistemological spectrum. Among its various topics the Qur'an contains very precise historical and scientific notions which led to the study of history and sciences. Roslyn Quinn's book *God's Argument,* which is about the logical structure of the Qur'an, offers a systematic exposition of how most of the classical form of Aristotelian syllogism and logic are present in the modes of arguments in the Qur'anic texts.[281] Such structure had actually inspired theology and philosophy among the Muslims.

---

[281] WR8.

A high-quality dialectical balance existed in the society between all the epistemologies. Thus, if there was any contradiction in the work of a scholar of any one discipline, the other scholars would debate and correct them. For instance, when the philosophers stepped out of line the theologians corrected them—as did al-Ghazali. When the Sufis crossed the line the ulema corrected them—as was during the time of early Sufis. When the rational scholars tried to dominate politics the legal scholars set them right as was done by Imam Hanbal. During that period of time, when such critique and 'corrections' were carried out, none of the great scholars actually said that the other disciplines were not required they simply corrected the mistakes. They never disrupted the balance of the 'Total Knowledge'.

To such scholars the Qur'an was fertile and open to multifarious types of reception. Caliph Ali once commented on the Qur'an, 'Allah has made the Qur'an a drink to quench the thirst of the learner, a spring for the hearts of the jurists, a guide for the pious, a proof for those who discourse it, an evidence for its adversaries, and a convincing proof for those who pass judgement'.[282]

Centuries later, in the modern age, Professor Laura Vaglieri echoes the same notion, 'On the whole we find in the Qur'an, a collection of wisdom which can be adopted by the most intelligent of men, the greatest of the philosophers, and the most skilful of politicians'.[283]

Intellection, Reason and Guidance

Original Islamic scholarship, comprised of the Qur'an and *Sunnah,* provides a body of *integrated intellect* containing a spectrum of epistemologies starting from formal worship, the gift

---

[282] Hasan, M., 2004, p. 606.

[283] *Ibid.,* p. 608.

of the spirit, the essential requisites of social, political, military and economic life, to the very needs of the individual—such as daily functions, obligations, cleanliness, purity—all in one massive practice.

It is a vast array of intelligence not just a mechanical regulatory body for social or ritual matters.[284] With specialisation, individual topics in the *integrated intellect* led to the development of individual disciplines like jurisprudence and the sciences. There was a progressive widening in the study and understanding of knowledge.

The purity of the *integrated intellect* was always essential. Any attempt to tamper with it, for example messing with the authority of ḥadīth, will cause a new religion to form as that is changing the root of the religion or, at least, a new sect to form. Traditional ulema scholars have preserved the unity of the *integrated intellect* to protect the individuals and the community from splitting up leading to segregated socio-religious entities.

While the theologians protect the community from misplaced ideas, many due to external influences, and the Sufis define a depth and meaning of soul, and the rationalists advance the sciences, the ulema safeguard the primary *integrated intellect*. They don't let the intellect and by extension the community to split. Thus, if scholars of theology, Sufism, rationalism and social sciences are necessary, the ulema remain fundamental - the peg to which all necessary ideas are tethered to, retaining it as a coherent mass and providing morality and guidance.

The ulema are the centre of all epistemology and, thus, they require to be the most dedicated and best versed. In this constantly changing world all other epistemologies have kept on changing, even the scriptures of past religions have been altered. It became the duty of the ulema to retain the absolute purity of the

---

[284] WR8.

integrated intellect. Through remarkable odds they have maintained that stupendous task up to now.

Intellect, *aql*, was always a broader term in Islamic disciplines than its current neurological definition. Muslims showed a high regard for the mind, in a versatile and intuitive way. For intellect to function properly it needs to be free of emotive influences. People have emotional tendencies or weakness like ego, prejudices, anger, envy, rancour, *etc.* These emotive aspects actually hinder insight and vision. In the development of any discipline—theology, *tafsīr* or in the modern cases the social sciences—one needs to understand and decide objectively. A good argument or a good theory choice is only possible if one has overcome the emotive weaknesses and prejudices that reside within. The self has to be completely neutral in terms of emotional turbulence or wrong choices will be made.

To control emotion the need to understand the self is paramount. Intellect, in Islam, is not just knowing the self but also controlling the self. Knowing one's ego includes restraining the ego. Spiritual practice that binds or restrains the ego is incorporated in Islamic intellectualism.

The early generations of Muslims (*Salaf*) did not look into intellectualism in just a scholastic way but also in a humanistic sense. Rationalism not simply liberated the early Muslims from superstition but also maintained their integrity. It became rational to be moral. It produced a coherent human being capable of self-knowledge and discipline, who could do justice in understanding the world and people without emotional prejudice or mental blocks. The absence of such humanistic influence on intellect leads to extreme fundamentalist views or extreme liberal tendencies driven by the influence of emotive urges. In such cases, conviction can become an ugly mirror to internal turbulences. Post-modern philosophy has a poor understanding of human selfhood which is causing much turmoil in human society.[285]

Sufism emerged to put some formal mechanism of restraint on ego and similar emotive problems. Thus, it meant to bring to people an understanding of what their soul was engaged in or should engage in by using the richness of the prophetic heritage — a theory of the soul. *Tasawwuf*, the source of Sufi practice, is rooted in the *sirah* of the Prophet,[286] his long contemplations in the cave of Makkah, his frugal way of life in Madinah and also the *zuhd* or austerity of the Rashidun Caliphs. Islamic theology, on the other hand, had emerged to deal with the negative aspect of ignorance, divisiveness, speculative philosophy and the imported-misperceived theological ideas that were gaining popularity among the unsuspecting mass.

There had existed mutual affirmation as well as conflict between the past scholars. That was quite normal and, in fact, helpful because it helped to root out errors and inaccuracies within the competing epistemologies. Ibn Taymiyyah's views, with Hanbali influence, conflicted with other models of epistemology. The point, probably, being that if the literalist dogma is not retained then mundane 'reason' will rationalise and change divine religion to the extent that it will no longer be recognisable. Moreover, reason does not necessarily lead to any unique solution. Ibn Sina, al-Ghazali and Ibn Rushd all used reason in their definition of metaphysics, but they all arrived at different systems, solutions or positions.

So, in this broad view of intellect, basing the entire code of life on just one aspect, even reason, could be perilous. It would give power but not the guidance to apply the power ethically. The ascent and evolution of humanity to the 'One' is not through standalone logic, which would make human beings inert like

---

[285] WR8.
[286] *Ibid.*

matter with fixed properties and convert human intellect into fixed processes like chemical reactions. To appreciate the Divine, which is above rationalism, human beings also require abstraction without computation.

SECTION TWO

Muslim Contributions
to the Renaissance

The early Muslim empires' strength dissipated due to conflict and infighting caused by internal disintegrational forces. This led to the breakup up of the empires into smaller sultanates and emirates. These weakened entities were then subject to sustained external invasions and practically annihilation.

All the knowledge the early Muslims had accumulated and developed was at risk of being lost during these invasions. Definitely, significant part had been lost but, fortunately, much of it was transplanted to Europe. European scholars came to Muslim lands and studied the Muslim knowledge and translated it into their own languages, mainly Latin in the initial phase, and spread the knowledge in Europe. As the Muslims had revived the lost philosophy of the classical Greeks, the Europeans retained the Muslim knowledge while the Muslims themselves fell into intellectual regression.

CHAPTER 8

Intellectualism in Medieval Europe

There were three sustained military invasions (Tri-Military Events) of the Muslim lands that had devastated the early Muslim empires—the Spanish *Reconquista*, the Crusades and the Mongol Scourge. Before going into details about these invasions and their effects on the Muslim society it is important to understand the relative intellectual levels of Europeans and Early Muslims, and their dominant epistemologies or guiding intellectual principles during the period when the first European encounters with Muslim knowledge took place.

A Comparision of Principle Epistomology between Mediaval Europe and Early Muslim Empires

In Europe, the central dominant thought since the 4th century was theology. After that, from the Renaissance (14th century) onwards theology was replaced by philosophy and rationalism. A brief historical background is required to understand this change in intellection.

Immediately after Christ, Christianity had evolved in

multifarious ways. There developed many Christian sects, different groups had different religious views. There was one group that considered themselves Jews but believed Jesus was a messiah. Some sects considered him a prophet while others considered him divine. There was another sect, followers of Marcion of Sinope, which considered that there were two gods. Arius of Alexandria claimed that God and Jesus were of different 'matter' as Jesus had a beginning but God was eternal. Another group believed that Jesus was born of Mary and her husband was Joseph, while the Ebionites considered that God had adopted Jesus as his son.

All the Christians were much persecuted in pagan Roman Empire. But Saint Constantine, Emperor of Rome, accepted Christianity as the religion of Rome which ended the persecution. He inaugurated the Council of Nicaea in the 4th century in which a rectification and unification of all these diverse beliefs needed to be carried out to arrive at a singular unified religious consent. This immense task carried out theologically resulted in the Trinity becoming the dominant belief in Christianity.

During the first three centuries of Christian era many Christian books were written. There were more gospels than the four which was later theologically canonised and became part of the Bible. The Bible was the product of theological consideration as to which of the religious books, gospels and epistles, were to be included and which to be rejected. Theological disagreements over time among different denominations led to different Bibles with some dissimilarities. Thus, the attempt to arrive at a unified religion and Bible was carried out by theological debates, political assertions and resolutions.

Only when the theological resolution was complete then Christianity played the unifying role in Europe. North and western Europe had many small kingdoms ruled by minor kings and tribal chieftains with pagan beliefs. Each had their own rules and morality. Christianity paved a uniform morality throughout Europe.

But, as time went by, Christian theology rejected natural philosophy and science. Much earlier, in Saint Paul's letter to the Galatians 'time reckoning' is discouraged,

> "But now after you have known God, or rather are known by God, how is it that you turn again to the weak and beggarly elements, to which you desire again to be in bondage. You observe days and months and seasons and years."

> —*Galatians*, 4:9-10

Perhaps, the context in which Paul had given such guidance was completely different, but later literal misunderstanding of such words led to a distancing from natural philosophy. In late 4th century, Saint Augustine of Hippo, a remarkable theologian and intellect, had foresworn science and arts, 'Men proceed to investigate the phenomena of nature, the part of nature not beyond us, though the knowledge is of no value to them: for they wish to know simply for the sake of knowing'.[287] Such was the theology dominated worldview that Europe possessed and practised.

The change of dominant worldview from theology to philosophy and natural science was initiated due to the influence of Muslims of Spain and Sicily. By the 9th century, the Muslim world had advanced in science and philosophy to a great extent. There was no conflict between science and religion for the Muslims. When European scholars came in contact with these disciplines they were amazed.

---

[287] Sheed, F. J., 1942, p. 247.

As the European intellects increasingly started to accept philosophy and science from the Muslim world, there developed an immense conflict between rational Europe and theological Europe. At this juncture, the intellectuals discovered the rational commentary of Ibn Rushd (Averroes) on Aristotle. Such were the weapons the intellectuals were searching for and accepted it with ardour. Ultimately, around the renaissance, philosophy won over theology and became the dominant intellectual force in Europe which allowed them the pursuance of natural science.

In the Muslim world, the central dominant thought and the way it developed was different from the European Christian model. In Europe, fundamental religious concepts like Trinity and the Bible were theologically debated and deduced over three centuries after Jesus. The Qur'an, on the other hand, was memorised and written during the time of the Prophet, and formally compiled within a year of his death. So, there was no scope for theology to play any dominant role—all the precepts were given. The traditions or sayings of the Prophet, the second most important Islamic scripture, was practised in schools as oral literature along with some uncompiled written traditions. In a couple of centuries ḥadīth was compiled from both of these sources first by jurists like Imam Malik and then specialised tradition or ḥadīth scholars like Imam Bukhari using a methodology based on the rational *isnad* referencing system. Again, no scope for theology.

Most important of all, unlike Christian theology of the same period, the Qur'an and Islamic tradition encouraged the seeking of knowledge of all kinds. So, the early Muslims studied religious disciplines as well as the natural sciences—there was no intrinsic conflict between revelation and reason. As there was no theology blocking the study of sciences, there was, in fact, no need for philosophical arguments in favour of sciences for the Muslims. They studied sciences *and* philosophy because their religion itself encouraged all knowledge.

Among the Muslims, theology came to *be* for different reasons. It did play a part in factors of lesser significance. It was used to explain unique perennial issues that other religions have faced such as 'Theodicy' or the presence of evil in the world. But mainly, theological debates ensued at stages to resolve finer abstruse opinions or political differences or to defend the intrusion of speculative ideas into the Muslim religious framework. So, neither theology nor philosophy were needed for the Muslims to investigate knowledge and specifically the sciences as it was encouraged in their own religion. Did they study theology and philosophy? Indeed, they did and produced remarkable theologians and the best philosophers since Aristotle. But the Muslims studied these like any other disciplines— mathematics, chemistry, optics, medicine, astronomy, *etc.*, and in which also they produced the best scholars.

This is the concept that the Western scholars find hard to grasp. They have come through a worldview dominated by theology that *rejected* natural sciences in which philosophy was a *necessity* to counter theology and enable natural sciences. They think that the Muslim enlightenment must have come via the very same model. But in the Muslim society the seeking of knowledge including natural sciences have been *encouraged* by the religion itself, and thus philosophy was not a requirement to study the sciences, it was just another discipline, albeit, that supported theoretical contemplation.

The first famous Muslim philosopher was al-Kindi (9th century). By his time Muslim scholars had already progressed into science. Al-Khwarizmi, founder of algebra, was born in 780, about 20 years before al-Kindi. Al-Jabir, founder of chemistry, did most of his work in the 8th century before philosophy became established in the Muslim domain.

Again, centuries later, a time came when the Muslims gave up the seeking of knowledge. Many Western scholars claim that the Muslims gave up natural sciences because they forsook philosophy. Some put the blame specifically on al-Ghazali who attacked philosophy in his work *Incoherence of the Philosophers*. But what they fail to realise is that as the Muslims had started to study all the disciplines at the same time, they also gave up studying everything at the same instance. They did not give up one because of the other.

Thus, the main difference was that while theology denied Europe of philosophy and science, the early Muslims were encouraged by their religion to delve into all aspects of knowledge including science.

European Intellectual Environment During Early Islam

During the time when enlightenment was being spread by the Muslims throughout the world, Europe was in its dark age. It needs to be understood that the 'dark age' was a localised European phenomenon. In Europe, a negative attitude towards natural sciences had prevailed. The wholesale disappearance of Greek as the language of learning in Europe also meant that Greek knowledge was wiped out from the collective Latin Europe. Roman patrician Boethus had intended to translate the classical Greek works to Latin but he was executed around 524 CE. The 6th century *Topographica Christiana* by Monk Cosmas Indicopleustes had on the front written, 'Against those, who while wishing to profess Christianity, think and imagine like the pagans that the heaven is spherical'.[288]

The Romans had invaded and for some time extended their rule in Europe up to Britain. But they were invaders and definitely

---

[288] Lyons, Jonathan, 2009, p. 46.

did not go there to teach Hellenic philosophy. Thus, classical knowledge was sparse in western Europe. The fall of Western Roman Empire to the barbarians further destroyed the formal education system in the west.

In the 11th century, Europe was in an intellectual and social mess with antiquated inheritance laws, primitive agriculture no longer keeping pace with demand, and gangs of brigands and thugs prowling the countryside.[289] As late as the 13th century, the Europeans could not tell the time. Monks in France used local observation markers aligned with the constellation to ascertain prayer times. In the Cistercian Abbey of Villars, in Belgium, the sun and stars were traced through different windows to give some indication of time.[290] A handful of cathedral schools managed a course of seven *Quadrivium* and *Trivium* subjects—grammar, rhetoric, logic, arithmetic, geometry, music and astronomy.[291] There were no advanced subjects and the quality of the material taught was limited.

The most prominent book of that time was the *Etymologies* by Saint Isodore, bishop of Seville (560-636). He laid out everything he knew in 20 volumes of the book: astronomy, zoology, agriculture, theology and military science. He was well read and industrious but lacked critical thinking and understanding. The bishop considered the world as a flat circle surrounded by water like the letter O. In the middle of the circular land mass was the Mediterranean Sea, its shape considered to be like the letter T, with Asia on top of the T and Europe and Africa on its two lower sides. This was the T-O map of the world. His teachings, like the 'the world was flat and resembled a wheel', held sway of European thinking well into the renaissance. The

---

[289] Lyons, Jonathan, 2009, p. 28.
[290] *Ibid.*, p. 31.
[291] *Ibid.*, p. 33-34.

Venerable Bede (d. 735) of northern England was a more sophisticated thinker. His *The Reckoning of Time* was an early attempt at the calculation of the hour. But his teachings were completely obscured by the vastly more popular Isodore.[292]

The first cathedral school in France appeared at Tours in the 8th century at the behest of Charlemagne. He was well aware and in touch with the splendours and knowledge of the Abbasids and the Spanish Umayyads. After that followed the cathedral schools in Chartres and Leon. While in the Muslim lands the golden age of the Abbasids had already been ushered in.

For a few centuries most of the cathedral schools were used to produce trained functionaries similar to the *abids* of the early Umayyads. These schools started to become popular around the 11th century for aspiring young students. But such schools only contained a dozen or two parchment books or volumes of mainly outdated learning.[293] Around that time, Europe did not have the rudimentary knowledge to understand the tables of Ptolemy.[294] Only in the 16th century did they gather enough science to understand time and reformation of the calendar.

There are two interesting facts about the famous medieval European maps of the world and the Caspian Sea. German scholar Albertus Magnus produced a world map in the 13th century. It depicted cities like Baghdad and Basra but not Paris proving that Muslim resources were used in the making of the map and at that time those cities were more important than Paris. The map of the Caspian has an even more interesting history. The 14th century European map, which was influenced by Muslim cartography, showed the correct north-south orientation of the Caspian Sea. But in the 16th century, the Caspian was portrayed as being oval

---

[292] Lyons, Jonathan, 2009, p. 35.
[293] *Ibid.*, p. 37.
[294] Eidelberg, Shlomo, 1977, p. 21.

in shape in a new map. This was because the European cartographers decided to use the incorrect Ptolemy's work as the basis of their map instead of the Muslim maps. It would be in the 18th century that this mistake would be finally rectified, about eight hundred years after the Muslims had correctly charted the Caspian.[295]

Generally, when the European scholars who came in touch with Muslim knowledge, for instance in Spain, they were amazed. Many such works were translated and taken back to Europe. After visiting the Muslim lands, Adelard of Bath, in *Questions on Natural Science*, criticised the European society, saying, 'I found the princes barbarous, the bishops bibulous, judges bribable, patrons unreliable, clients sycophants, promisers liars, friends envious and almost everybody full of ambition'.[296]

The growing popularity of Muslim sciences caused a severe backlash from the conservative circles in Europe. In the early 13th century, the University of Paris would repeatedly ban the natural philosophy of Aristotle, translated to Latin from Arabic, threatening excommunication for offenders. The body of Amaury, a local student who studied Aristotle, was removed from the cemetery and thrown to 'unconsecrated' ground and excommunicated by all the Churches of the province.[297] A freshly written Latin translation of Abu Ma'shar Ja'far ibn Muhammad's (Albumazar) book on astrology was appended by the European translater-scribe, 'Finished, with praise to God for his help and a curse on Mahomet (Muhammad) and his followers'.[298]

But all the restrictions would be of no avail for the European scholars had tasted ambrosia. They were not just reading

---

[295] Owen Gingerich, 1986.
[296] Charles Burnett, 1998, p. 83.
[297] Lyons, Jonathan, 2009, p. 134.
[298] S. J., Tester, 1987, p. 153.

translated knowledge but also inheriting a passion from the Muslims, that unquenchable thirst for knowledge—the spirit of science. As for the Muslims themselves things were about to change for the worse.

CHAPTER 9

The Tri-Military Events and the Fall

Political infighting had caused the Muslim empires to break down into smaller sultanates, emirates and kingdoms. This disintegration weakened the Muslims considerably. As they became weak external forces saw the opportunity to attack them. The aggressions against them occurred time and again but three major invasions would prove to be very destructive and conclusive. Destruction would be so severe that every aspect of Muslim life would be affected. These events would even redefine the epistemological model of the Muslim societies and its negative affect would linger on up to the present time. The fall of the early Muslim was brought about by the following three military events.

1. The Spanish *Reconquista* or ouster of the Muslims from Spain (initiating in the 11th century but mainly carried out in the 12th and 13th centuries)

2. The Crusades (from the end of the 11th century to the 13th century)

3. The Mongol invasion (13th century)

Muslims had lived and spread enlightenment in Spain for many centuries. Their ouster took place over time by the Spanish

Reconquista. It was not truly a reconquest but the driving out of a people who had resided there for nearly nine centuries. Once the military defeat had finally perpetuated then the Spanish Inquisition, the realm's drive against Muslims and Jews, completely shattered and cast out the Muslims from the Iberian Peninsula.

In about the same historical time, the First Crusades in the Levant-Mediterranean region caused more rapid destruction. Instability set in and all the centres of learning in the Levant were marred and damaged. One crusade after another followed. Due to the military and political instability of the region, sponsorship for academic centres and scholars became significantly less available. These two events or invasions came from the west. Then from the east came the final and the more apocalyptic destruction. From Persia up to the Syriac-Levant the Mongols completely destroyed the Muslims, their way of life and their institutions. Millions were killed, libraries burnt and towns after towns destroyed.

Knowledge researched and accumulated over centuries was ruined, institutions obliterated and scholars killed. Muslims became poor, among the scholars only ascetic scholars like the Sufis could manage to continue to work. Those type of scholars who needed finance were left in the lurch.

Besides the Hejaz, a region for spiritual enrichment, the only Muslim ruled regions that were not destroyed by these Tri-Military Events were Egypt and India. Egypt had been attacked by the Crusaders which cost the Egyptians much resource but were not completely destroyed. In the all-around upheaval they would face continuous political instability. Egypt and the rest of North Africa, at that time, had centres of various disciplines but science was not one of their main focuses.

While in India, the Muslims were relatively new there and the quest for knowledge had just begun with the establishment of basic schools and madrasahs. But, at the time of the Mongol attacked the Muslim world, advanced scientific academic institutions had not yet been introduced in India. Those were located in Central Asia, Middle East and Spain, and were all destroyed. So Indian Muslims were yet to develop or were developing advanced scientific institutions when all the calamities struck the Muslim world.

Further details of the above mentioned three military events follows.

The Spanish *Reconquista* and Inquisition

After having ruled for centuries, internal revolt caused the fall of the Umayyad Caliphate of Andalusia in 1031. Muslim Spain fragmented into numerous independent principalities and petty states. Squabbling and infighting became common among them. Towards the end of the 11th century, the Iberian Christians rallied together to invade the squabbling Muslims.

But with the support of the powerful al-Moravid and after that the al-Mohad rulers of North Africa the Muslims defeated this aggression. For about a century a status quo prevailed. But Muslim Spain never really unified against the *Reconquista* of the allied Christians and saw their territories increasingly eroded. Gradually, the Muslims first lost northern regions and then the southern regions and by 1236 only Granada remained under Muslim rule but mostly as a vassal state. It still maintained its ideal as a centre of learning with scholars writing books on various subjects along with beautiful poetry. The Nasrid princes lived in the famous al-Hambra palace on a hilltop overlooking beautiful gardens.

In 1492, the rule of Granada was finally surrendered to the joint forces of King Ferdinand and Queen Isabella, Catholic monarchs of Leon and Castille. Up to this time, Muslims still lived under the Christian rulers of Spain. The condition of surrender was that the Muslims would be allowed to pursue their culture and religion without persecution. But within two years the king went back on his word. Muslims and Jews were forcefully converted to Christianity or evicted from the country. Islamic culture was prohibited, graves desecrated and libraries burnt. To root out any hidden dissidence the authorities proclaimed an inquisition. They searched for Muslims who practised their religion in hiding and most were exterminated. This inquisition brought back the religious intolerance of the pre-Islamic days.

A major portion of the Muslim population left Spain. Those who had any skills that could be utilised in foreign lands departed. Those who stayed and converted were still discriminated against and were not given any important office. In 1609, Phillip II finally expelled all the remaining Muslims.

Due to the Spanish Inquisition a region with major Muslim centres of learning and enlightenment became history. The Muslims left Spain leaving behind an enduring legacy. The 'jewel' that they had created in the Iberian Peninsula was not only of the material kind but was a superb example of harmonious coexistence and illuminating knowledge as well. Muslim Spain was richer and more progressive than the Franks and the Byzantines, the two other contemporary powers of Europe.

Like Muslims the world over, the Muslims of Spain patronised scholars and their thirst for knowledge. They had produced an enormous quantity of the most advanced works which were recorded in books. From the 11th century onwards these works were translated to Latin. The enlightening knowledge gradually spread from Spain to the rest of Renaissance Europe. It was the inheritance of this knowledge and the advanced economic system from the Muslims that enabled Spain to be the first colonial power of Europe till the 17th century after which newer powers were to rise.

The Crusades

From the time of Emperor Saint Constantine (4th century) to that of King Charlemagne (9th century) Christianity gradually set a uniform moral ground and law all over Europe. At the start of the 11th century, when the Muslim Abbasid Empire were slowly disintegrating, the barbarians in Europe, such as the Vikings and Magyars, were being converted to Christianity and a large portion of the European population could unite under a common identity. Up to then, the Byzantines, had been bearing the brunt and impact of the Muslim empires. Now there were some Christian successes in Spain and the Mediterranean Islands, which finally were causes for encouragement to go on the military offensive.

In 1095, Pope Urban II proclaimed a call to arms for Christian Europe—a crusade to remove the Muslims from the holy land of Jerusalem. The cry rose from every pulpit declaring that anyone who participates in the crusade would earn the blessing of the Church and full remission of all sins. About 150,000 people responded to the call. They included significant numbers of Franks and Normans who already knew of success in Spain and Sicily. This also indicates the dynamic rallying power of the Pope and the relative political incompetency of the then Muslim caliph in Baghdad.

The highly motivated army started its march and in the first encounter defeated the Seljuk Sultan Qilij and annexed his capital Nicaea. The sultan retreated to Anatolia. Then the army marched again taking Armenia and Syria. The Fatimid Shi'ah caliph of Egypt was quite content to see the discomfiture of the rival Sunni Abbasid-Seljuks but was devastated when the Crusaders moved towards Egypt's direction annexing Tripoli, Jerusalem and Galilee. The disunited Muslims were unable to offer any resistance against the united Europe. In Jerusalem the Crusaders massacred a large number of the Muslim and the minority Jewish population. The

Crusaders boasted that 'their blood rose to ankle depth'.

After their victory, the Crusaders formed four independent principalities in the occupied region—the Kingdom of Jerusalem, the Principality of Antioch, the State of Edessa and the State of Tripoli. These were set up along the littoral east of the Mediterranean Sea connected by a fifty mile wide corridor up to Jerusalem.

For fifty years this impasse continued. Then Imad al-Dinn Jangi, the ruler of Mosul (modern-day northern Iraq), launched a jihad against the crusaders. In 1144, he marched through Armenia and captured Edessa, the first crusader state. But he died in 1146 and Edessa was lost for some time till his son Nur al-Din Jangi recaptured it.

The fall of Edessa, not once but twice, was distressing to Europe, and Pope Eugene III proclaimed the Second Crusade (1144-1155). Muslim monarchs like Nur al-Din Jangi and Salah al-Din al-Ayyubi (Saladin) fought back taking Jerusalem after 88 years of Christian rule. But there would be more Crusades and the volatility of the region caused the learning centres like Damascus and Aleppo to degrade, never to reach their previous glory.

Aftermath of the Crusades

All the subsequent Crusades ended in failure to attain their military objective. But politically the success of the whole episode was stupendous—the fusion of a European identity under the common cause of Christianity. The other obvious outcome was it caused the further weakening, political fragmentation and instability of the already disintegrated Muslim domains.

The enhanced contact with the Muslims was also of prime importance to Europe. The porous activity of the merchants brought about a lot of information about development in various sectors of Muslim domains. When the Crusaders and pilgrims returned from the Muslim lands they brought back tales of incredible cities and progress that awakened the interest of Europe. Large scale translation of Muslim science, arts and philosophy had already begun in Spain, Portugal, France and Sicily. Now further contacts with the cultured modern outlook and high quality urban life of the Muslims influenced Europe and initiated the breakdown of the rigid society and established the foundation of progressive social groups and communities establishing durable modern institutions.

Once the foundation of society had been laid down by Christianity, morality alone was no longer capable of enacting social progress. The need for pragmatic and rationalistic views and policies, a system for further progress, became apparent. That need was satisfied by the inheritance of Muslim passion for knowledge and its vast sweeping culture. But the incoming seepage of the alien Muslim culture and their knowledge was not deemed well by the Church. While the Church was agreeable in incorporating arts into their domain they stood firmly against the admission of science and changes in commerce. The clergy establishment was a beneficiary of the existing commercial system and thus the status quo was more profitable to them. But this stance, in the long run, caused disillusionment among the people towards the Church as it failed to align with the new necessities of the environment.

The dynamic changes imparted on Europe a readiness for the next stage of socio-cultural development that would lead to the Renaissance and the subsequent scientific and industrial evolution of Europe. For the Muslims, though, the story would be just the opposite.

The Mongol Scourge

In 1206 CE, in far-off Mongolia, Taimujin was elected the chief of the Mongols. He united the many nomadic Mongol tribes of northeast Asia. He took on the title of Chengiz Khan and from his capital in Karakorum, he embarked on one of the most spectacular careers of conquest that the world has ever seen. During his life, the Mongol Empire would eventually occupy a large part of Asia, and his descendants would make the Mongol Empire the largest contiguous empire in history by conquering China, Russia, Eastern Europe and a significant part of Asia and the Middle East.

After establishing Mongol rule in China, Chengiz moved west. Obliterating the Kara Khitayas of Transoxiana (Central Asia) he reached Khwarizm (Uzbekistan region) in 1218. There he sent a Mongol trade delegation. In the border town of Utrar, the Khwarizm governor suspected the delegation of spying and had them executed. When Chengiz Khan demanded compensation the Khwarizm shah refused. The Mongols then unleashed a ferocious multi-pronged attack on Khwarizm. One of their legions decimated Utrar and massacred all of its population. Molten gold was poured down the throat of the governor who had executed the trade delegation. Another legion led by Chengiz himself captured Bukhara where he assembled the vanquished people to the main mosque. From the pulpit he declared, 'I am the Scourge of God, come to punish you for your sins'.[299]

All the assembled people were executed and then the Mongols proceeded to Samarqand. The city fell after a weak resistance. The people were gathered in an open field outside the city where they were butchered. A pyramid of severed human heads, the symbol of Mongol victory, rose in the field. Two more legions destroyed Khojend and Gurganj. After the fall of Gurganj, the Mongols breached its dam and flooded the town. The people drowned and those who tried to escape were massacred. The

---

[299] Hasan, Masudul, 1998, p. 2.

Khwarizm King Ala ad-Din Muhammad Shah fled on the face of the brutal onslaught.[300]

The Mongols crossed the River Oxus (Amu Darya) and reached Khorasan in 1221. Whatever came in their path was destroyed and devastated leaving in their wake a hallmark trail of destruction. City after city were razed and hundreds of thousands of people were slaughtered in each of them. Tirmiz, Balkh, Merv and Sanjar, the Seljuk capital, were all reduced to dust and blood. In Merv alone 700,000 people were massacred. In Nishapur a son-in-law of Chengiz was killed. Extra Mongol troops were dispatched there and the entire population of the city was butchered turning it into a carnival of blood, bones and butchery presided over by the widow.[301]

The Mongol conquest continued after the death of Chengiz in 1227. Korea, Georgia and Armenia were turned into vassals and large parts of Persia and China had already been annexed. Next, they moved towards Europe and captured almost all the regions from Russia to Hungary and Poland. When Europe was ready to fall, succession dissension among the Mongols caused them to pull out of Poland and Hungary, which caused the cessation of invasion in this region and Europe was spared.

In 1248, Halaku Khan, the grandson of Chengiz, was given charge for the conquest of the Middle East. From Samarqand the forces of Halaku Khan crossed the River Oxus in 1256. Halaku set his sights on the mountainous forts of Alamaut. This region was under the control of Nizari Isma'ili Shi'ahs infamously known as the Assassins. He sent an ultimatum to the Assassins to demolish their fortress and surrender. The Assassins were under the impression that their mountainous fortress was impregnable and evaded any reply. But under the Mongol onslaught the Assassins

---

[300] *Ibid.*, p. 2-3.
[301] Hasan, Masudul, 1998, p. 2.

fell and their fortresses were destroyed.

While attacking the Assassins, Halaku had asked Caliph al-Musta'sim to send a contingent against the Assassins as well. But al-Musta'sim had refrained hoping that the two devils, Mongols and Assassins, would undo each other. Now Halaku used the non-cooperation as a pretext to send an ultimatum to the Caliph. In 1258, the Mongols besieged Baghdad and after a token resistance Baghdad fell. The palace of the caliph was plundered and the caliph was made a captive.

The caliph was put into a sack and trampled to death under horse's hooves. After plundering of the city was over it was put to the torch. Thus, burnt the universities, libraries and all the institutions of learning and knowledge built up through ages. A large number of books and scrolls were also thrown into the river. A significant portion of the population of Baghdad was marched to a field outside the city. Here, they were slaughtered regardless of age or gender and a mountain of skulls was piled up.[302] Six centuries of accumulated knowledge, libraries, madrasahs, mosques, *kuttab* and hospitals, along with scholars and students—the entire heritage—were destroyed.

The unstoppable Mongol wake of destruction continued to progress through the Muslim domains. In two years' time all the regions that comprises Iran, Iraq and Syria fell. Damascus and Homs were captured, Aleppo destroyed and all its population numbering 50,000 were massacred.[303] Then they turned towards the still standing Muslim bastion—The Mamluk Egypt.

In 1260, on reaching Gaza, Halaku sent an ultimatum to the Egyptian Mamluk King Kutuz. It was an insolent, threatening and humiliating message that enraged Kutuz so much that he had the Mongol ambassadors executed and their bodies hung at the gates

---

[302] Hasan, Masudul, 1998, Lahore, p. 6.
[303] *Ibid.*, p.14.

of the city. Then he marched the Egyptian army to measure swords with the Mongols. Baybras, the ablest and the bravest of the Mamluk generals, lead the vanguard. In the meantime Mongke, the Great Khan, had died and Halaku returned leaving command in the hands of his step brother Ketgugha.

The two armies clashed in a titanic and historical battle at Ayn Jalut in Palestine. The Mamluks rose to the occasion and comprehensively defeated the Mongols, shattering the myth of Mongol invincibility. In 1280, the Mamluks delivered another crushing defeat to the Mongols in Syria. The Mamluks of India did not languish behind. Under Sultan Giyath al-Din Balban, the Mamluks of India defeated two Mongol attacks in Multan in 1279 and 1286. In the second battle, Muhammad the son of Sultan Balban died while chasing the Mongols. The Mongols returned to India thrice in the beginning of the 14th century. But thrice they were repulsed by the Khilji sultans. These defeats plugged any further Mongol advance into India. Thus, only India and Egypt were spared from total destruction.[304]

Mongol Assimilation

After the death of Chengiz, the Mongol Empire was divided into four domains among his sons. With time these subdivisions transformed into three major domains, those of the Il-Khans of Persia, The Chagtais of Transoxiana and the Golden Horde Khanate of Russia and Eastern Europe.

The changes in the Mongol's culture and attitude came from within. While their sword had broken the back of the Muslims, the intellectual and spiritual superiority of the Muslims overcame the Mongols. The first of the Mongols to accept Islam were the Golden Horde. Gradually, all the Mongols who settled down in

---

[304] Hasan, Masudul, 1998, p. 8.

the Muslim domains were assimilated. And at one stage, amazingly, they became the torch bearers of Islam. Among their descendants were the Great Moghuls of India and the mighty Taimur (Tamerlane) of Samarqand.

When the Mongols were fighting the Muslims, a loose alliance was formed between the Mongols and European rulers. After their second humiliating defeat in 1280 at the hands of the Mamluk, the Mongols tried to incite their European allies to launch another Crusade, promising them a huge cavalry support and restoration of the Holy Lands. But they were snubbed by France, England and the Pope as well. They were in no position to further continue the Crusades. In 1291, Sultan al-Ashraf Khalil of Egypt occupied Acre, the last stronghold of the Crusaders, which closed the chapter of the Crusades in the Muslim lands.

Gradually, as the Mongols converted to Islam the state of affairs in the Muslim domains showed a return to normalcy. But the loss of Spain and Portugal, the battering sustained during the Crusades and the ease with which the Mongol onslaught had demolished the Muslims, destroyed the Abbasid Caliphate and the subsequent horrifying experiences left their mark on the Muslim psyche. These onslaughts had destroyed them economically, socially and intellectually. All their famous academic institutions were gone and scholars dead or displaced. As a reaction the Muslims began to rethink and realign their politics and philosophy.

As the Mongols assimilated, they took up Islamic values, but the Mongol tribal conflicts and conquest mentality were also retained to some extent. During this period, Islamic astronomical research had reached its zenith in the works of al-Tusi and al-Shatir. But they were the last brilliant individuals contributing their last scientific bequests in a world where the scientific network had been destroyed. Their works were taken over by the European scholars.

Mamluk Egypt

Egypt boasted of grand academic institutions like al-Azhar University, Nasir al-Din Madrasah, Ashrafiyyah Madrasah and Mu'ayyadiyyah Mosque. These institutions were large and composite, for instance, the Asharfiyyah Madrasah was a multi storied complex where the madrasah *kuttab*s (classes) and four great halls surrounded the central courtyard with a public fountain. The Mu'ayyadiyyah Mosque employed more than 150 non-academic staff to support the academics and teachers. The famous polymath scholar al-Mahalli taught jurisprudence in this mosque. Madrasahs, mosques, khanqahs and hospitals were all used for academic purposes. According to Berkey, 'The life of the academic world blended thoroughly with the urban metropolis world around it'.[305]

A madrasah for women was established in Egypt, just before the fall of Baghdad, by Khatun, daughter of Amir Ashraf Musa of Damascus, and in 1354 it was endowed by Oghl Khatun daughter of Shamsuddin Muhammad ibn Sayf al-Din of Baghdad.[306]

The Egyptian academic institutes specialised in teaching legal studies, military sciences, all the literary or *adab* disciplines, medicine and the ulemaic disciplines. Pure science was not a speciality in this region even though scholars like al-Haytham had settled in Egypt for some time.[307]

The decline of the Mamluk Egypt's economy and education is considered by many historians due to the 'Black Death' plague that caused the death of almost 40% of its population. But that was not the only cause of its intellectual decay. The Black Death had also affected Europe as devastatingly compounded by political instability. But Europe had continued to forge ahead with its

---

[305] Berkey, Jonathan P., 1992, p. 189-193.
[306] Hossain, M. Amjad, 2013. p. 146.
[307] *Ibid.*, p. 143-146.

intellectual advancement amid these cataclysms. This, in the case of Egypts, indicates a bewilderment at the devastations the Muslims had suffered, a lack of appropriate schools and scholars for science, and a probable lack of political vision as the root causes.

Before their fall, towns like Cordoba, Baghdad had a variety of scholars. Each discipline had their own specialist—scientists, philosophers, ulema, *etc*. But with the fall of all those towns these scientists, their scientific works and institutions, on which Egypt or India could depend on, were gone. This intellectual deterioration was, certainly, aggravated by the political instability, corruption, economic constraint, and deadly health crisis like the plague.

Under devastating circumstances, people have a tendency to turn towards some form of spiritual relief as did the Egyptians. Earlier, *tasawwuf* or Sufism was practised by individuals or small groups up to the 12th century. Most of the Sufis were erudite individuals and wielded high spiritual, literary and cultural influence. This led to the development of a popular Muslim culture[308] which gradually became dominant. But from the 13th century onwards ill-educated pseudo-Sufis and charlatans, pretending to be scholars, started to take advantage of this culture. Some could be very charismatic and lead a large group of followers into religious innovations. This ultimately led to the development a 'popular religion' accepted by many as a substitute for the genuine religion. It demotivated the general mass away from the ulemaic and scientific disciplines and developed an imbalance in the sphere of Total Knowledge.

Scholars such as Ibn Taymiyyah and Ibn Baydakin al-Turkmani wrote numerous treatises against such innovations.[309]

---

[308] Berkey, Jonathan P., 2001, p. 4.
[309] Hossain, M. Amjad, 2013, p. 154-155.

But from the 14th century onwards this popular religion became rife in Mamluk Egypt further distancing from ulemaic disciplines and scientific intellectualism. In the 16th century the Ottomans conquered Egypt.

Muslim Intellectual Imbalance

The Medieval age is approximately from the 5th to 15th centuries CE. For Europe, the period was the Dark Ages starting from the fall of the Western Roman Empire up to the Renaissance. But the rest of the known world—Middle East, Central Asia, Spain, North Africa and China—saw a tremendous upsurge in knowledge, learning and improvement of human social conditions.

The development of thought influenced, as expected, the development of society in the empires and kingdoms. Irrespective of the governing political entity, wherever the Muslims travelled in
that vast central tract of civilised region between China and Byzantium, they were always under the same harmonious environment with the same God, the same prayers, the same laws and the same custom. For the common Muslim a practical code of citizenship guaranteed her or him freedom of movement and expression throughout most of the civilised world.

The study of history of the Umayyad and Abbasid period discloses the usual wars and revolts that empires face. But the general society and the civilians were far removed from all such calamities. Once the initial Muslim empire had been formed and political administration settled, the battles and the revolts, to the masses, were between political opponents trying to undo each other. The general public would get involved only under exceptional cases. The average Muslims viewed the intrigues and battles from a 'long distance' perspective. All this was 'news' to them and it did not matter much to their daily life, which consisted of education, commerce and a progressive culture typical to the Muslim world.

The average Muslims led a stable life throughout this period. They were the most progressive demographic group in the entire world living a modern way of life with advanced civic sense and education. Their commerce was the best as they controlled a huge free trade zone in the centre of the civilised world.

But the Tri-Military Events, which directly devastated the masses, would change the psyche of the Muslims. The first two events, the loss of Spain and the Crusades, had dented and damaged the Muslim domains from the west. The last and the greatest shock was the destruction, humiliation and suffering inflicted by the Mongol scourge. Except for Egypt and India, much of the Muslim world was at throes for their very survival. With the all-around destruction, the Muslim world's trade and economy had fallen apart. Resources were needed more to protect themselves rather than sponsor academic institutions.

At that instance of history, the futility of science and scholarship appeared pronounced. When survival in the face of the sword was the main issue, the scientists and scholars— debating with perishable books over invisible germs, algebra, chemical reactions and physical laws—had proved themselves, seemingly, to be most worthless. So, it appeared that the pursuit of knowledge and learning were all too futile and ephemeral. This pursuit had not been able to save a single life, it had not sharpened a single sword against the onslaught of the enemies, it had not emboldened a single person to stand and face this scourge. To survive and rebuild the empire, warriors were needed—or so it seemed.

The immensity of the Mongol tragedy, including the cruel death of the caliph, sent shock waves all over the Muslim world. A stormy unsanctioned but undisputed reassessment of the Muslim culture and history took place. The scourge had obliterated centuries of advancement. Apparently, the only thing that could conquer and save empires were men of metal, men who feared nothing not even death, men who could forge ahead irrespective of what lay in front—a sword, an army, a storm, a mountain or a sea. Thus, a cultural change appeared in the psychological outlook of the Muslims.

Up to that juncture there had existed a crucial balance between rationalism and orthodoxy. Now martial orthodoxy and mysticism prevailed over pure and social sciences. Scientists like Ibn Haytham and al-Biruni ceased to be produced. The passion for knowledge was transformed to a passion for defence. There was not much will in rebuilding the scientific network that could so easily be destroyed.

In the face of such external adversity, Muslims also attempted to hang on to their religion more firmly as can be seen in the works of Ibn Taymiyyah. The Hanbali literalist view of scriptures became more important. To counter the external 'cultural' threat, female scholars stepped up their efforts in protecting the Muslim way of life. During this period, while the men were fighting the invasion or attempting to negotiate with the new hostile environment, there was a sharp increase in women studying, teaching and transmitting ḥadīth[310] among the Muslims.

As the study of sciences and social sciences came to an end, the Muslims, a nation of scholars by tradition, toiled hard to retain the basic form of scholarship, Qur'an and ḥadīth. There grew a large number of madrasahs and Sufi khanqa as school of sciences became unaffordable due to the inability to sponsor and also due the destruction of the network of rational scholars.

Some modern scholars have noticed this great change[311] but have not been able to fathom the reasons behind it. Muslims had

---

[310] Nadwi, M. A., 2013, p. 246.
[311] WR 22.

latched on to religious and Sufi studies to save themselves from a complete scholastic demise. There also must have been some apprehension about the culture of the invaders and the desire to protect the way of life from it, which led to religious studies. It is probably true that at a later stage the anti-rationalist scholars within the orthodoxy became more influential. The environment became less congenial for the study of sciences even when the Muslims, subsequently, were able to control their political instability and re-emerge as powerful empires. At least, they remained far behind the European scientific progress.

Earlier in the 10th century, after the finalising of jurisprudence by the four Imams, a ban against any further research or development of 'law' appears to have been invoked. This ban came to be known as 'Closing the Gates of *Ijtihad*', with *ijtihad* loosely translated as 'personal research'. Historically, it is still unclear who were behind the ban but it was probably to stop the willy-nilly development of law in the Muslim domains and retain the uniformity of the legal system. After the Tri-Military Events, it appears that the Muslims, under the invaders' rule, became very concerned that they would lose complete control over the academic and social culture. So, this ban appears to have been revitalised.

By this time Christianity had established a moral framework throughout Europe. It was waiting for an impetus to take the next step towards rationalism. Thus, as the Christian West was moving toward rationalism the Muslim East was moving away from it. The works of Ibn Rushd and al-Ghazali had become well known in both Europe and the Muslim world. Ibn Rushd's rationalism triumphed in Europe and al-Ghazali's theology in the East.

These were temporal socio-political exigencies that were necessary for the next stage of development. Al-Ghazali's works gave Muslims the instant spiritual and psychological strength and unity needed to fight back the many crises that they had been subjected to and, again, build mighty and grand empires. Ibn Rushd's rationalism led Europe to the Renaissance in its fight against laid-back institutions, socio-cultural backwardness and dogmatic way of life. The new European philosophical organisation would, in the long run, take them to great new heights of empire building and further into modern statehood.

Meanwhile, a parting of ways took place between 'rational sciences' from Muslim psyche. Rational studies no longer existed in schools of consequence where, from then on, mainly ulemaic, Sufi and some theological-philosophical thoughts were to prevail. After that a 'popular religion' would start to dominate the masses pushing the orthodox ulemas to the sidelines. The rational vacuum was exacerbated due to the fact that most of the libraries of importance and learning centres of the Middle East and Central Asia had been destroyed by the Tri-Military Events.

After the fall of Baghdad, the Mongols had either burnt or emptied its libraries into the Euphrates. The millions of volumes caused a bridge across the river and for days the river water was stained black from the ink washed out of the books. Spain and Portugal along with its libraries and institutions were lost forever. The Crusades had damaged the Syriaic-Levant Mediterranean region. All over the Muslim world the academic institutions, the books, and the scholars were lost or annihilated. Research and development in the Muslim domain would slow down and grind to a halt.

CHAPTER 10

Rise of European Intellectualism

The European intellectual awakening was parallel in time with the latter Muslim empires. These Muslim empires were vast, bigger than the European entities. But the rising Europeans had harnessed knowledge that led to the Renaissance. After the Renaissance the Europeans would gradually become highly advanced in trade and technology giving rise to the Modern Age. Their industrial and armament technology would become much superior to the Muslim empires. During this time, the Muslims would regress and, ultimately, fall to the rising European colonial powers.

The Latter Muslim Empires

After the Tri-Military debacle the Muslims changed their scholastic approach to life and became more interested in rebuilding politically. The Muslim domains had become indefensible against invasions. Under the circumstances, rationally thinking, the fightback by the Muslims was the right direction *for that time*. The change in focus from the scholastic to empire-building led the Ottomans to build the Janissary, one of the finest armies the world had ever seen, and reconquer whatever glory the Muslims had lost and even more. The Ottoman sultan became the caliph of the Muslims. They became the longest reigning dynasty ever in the history of the world. The other two great Muslim empires that arose were the Safavids of Persia and the Moghuls of India.

Besides these three great empires of the latter period many other kingdoms and emirates rose and fell from the 13th to 15th centuries. They included the Zayanid of Algeria, the Marinid of Morocco, the Khiljis of India, the Ilyas Shahis of Bengal, the Muslim legacy of Mongol Persia—Sarbadarans, Jalayars and Muzaffarids—the Malay Sultanate of Malacca, the Indonesian Samudra Darussalam, the Sultanate of Demak, the Aceh Sultanate and many more. But none of these Muslim domains, all comparatively small in geographical extent, took any great interest in pure sciences. Most were busy existing in a changing world. A significant part of the Arab populace would regress to a tribal way of life in deserts or live in antiquated town environments. They would remain there for centuries re-emerging only in the 20th century.

The Ottomans, Safavids and Moghuls for centuries up to the modern age would remain the most powerful and greatest empires. These empires produced great rulers, administrators, generals, grand builders and conquerors. Most of them sponsored fine arts, architecture, commerce and social studies. They had the best schooling systems in the world. Science and social science were studied in the vast empires but when attempts were made to establish the scientific network, internal and external factors caused it to fail (see Appendix 6 for more details). In the long run, the reorientation caused an imbalance in the Total Knowledge framework of intellectual Islam. The Muslim success story would have continued to the modern age had the Muslims returned to their Total Knowledge framework once they had become politically stable again.

While these empires had a large demographic variety and were much more extensive and richer than their European counterparts, the 15th and 16th centuries were also the time during which lived people like Copernicus, Tycho Brahe and Kepler in Europe. They led the way for more remarkable scholars to follow—people whose works were fundamental to the Renaissance that would change Europe and, subsequently, the world.

The Italian Renaissance and the Aftermath

In the 12th and 13th centuries, religious studies became institutionalised in Europe and mass translation of Muslim works began which introduced a different form of theology and philosophy which was more advanced than anything that Europe had witnessed.

In studying the stupendous amount of scholastic work done by the early Muslims, the Italians found a link to their own Greco-Roman legacy—Aristotle, Plato, Socrates and others whose 'pagan' names and thoughts had been purged from history by the Holy See. The passion for knowledge now inflamed the Italians and the French—art flourished, philosophy flourished, rationalism flourished, schools and universities were established. Due to political and religious bias Europe could not credit Muslims for all the knowledge they inherited from them. Instead Europe aligned their identity along with the Greco-Roman legacy without mentioning the Muslim contributions.

The Renaissance took place in the period from the 14th to the 17th century. This was the time when the passion for knowledge inherited from the Muslims was put into practice. This period saw the rise of the spirit of science, arts, and literature in Europe. It was an uplifting cultural shift that brought to an end the Dark Ages and became the harbinger of the early Modern Age.

The Renaissance started after a calamitous period. After the Mongol calamity in Eastern Europe, one disaster after another ravaged Europe till the middle of the 15th century. The Black Death plague appeared and by the mid-14th century it swept through Europe with devastating speed killing at least thirty percent of the populace. The Renaissance had started after the win against the Muslims in Spain and just after the major Crusades had ended. But conflicts and wars in Europe were endemic during the end of the Middle Ages. Internal conflicts continued in varying forms from feuds between nobles with private armies to those between states. The most protracted one was the 'Hundred Years War' fought between England and France raging from 1337 to 1453.

But the passion for the sciences was so great that it sustained over all these calamities and maybe as an angst against such calamities. The sponsorship of knowledge by sovereigns like King Roger II of Sicily and Emperor Frederic II placed Italy among the leading countries in Europe. By the end of the 15th century, the rest of Europe caught up with Italy in literate manpower and had overtaken it in demand for books due to establishment of numerous universities.

A book revolution had started in Paris in the 13th century. The subsequent establishment of universities in Prague, Vienna, Caen, Bordeaux, Dole and Louvain increased the demand for different types of books. Gutenberg's invention of types in the mid-15th century gave a tremendous boost to printing and book publishing. Machine took over the printing of books from the copyists.

Spain and Portugal set up the first colonies, a path that was to be followed by other European countries. Mining, metallurgy and shipbuilding became very important. Most large European towns would have a public clock by the 16th century. Europe was forging forward, but it was England that started to accelerate ahead of all.

By the first half of the 17th century the first fire engines were made and the first postal service between London and Edinburgh was established.

From the myriad confusion of the past emerged a new kind of civilisation with its power based on freedom of thought and its wealth based on the emergence of machinery based industry and improvement of agriculture. European national demarcation became culturally defined by the rise of various modern languages —French, Italian, English, Flemish, Catalonian, Czech, *etc.*

Stalwarts of the Renaissance

The Renaissance would spawn a huge number of stalwarts in different fields of arts and science. A few important ones, along with some reference to relevant Muslim works, are listed below.

Roger Bacon

Roger Bacon (1214-1292), an English philosopher and Franciscan Friar, is the originator of the experimental method in Europe. He was actually an apostle of the Muslim sciences and had transmitted the experimental method to Europe from them.[312] Bacon had studied Muslim works from Cordoba and was influenced by the works of Muslim scholars like Ibn Haytham, al-Kindi, Ibn Firnas (who had proposed the flying machine idea— the ornithoptor) and Ibn Sina. Bacon quoted Ibn Haytham extensively in his work on optics in *Opus Maius*. A great impact on him was the work of al-Razi *The Book of the Secret of the Secrets* translated into Latin as *Secretum Secretorum*. Roger Bacon could speak Arabic and would publicly praise the works of Arab Muslims.[313]

---

[312] Hasan, M., 2004, p. 598.
[313] Al-Hassani, 2007, p. 322.

Petrarch

Francesco Petrarca (1304-1374), known as Petrarch, is considered by many to be the 'Father of the Renaissance Humanism.' An Italian scholar, he is best known for his poems, the *Canzoniere* and the *Trionfi*, and his translation of ancient works. The poems of Petrarch were based on Arab lyrics.[314] Petrach was initially a priest but gave up the vocation. In the Church he saw a lovely woman named Laura and fell in love. She was already married and there was little or no contact with her. But he wrote of her in his poems and harboured her in his heart forever.

Petrarch was the model for the Humanist Movement, an eclectic search into knowledge. The intellectual movement began in Florence at the end of the 14th century. Initially, the humanists were simply teachers of Latin literature but over time, their knowledge improved when they came in contact with the knowledge that had been translated to Latin. The work of translation was considered so important that they markedly developed modern philology. By the mid-15th century, humanists were teaching moral philosophy, grammar, rhetoric, poetry and history.

Translation was a major skill in demand and Petrarch was very concerned with the accuracy of translated manuscripts. He checked all the translations himself and said, 'I prefer to observe with my own eyes than those of others.' His *Secretum Meum* (*The Secret Book*) is a self-examination of his Christian faith in dialogue. It was found after his death. In it his secular achievements did not preclude God. According to him God had given intellect and creative potential to humans to be utilised to their fullest.

---

[314] Hasan, M., 2004, p. 598.

Da Vinci

Leonardo Da Vinci (1452-1519) was an Italian polymath. He is considered a mathematician, engineer, inventor, anatomist, painter, sculptor, botanist, writer and musician. He lived in Florence when Lorenzo Medici governed it. Michelangelo, Raphael and Niccolo Machiavelli flourished at the same time as Da Vinci. He learned painting in the studio of artist Verrochio. He painted one of the angels in 'Baptism of Christ' by Verrochio. When Verrochio saw his student's work has surpassed his own he decided it was time to retire. Of the twelve Da Vinci paintings that have survived the most famous is 'Mona Lisa'. Much has been written about the painting and the mysterious smile of the lady in the painting, but the real genius of the painting is in the subtle play with the shades of colours that makes the face look lifelike, almost a photograph rather than a painting. His other famous painting is the 'Last Supper' which shows Jesus and his disciples on the table eating their last supper together.

Da Vinci's fame also lies in his notebooks with 5000 pages of notes and sketches. These notebooks are filled with various types of sketches: fossils, skeletons, plants, muscles, embryos and eye structures. There are designs for irrigation and notes on the strength of materials. There are highly imaginative sketches of flying machines and military weaponry. It also includes sketches of pumps, lathes, cranes and steam engines. He made clever devices (for example a mechanical lion) for the King Francis I of France and died still in his employment. Some of his works are reminiscent of the 9th century Banu Musa brothers of the Abbasid-Ma'mun era and al-Jazari, engineer of the 12th century.

Da Vinci also drew the Vitruvian Man, a man of perfect proportion from the Roman Canon of Vitruvius. Da Vinci's illustration was considered innovative because it showed that the centre of the man lay not at the navel but lower. The same conclusion had been reached by Muslim scholars of the *Ikhwan al-Safa* (Brethren of Purity) five centuries earlier.[315] Da Vinci completed the work on the camera obscura invented by Ibn Haytham and developed a full design. *Al-Shifa* was a source of inspiration for Da Vinci's geometrical thought.[316]

Machiavelli

Niccolo di Bernardo dei Machiavelli (1469-1527) was a diplomat, political philosopher, musician, poet and playwright. He was a Florentine diplomat and visited the French court on several missions. He became the right-hand man of the Borgia ruler of Florence and had led a band of soldiers against Pisa. There is a similarity between the life and work of Machiavelli and the 11th century political scientist al-Mawardi.

Machiavelli's famous work *The Prince* proposes that a ruler should do all within his means, morality notwithstanding, to govern and control the state and people. The departure from moral was opposite to that of the 11th century *Dastur al-Wuzara'* and *Siyasat Nameh* of Nizam al-Mulk. These two books advised the rulers to rule on the basis of morality. On the other hand, the stupendous 14th century work of Ibn Khaldun *The Proglemena* was, among other things, more an objective sociological and historical study into statecraft and society rather than advice to rulers.

Copernicus

Nicolaus Copernicus (1473-1543) is the first astronomer to postulate the scientifically based heliocentric theory that put the sun in the centre of the solar system. For thirty years, he read and

---

[315] Al Hassani, 2007, p. 79.

[316] *Ibid.*, p. 323.

re-read the translations of Arab and Greek works and carefully studied the stars. Then in the middle of the 16th century he declared that the earth was not the centre of the universe but, in fact, the earth moved round the sun. Seventy years after the publication of his famous book *On the Revolutions of the Celestial Spheres* the Church declared him a heretic.

His theories were based on Nasir al-Din Tusi and Ibn al-Shatir's works and was also influenced by al-Zarqali's Toledan Astronomical Tables and al-Battani's comprehensive astronomical treatise that included star catalogues and planetary tables. His planetary model and theories were mathematically identical to that of Ibn al-Shatir, prepared a century earlier.[317]

Kepler

Johannes Kepler (1571-1630) the German astronomer, mathematician and astrologer is famous for the eponymous laws of planetary motion. In optics, Ibn Haytham's six century older work influenced him. He also improved Ibn Haytham's camera obscura by further enlarging the projected image. According to the *Historian's History* it was from Ibn Haytham's *Twilight* that he acquired his idea of atmospheric refraction.[318]

Tycho Brahe

The Danish scholar Tycho Brahe (1546-1601) was the most famous astronomer of the Renaissance. He is renowned for his work on the moon's variation which was first discovered about six hundred years ago by Abu al-Wafa Buzjani. He was aware of the works done by the Ottoman scientist Taqi al-Din.[319] The

---

[317] Al Hassani, 2007, p. 323.

[318] Hasan, M., 2004, p. 598; Al Hassani, 2007, p. 323.

[319] Agoston and Masters, 2009, p. 552.

instruments he used were very similar to those used by Muslim scientists especially those used by Taqi al-Din.[320]

The work of the scholars like those mentioned above are indeed milestones in scientific history. But the Renaissance that changed Europe forever did not start with them, as it is mistakenly assumed, nor did it start in Italy or France. This European upliftment, in fact, started somewhat earlier in Spain and Sicily and progressed inwards into Italy, France and the rest of Europe.

The Real Origin of the Renaissance

The European renaissance started from Spain and Sicily when Muslims ruled there. From these two regions enlightenment would flow into the rest of Europe including France, Italy, Germany and England. Some details of this phenomenon are given below.

The Spanish Connection

The Muslims ruled in al-Andalus, *i.e.*, whole or parts of Spain and Portugal from the 8th to the 15th century CE. A time came when the Muslim rule in Spain disintegrated into principalities and autonomous zones. In the final two centuries they only ruled in Granada on the south of Spain. The Christian *Reconquista* had gradually taken over the Muslim political entities first in the north driving the Muslims to the south. Finally, the Muslims were forced to leave Spain, but they left behind an enduring legacy. Muslim Spain was materially rich, intellectually superior and socially progressive with hallmark coexistence between races and religions. They were far ahead than any of the existing European powers including the Franks and the Byzantines, the two other

---

[320] Al Hassani, 2007, p. 323.

contemporary powers of Europe.

Like Muslims the world over, the Muslims of Spain had patronised scholars and their thirst for knowledge. Scholars produced a huge amount of very advanced works in different disciplines which were recorded in books. This, here in Spain, was the true start of European Renaissance. As the Christians took over the disintegrated Muslims principalities, the scholars and their works came under the suzerainty of the new rulers. From the 11th century onwards these works were translated to Latin. The enlightened knowledge spread from Spain to France, Italy and the rest of Europe. It was this inherited knowledge and intellectual system that made Spain the great global power of the colonial world till the 17th century.

S. P. Scott, the 19th century American historian, described the Spanish Muslim agriculture and irrigation system as 'the most complex, the most scientific, the most perfect, ever devised by the ingenuity of man'.[321] Professor Phillip K. Hitti of Princeton University in his *History of the Arabs* states, 'Muslim Spain wrote one of the brightest chapters in the intellectual history of medieval Europe. Between the middle of the eighth and the beginning of the 13th centuries the Arabic speaking people were the main bearers of the torch of culture and civilisation throughout the world. They were the medium through which ancient science and philosophy were recovered, supplemented and transmitted in such a way as to make possible the Renaissance of Western Europe'.[322]

In the 9th and 10th centuries, the earliest intellectual activity of Europe would start from the religious schools of the Kingdom of Lotharingia, which comprised parts of Western Germany, France, Belgium and the Netherlands. During this time England

---

[321] Scott, S. P., 1904, p. 598.
[322] Hassan, 2004, p. 597.

did not have sufficient institutions to produce their own clerics and relied on scholars trained in Lotharingia. These schools and monasteries of Lotharangia, commenced at the time of Charlemagne, emerged as the first tentative repository of Muslim science and technology.[323]

One of the remarkable intellects of this period was Gerbert d'Aurillac (d. 1003) who would later become Pope Sylvester II. As a young monk-in-training, Gerbert outgrew the meagre learning available in France. His superiors sent him for three years training to the Vich monastery in Catalonia, Spain. Catalonia had been ruled by the Umayyad Muslims in the 8th century and was now a frontier Christian outpost adjoining Muslim Spain. It enjoyed good trading relationship with Cordoba, the capital of the Muslim Spain Caliphate. Gerbert also went to Cordoba to study under Muslim scholars.[324] Muslim cultural trends like chess, inventions like the astrolabe, water clock, abacus, scholarly ideas like Hindu-Arabic numerals, and a variety of books were available in Catalonia[325] and Cordoba.

Catalonian Monks of *Santa Maria de Ripoll* had access to a relatively large number of Arabic texts and translations. After studying in Ripoll Gerbert went back to France and took up a series of teaching position of the *quadrivium* that he had learned in Catalonia. It was here that Gerbert fell out of the flat-earth theory. Gerbert's mission was just a small intimation of the vast learning of Muslims that awaited discovery by Europe. It would take another 150 years for Europe to become well acquainted with ideas like Arabic numbers with its 10 units and positional system of tens, hundreds and thousands.

Gerbert was the first to introduce the astrolabe to France to

---

[323] Lyons, Johnathan, 2009, p. 36.
[324] Al Hassani, 2007, p. 66.
[325] Lyons, Johnathan, 2009, p. 37.

obtain the monastic prayer times of the day. A portable instrument made of bronze with disk and calibrations the astrolabe was the most potent analogue computer for time measurement. Besides time, it could be used to determine the latitudes and geographic direction, work out the position of stars and sun, and also determine the height of a construction or the depth of a well.

Gerbert faced two types of resistance. One was from the religious circle who were wary about the Muslim 'sorcery' that Gerbert had imported and the other was one of general ignorance. A couple of students whom he had taught could not work out even the interior angle of a triangle. But Gerbert's influence was strong in the Lotharangia region and from there Muslim scholarship would pass to England, France and Germany.[326] He had prepared the grounds for incorporating the Muslim sciences that was to come.

Adelard, from the city of Bath in England, picked up where Gerbert had left off in the pursuit of Muslim knowledge. He left home in the 12th century for education in France. In Tours he had a vision of two women, one of whom offered him wealth, fame and power and the other offered knowledge of the seven disciplines included in the *Quadrivium* and *Trivium*. Despite human temptations he opted for and embarked on the road for knowledge.

He arrived in Syracuse, an Island of Sicily, which not long ago was a Muslim ruled domain. He was amazed at the mathematical skill of his host Bishop William. Later when he wrote the book *On the Same and the Different* he dedicated it to the Bishop. This book provides information of prevailing European knowledge level in the 12th century when encounters with the Muslim world

---

[326] Lyons, Johnathan, 2009, p. 40.

of knowledge increased.[327]

A few years before Adelard's arrival in Antioch (city in Syria), the combined Normans and Genoese forces had captured the nearby city of Tripoli from the refined Bannu Ammar Prince. The *Damascus Chronicle of the Crusades,* a contemporary Arab account, recorded that among the booty carted off from Tripoli by the victorious Christians were 'the books of its college and libraries of private collectors'.[328] Thousands of these works ended up with Antioch's merchants and became accessible to the itinerant Englishman Adelard.[329]

Adelard studied under Muslim masters and extensively translated to Latin the works on geometry, astronomy and philosophy. In alchemy he learned the processes to produce colour pigments, dyed leather and tinted glass. About a dozen of his work still survive which range from applied chemistry, geometry, astronomical geometry (al-Khwarizmi's *Sindbind*) to the art of falconry and cosmology. He translated Euclid's work the *Elements* from Arabic to Latin[330] and also wrote on how to use the astrolabe.[331]

Unlike the Crusaders, who were inclined towards conquest of the Muslim lands, Adelard held the unorthodox view that the knowledge available in the Muslim East would cure all the ills of Europe. His works, learned from Muslim mentors, acknowledged 'my Arab masters'. These works soon spread out to many of the European schools amidst significant commotion.[332]

Muslim Spain was a region of scholars and repositories of knowledge. Following the example of Adelard, young European

---

[327] Lyons, Jonathan, 2009, p. 43.

[328] Ibn Al-Qalanisi, 1998, p. 89.

[329] Lyons, Jonathan, 2009, p. 2.

[330] *Ibid.,* p. 116.

[331] *Ibid.,* p. 105.

[332] *Ibid.,* p. 122-123.

scholars began to spread out to Spain, Sicily and Southern Italy. As Muslims were forced to withdraw from Spain there was a rush of such young people going there, pouring over Arabic texts, sometimes in groups, and translating those to take credit for the discovery. The translators, who studied under Muslims of Spain, included a range of Europeans including Englishmen, Germans, French, Slavs, Italians and others.[333] Their translated works were taken back to the regions of their origin and helped in the formation of the earliest European universities in Bologna, Paris and Oxford.[334]

Stephen of Pisa, Italian translator and scholar, also known as the 'Philosopher', translated al-Abbas al-Majusi's medical encyclopaedia *The Royal Book*. The Latin version soon became a European standard.[335] Michael Scot, born in Scotland in the late 12th century, came to be known as one of the renowned intellectuals of his time. Michael became part of the translation movement that brought him fame. Among his substantial contribution was the translation of Ibn Rushd's philosophical works. Rationalism was introduced to Europe through the translation of this work. Ibn Sina's (Avicenna) Canon of Medicine remained a standard European text into the 1600s. Arab books on optics, chemistry and geography were equally long-lived.[336] The Italian scholar Gerard of Cremona working in Toledo of Spain translated a large number of scientific books from Arabic to Latin.

The famous mathematician Leonardo Fibonacci of Pisa, known for his Fibonacci Sequence, learned mathematics and (double entry) accounting from Muslims in what is now Algeria. He also travelled to Egypt, Sicily, France and Constantinople and

---

[333] Lyons, Johnathan, 2009, p. 160.

[334] *Ibid.*, p. 161.

[335] *Ibid.*, p. 104.

[336] *Ibid.*, p. 3.

wrote his first comprehensive book on algebra and geometry after returning to Europe in 1220.[337]

The arrival of Muslim science and philosophy, the legacy of Gerbert-Adelard and those who followed their model of seeking knowledge, gradually transmuted the archaic Europe into a scientific and technological authority. Its reach extended into the 16th century and beyond, shaping the ground breaking work of Copernicus and Galileo.[338]

The power of Muslim learning refashioned Europe's intellectual landscape. Without accurate control over clock and calendar, the rational organisation of society was unthinkable. Such developments provided for the progress of science, technology, and industry, as well as the liberation of man from the thrall of nature. Arab science and philosophy helped rescue Europe from ignorance and made possible the very idea of the West.[339]

Sicilian Connection

The first Muslim excursions to Sicily were made during the rule of Mu'awiyah (602-680 CE), founder of the Umayyad Dynasty, whose navy is known to have undertaken such expeditions. But it was the Abbasid Caliph al-Mu'tasim's navy that captured Messina in Sicily and then took the southern tip of Italy in the 9th century.

The Muslim rule in Sicily started in 827 and lasted for 264 years. West Sicily was under the Aglabids of North Africa and then the Fatimids after they overthrew the Aglabids. The Byzantines ruled the eastern part of Sicily but were forced away in 966 leaving the entire island to the Fatimids. Soon the island became a centre of culture and education. From the end of the

---

[337] King, Charles, 1994, p. 252.
[338] Lyons, Johnathan, 2009, p. 3.
[339] *Ibid.*, p. 2.

10th century up to the first half of the 11th was a golden age in the history of Sicily. Modernisation of agriculture, promotion of knowledge and commerce made the island prosperous. About 300 schools and a similar number of mosques were established in the city of Palermo.

According to Professor Francesco Gabrieli, in *Muhammad and the Conquest of Islam,* during this period the Muslims had also established at least three Principalities in the southern extreme of mainland Italy.[340] By the beginning of the 10th century these principalities were annexed by the Italians.

During the second half of the 11th century the emirs of Sicily lost their political control leading to anarchy and the finally the island was captured by the (French) Normans. The Normans did not bring about any drastic change in the administration but just replaced the emirs. In fact, Muslims still occupied the highest positions under them.

Besides the European scholars, few European monarchs were also developing interest in Muslim knowledge. Two of the monarchs who were responsible for the propagation of knowledge into pre-Renaissance Italy were the Norman King Roger II of Sicily and his grandson Frederick II, emperor of Italy and king of Sicily.

Roger II and al-Idrisi

King Roger II (1097-1154) consolidated all the Norman conquests in Sicily and Southern Italy into one kingdom that he ruled from Palermo, a predominantly Muslim city with Muslim culture and knowledge.[341]

He was an enlightened person whose palatial court welcomed Muslim and other scholars and professionals. The Englishman

---

[340] Hasan, 2004, p. 588.
[341] Lyons, Johnson, 2009, p. 92.

Thomas Brun was the *qa'id* (Arabic: leader) of his royal *diwan* (governing body). The title of his prime minister, George of Antioch, also in charge of the fleet, was the 'amir of amirs' (*ammiratus ammiratorum*) from which the word 'admiral' was derived. George was formerly under the employment of a Muslim prince of Mahdia (in present-day Tunisia). Roger ran an Islamised system of government and could speak Arabic. His court resembled the courts of Muslim rulers. For this some European historian would call him 'The Pagan' probably meaning 'The Muslim'.

Roger sponsored a project to develop a map of the world[342] in which he engaged al-Idrisi to lead. Roger must have heard about the experience and knowledge of al-Idrisi to have proposed him to lead the project. Al-Idrisi, who was initially reticent to join, vindicated his appointment and produced a remarkable map of the world.

Abdullah al-Sharif al-Idrisi al-Qurtubi, one of the greatest geographers, botanists and cartographers of the Middle Ages, was born in Cueta (North Africa) in 1099. He was educated in Cordoba, after which he embarked on a journey of the world seeking and teaching knowledge.[343] He visited many regions including Central Asia, Middle East, Constantinople, France and England.

After joining the King Roger sponsored project to record all the known places of the world, al-Idrisi and others under him toiled for fifteen years to produce the book which he named *Al-Kitab al-Rujiri* (*The Book of Roger*). Roger, not after any personal fame, wanted to name the book *Nuzhah al-Mushtaq fi Ikhtiraq al-Afaq* (*Delights of Him Who Desires to Journey through the Climes*). However, al-Idrisi retained the name of *Al-Kitab al-Rujiri* as a

---

[342] Lyons, Johnson, 2009, p. 91.
[343] Said, H. M., 1991, p. 21.

respect to his sponsor.

Al-Idrisi's book was the best geography book of his age showing details never known previously.[344] He postulated concepts like the earth was spherical and that the water body remained undisturbed in this spherical surface due to 'an equilibrium of no variation'. Muslim geographers had recognised that the earth was spherical and al-Idrisi was the first to construct a reliable spherical globe of the world. Al-Idrisi's maps would find its way to European libraries and navigation centres, including Spain and Portugal, and be retained for centuries. Due to their accuracy his maps would be copied for three centuries by geographers without alterations.[345]

Roger's love for knowledge would retain Muslim knowledge in Sicily and propagate it to Italy.

Emperor Frederick II

Frederick II (1194-1250), who was called the 'Stupor Mundi', wonder of the world, was a very enlightened person. He was multilingual, knew Arabic and was a voracious reader. His court became the centre of the new emerging intellectual and cultural Europe.

Frederick's court was literally filled with Muslims. He had a Muslim physician, Muslim dialectician, Muslim pages and valets, and Muslim tutors. The Muslim call to prayer, the *adhan*, was regularly held in his court.[346] He patterned his court like his grandfather King Roger, *i.e.* in the style of contemporary Muslim rulers, and was in communication with learned figures in North Africa, Spain and other Muslim regions.[347]

---

[344] Hasan, 2004, p. 642.

[345] Al Hassani, 2007, p. 254.

[346] Lyons, Johnson, 2009, p. 165.

[347] *Ibid.*, p. 168.

Politically, he got involved in conflicts, even armed conflicts, with the popes. All this led to him being disliked by some European political powers who spread rumours about him in lifetime and carried out a character assassination after his death.

He supported Muslims as well as European scholars like Michael Scot and Leonardo Fibonacci. The Scottish scholar Michael Scot after gaining fame from his work in Spain joined Frederick's court. His name was also maligned by those who disliked his association with Muslims in Spain and with Frederick in Sicily. Nevertheless, their works were instrumental in enlightening the emerging universities in Italy and France. Latter kings like Charles I of Anjou, of French lineage and king of Sicily by conquest from 1266, also continued the translation of Muslim works. He sponsored the translation of al-Razi's work *Al-Hawi* which was named *Continens*.

Muslim Influence on the Stages of European Intellectual Development

Thus, the development of European knowledge started from Muslim Spain and Sicily. From there the illumination moved to Italy and France. The Italian Renaissance was influenced significantly by Muslim Sicily and the sponsorship of knowledge by King Roger II and his grandson Emperor Frederik II. France was a country having borders with both Spain and Italy so they were also one of the early ones to come in contact with Muslim knowledge. Finally, the illumination moved to the west and north Europe. It was not just academic knowledge that was transferred across to Europe but a whole culture, a way of life and a new manner of thinking.

Robert Briffault—social anthropologist, surgeon and novelist of early 20th century UK—states that:

"It was under the influence of Moorish (Spanish Muslim) revival of culture and not in the 15th century that the real renaissance took place. Spain and not Italy was the cradle of the rebirth of Europe. After sinking lower and lower in barbarism, it had reached the darkest depths of ignorance and degradation when the cities of Saracenic world, Baghdad, Cairo, Cordoba, Toledo, *etc.*, were growing centres of civilisation and intellectual activity. It was there that the new life arose which was to grow into a new phase of human evolution. From the time when the influence of their culture made itself felt began the stirring of new life".[348]

When the Muslims, after the Mongol scourge, regressed from rational science, its seeds had already been transported and were waiting for the roots to germinate in Europe. There were three stages in the transfer and assimilation of knowledge from Muslims lands to the West.

1. Translation of Muslim works to European languages, mainly Latin.

2. Assimilation of the translated knowledge all over Europe and into various languages.

3. Research and works by the subsequent groups of Western scholars.

There were, obviously, overlaps in the three stages.

1. Translation of Muslim Works

The initial translation activity of Muslim texts had started by the time of Gerbert d'Aurillac (d. 1003) and Fulbert of Chartres (d. 1028). But it was after Adelard of Bath's (d. 1152) sojourn into

---

[348] Hasan, M., 2004, p. 597.

Spain, Sicily and Syria that a large scale translation movement of Muslim Arabic text to Latin started and continued through to the Renaissance. The main centres of translation were in Spain and Sicily. Professor Hasan presents a list of these translations in his *History of Islam,*[349] a summary of which is provided below.

Gerard of Cremona (1187) alone had more than 90 books translated from Arabic which included scientific, philosophical and various other works of Thabit ibn Qurrah, Hunayn ibn Ishaq, Al-Zarqali, Banu Musa brothers, Abu Kamil, Abu al-Qasim, al-Kindi, al-Farabi and Ibn al-Haytham. He also translated al-Razi's medical and chemical works, Jabir ibn Aflah's *Elementa Astronomica*, the *Almagest*, al-Khwarizmi's *On Algebra and al-Muqabalah*, the Arabic texts of Archimedes' *On the Measurement of the Circle*, Aristotle's *On the Heavens* and Euclid's *Elements of Geometry*.

Gerard edited the *Tables of Toledo*, the most accurate compilation of astronomical data of the time. Those tables had been completed by al-Zarqali, known to the West as Arzachel, the 11th century mathematician and astronomer of Cordoba. Gerard's Latin translation of al-Farabi's book on the sciences, *Kitab Ihsa al-Ulum*, which discussed classification and fundamental principles of science was named *De scientiis (On the Sciences)*. He also translated Ahmad ibn Muhammad ibn Kathir al-Farghani's (Alfraganus) *Elements of Astronomy.*[350] Gerard also wrote original treatises on arithmetic, algebra and astrology.

Michael Scot (d. 1232) and his successor Herman the German translated Ibn Rushd's summaries and commentaries on Aristotle in the late 12th century. Constantine the African monk translated the medical treaties including *Al-Kitab al-Maliki* by Ali ibn Abbas in the 11th century. Many of the books he translated

---

[349] Hasan, M., 2004, p. 596.
[350] Grant, Edward, 1974, p. 35-38; Burnett, Charles, 2001, p. 275-281.

were from the al-Qayrawan Mosque University complex.[351] Faraj
ibn Salim, a Jew from Sicily, translated al-Razi's *Al-Hawi* and
Taqwim al-Buldan of Ibn Jazlah. Astronomical tables of Majriti
and works of al-Khwarizmi and Abu Ma'shar Ja'far were
translated in the 12th century by Adelard of Bath. Robert of
Chester translated al-Khwarizmi's *Algebra*, while Abraham ibn
Ezra translated al-Biruni's *Commentary on al-Khwarizmi's Tables*.
John of Seville translated the medical and philosophical works of
al-Farghani, al-Kindi and al-Ghazali. Tivolo of Spain translated
the astronomical works of al-Battani while Stephen of Sicily
translated the medical works of al-Majusi. According to
Historian's History the theories of Kepler on atmospheric
refraction were derived from Ibn al-Haytham's *Twilight*.

In Italy, Burgundio of Pisa translated the works of Ibn Rushd
in the 12th century. Paravisius translated the *Taysir* of Ibn Zuhr.
Qabus Nameh, a major Persian work from the 11th century was
written by Unsur al-Ma'ali Kaykavus, the Ziyarid ruler of Persia.
This work contains 44 chapters and outlines princely education,
manners, and conduct set as moral instructions in prose in
original style and tone (This book influenced the *Dastur al-
Wuzara* of Nizam al-Mulk). It has been translated to German
from Turkish in the early 19th century and to English, French,
Japanese, Russian and Arabic in the 20th centuries.

Early translated works were, at times, passed off as the work
of the European translators. Some Muslim scholars even reacted
to it as can be seen in 11th century Spain when Ibn Abdun
admonished, "You must not sell books of science to Jews and
Christians ... because they translate these scientific books and
attribute them to their own people and to their bishops, when
they are indeed Muslim works"[352]. This was not always an act of

---

[351] Al Hassani, 2007.
[352] d'Alverny, Marie-Therese, 1982, p. 440.

gleeful plagiarism but happened due to the existing anti-Muslim phobia in the political environment that was reflected in the crusades.

Besides the above-mentioned works there had been many other translations which are now lost and no longer known, while certain works have been translated multiple times by different scholars. In Europe, renaissance took place due to a number of factors. But if a single enabling factor is to be stated, it would be that the Renaissance is the transliteration of Muslim works and thoughts to European languages and consciousness.

2. Assimilation of the Translated Knowledge

Along with the translation of Arabic texts by the Europeans came the assimilation of this knowledge. Up to the 15th century a major part of scientific activity of Europe consisted of assimilation of the Muslim sciences and other disciplines and systematisation of it. Among the great Western scholars and luminaries who played a major role in assimilation of Muslim knowledge include Alexander of Halle, St. Thomas Aquinas, Albertus Magnus, Robert Grosseteste, Roger Bacon, Arnold of Villanove and Peter of Abano.

With the appropriation of Muslim knowledge, the scope of European learning rapidly expanded. The works of Ibn Rushd, Ibn Haytham and other Muslim scholars were instrumental in new thoughts and, thus, new institutions to appear in France. The learning centres had moved from the monasteries to the cathedral schools. Two of the most famous schools were at Chartres and Notre Dame. The monk-philosopher-intellectual Theirry of Chartres taught that science was compatible with religion. By the end of the 12th century these schools started to develop into universities. And before the end of the 13th century these universities were granted royal charters.

The arrival of Constantine the African monk in southern Italy with huge number of translations gave the impetus to the blossoming of knowledge in the University in Salerno (*Schola Medica Salernitana*), which became famous for its medical schools. Muslim knowledge also stimulated the universities in Padua and Bologna in Italy. The University of Bologna, which was famous for legal studies, was given its charter by Emperor Frederick Barbarossa in 1158. The University of Naples was established in 1224 and is one of the oldest continuous functioning academic institutions of the world. It was established by Emperor Frederick II, who is known for his great respect for Muslim knowledge. Emperor Frederick ensured that the translated works, such as those of Ibn Rushd, were sent to the Italian universities.[353]

3. Research and Works by the Subsequent Groups of Western Scholars

In the European universities the translated works of Muslims remained the main teaching text, some till the 18th century. Based on these acquired knowledges the Europeans then started to write original works which are well recognised today.

One of the earliest of such texts was written by Fibonacci, who was born in 1170. Also known as Leonardo of Pisa, he went to Bougie in Algeria to learn mathematics from a master called Sidi Umar. His study included algebraic and simultaneous equations. He also visited the libraries at Alexandria, Cairo and Damascus, after which he wrote his famous *Liber Abaci*.[354]

Before Islam, knowledge was mostly theoretical, scientific experimentation was negligible, and scientific inventions

---

[353] Lyons, Jonathan, 2009, p. 184.
[354] Al Hassani, 2007, p. 67.

harboured more on accidents. The Greeks were theoretical geniuses but as noted by H. G. Wells in *An Outline of History* they lacked scientific experimentation. It was the Muslims who really started protracted scientific experimentations and developed a scientific methodology. Roger Bacon, according to Robert Briffault, studied Muslim sciences and transmitted the experimental method to Europe.[355]

The initial group of European scholars carried out their work based on Muslim knowledge. As the number of books by European authors increased, subsequent scholars could then base their research on the European books alone. After this point, arbitrarily the 17th century, Europe saw a remarkable rise in learning and development of knowledge. However, works like those of Ibn Khaldun, al-Razi and Ibn Sina would still be continued to be published up to the 19th century.

At this stage, though, the contributions of the Muslims were forgotten or erased in a gradual process. In the political fields of Europe, from time to time, there has been a feeling of enmity towards the Muslims. Over generations, the contributions of the Muslims were gradually forgotten. As Europe rose and the Muslims stagnated, the lack of understanding of Muslim contributions led the anti-Muslim feeling to change its hue from enmity to one of condescension. Thus, politics masked Europe's intellectual debt to Islam. Finally, a great harm to the history of knowledge was committed when a cruel fable was invented that Muslims had been just 'keepers' of knowledge from past civilisations and had simply passed them on to Europe without themselves doing any work.

The modern scientific methodology for researching in any subject is that a scholar must investigate all the previous works on the same or similar subjects and then progress with his or her

---

[355] Hasan, M., 2004, p. 598.

research which provides original output. This empirical system was set up by the early Muslim scholars. They investigated the ancient Greek, Indian, Persian, Chinese and any other source of knowledge they could find and then proceeded with their own research developing remarkable new knowledges. In their works they gave references to the old works. Some recent scholars misunderstand the methodology and tend to give more credence and weight to the ancient references rather than the Muslim work itself.

During the compilation of the ḥadīth the Muslim scholars had started a reference system, the *isnad*, to judge the authenticity of each ḥadīth. These gave credit to the scholars who were the narrators of each ḥadīth. In rational science, as well, Muslim scholars credited previous works, like those of Aristotle, or those coming from India. Thus, the old names were passed on and the old masters got their due credit. But when their turn came, the European scholars overlooked the Muslim names in the reference system except for a tiny minority. The Muslim contributions were either erased or remained Latinised, like Geber for al-Jabir, in overlooked historical-academic records. In the *Intellectual Development of Europe*, Professor John William Draper laments:

"I have to deplore the systematic manner in which the literature of Europe has continued to put out to sight our obligations to the Mohammedans. Surely they cannot be much longer hidden. Injustice founded on religious rancour and national conceit cannot be perpetrated forever. The Arab has left his intellectual impress on Europe. He has indelibly written it on the heavens as any one may see who reads the names of the stars on a common celestial globe".[356]

---

[356] Draper, John William, 1864, p. 42.

Scholarly Views about Early Muslim Knowledge

Many famous scholars who have truly studied historical Muslim intellectualism and are above prejudice or politics have given their views about Islam and its effect on knowledge. A few of those comments are presented below:

> "And if the reader entertains any delusions about a fine civilisation, either Persian, Roman, Hellenic or Egyptian being submerged by Islam, the sooner he dismisses such ideas the better. Islam prevailed because it was the best social and political order. Islam was the broadest, freshest, and cleanest political idea that had yet come into actual activity in the world, and it offered terms better than any other to the masses of mankind."

> —H. G. Wells, *History of the World*

> "Muslims historiography has at all times been united by the closest ties with the general development of scholarship in Islam, and the position of historical knowledge in Muslim education has exercised a decisive influence upon the intellectual level of historical learning and writing. The Muslims achieved a definite advance beyond previous historical writings in the sociological understanding of history and its systematisation. The development of modern historical writing seems to have gained considerably in speed and substance through the utilisation of Muslim literature which enabled the Western historians from the 17th century on, to see a large section of the world through foreign eyes. The Muslim historiography helped indirectly to shape the present day historical thinking."

> —Franz Rosenthal, *History of Muslim Historiography*

"The science of chemistry owes its origin and improvements to the industry of the Saracens (Muslims). It was they who first invented and named the alembic for the purpose of distillation, analysed the substance of three kingdoms of nature, defined the distinction and affinities of alkalies and acids and converted the poisonous minerals into soft and salutary medicines."

—Edward Gibbon, *Decline and Fall of the Roman Empire*

"Horticulture improvements constituted the finest legacies of Islam, and the gardens of Spain proclaim to this day one of the noblest virtues of her Muslims conquerors. The development of agriculture and horticulture were some of the glories of Muslim Spain."

—George Sarton, *An Introduction to the History of Science*

"For although there is not a single aspect of European growth in which the decisive influence of Islamic culture is not traceable, nowhere it is so clear and momentous as in the genesis of the power which constitutes the permanent distinctive force of the modern world and the supreme source of victory—natural science and the scientific spirit."

—Prof. R. Briffault, *The Making of Humanity*

"Arab astronomers have left on the sky immortal traces of their industry which everyone who reads the names of the stars on an ordinary celestial sphere can readily discern."

—Prof. P. Hitti, *History of the Arabs*

"Proceeding from the known to the unknown, taking precise account of celestial phenomena, accepting nothing as true which is not confirmed by experiences or established experiment, such were the fundamental principles taught and claimed by the Muslim masters of astronomy."

—Prof. Louis Pierre Eugene Sedillot, *Histoire Des Arabes...*

"... but for the Arab astronomy, there would have been no Copernicus and Newton."

—Prof. R. Briffault, *The Making of Humanity*

"In much the same way that the Muslim scholars transmitted to posterity a large fund of ancient learning. Muslim artisans preserved, developed and spread abroad the traditional workshop practice of arts in the orient, which had either never penetrated Europe, or, if known there in former times had decayed during the period of stress that ushered in the Middle Ages."

—A. H. Christie, *Legacy of Islam*

"The debt of our science to the Arabs does not consist in startling discoveries or revolutionary theories. Science owes a great deal more to the Arab culture: it owes its existence."

—R. Briffault, *The Making of Humanity*

"For a thousand years this civilisation was the central light whose rays illumined the world. It was the mother of European culture, for men reared in this civilisation were the masters in the Middle Ages at whose feet Spaniards, the French, the English, the Italians, and the Germans sat to learn philosophy, sciences of mathematics, astronomy, chemistry, physics, medicine and industrial techniques. Their names are household names."

—Dr. Tara Chand, All India Islamic Studies Conference
December 1964, Osmania University

"... forebodings of even the Newtonian law of gravitation are found among the Arabs."

—Prof. Frederich Heinrich Dieterici

"... the Court of the Abbasids the centre of the highest culture, to which the learned and the gifted flocked from East and West."

—E. Denison Ross, *Islam*, 1928

"Samarqand and Bukhara (in former USSR) became the centres of civilisation, learning, art and scholarship for a large part of the Muslim world."

—E. Denison Ross, *Islam*, 1928

"The Greeks systematised, generalised and theorised but the patient ways of investigation, the accumulation of positive knowledge, the minute methods of science, detailed and prolonged observation, experimental enquiry, were altogether alien to Greek temperament. What we call science arose in Europe as a result of new methods of investigation, of the method of experiment, observation, measurement, of the development of mathematics in form unknown to the Greeks ... That spirit and these methods were introduced into the European world by the Arabs."

—R. Briffault, *The Making of Humanity*

"[In Cordoba of Muslim Spain] After sunset a man might walk through its solidly paved streets in a straight line for ten miles by the light of public lamps' whereas, there was not much as one public lamp in London, and in Paris, for centuries subsequently, whoever stepped over his threshold on a rainy day stepped up to his ankles in mud."

—John. W. Draper,
A History of Intellectual Development of Europe, 1910

"Beautiful as were the palaces and gardens of Cordoba (Muslim Spain), her claims to administration in higher matters were no less strong. The mind was as lovely as the body. Her professors and teachers made her the centre of European culture: students would come from all parts of Europe to study under her famous doctors, and even the German nun Hroswitha far away in her Saxton convent of Gaudershiem, when she told of the martyrdom of Eulogius, could not refrain from singing the praises of Cordoba, 'the brightest splendour of the world."

—Stanley Lane-Poole, *The Moors in Spain*

The Mohammedan Theory of Evolution

After the Renaissance, Europe gradually started to become the hub of many new ideas, many theories and systems started to proliferate. One such theory was the 'evolution of life' by natural selection.

It was Darwin's famous work *On the Origin of Species* published in 1859 that made the evolution of life concept by natural selection famous in Europe. The general theory is that life originated as a simple organism which over a very long timespan slowly changed and evolved into new species becoming more complex. These species kept on evolving further forming newer animals until finally developing into human beings. Thus, the evolution of man is considered to be from human-like apes (primates) by such scientists.

The fossils of human-like primates have been found in recent times. Such human-like forms include the *Australopithecines* (from 3-6 million years ago), *Homo habilis* (1.5-2.8 million years ago), *Homo erectus* (Java Man and Peking Man, 70,000-1.9 million years ago), *Homo sapiens neanderthalensis* (Neanderthal Man, 40,000-400,000 years ago). The *Homo sapiens* (modern men) are 35,000 years old (and according to some biologists 100,000 to 500,000 years old). Other fossils are still being investigated. Natural scientists like palaeontologists used this information to claim that human beings may have evolved from the primates gradually. But there is no general agreement regarding the precise relationship between modern man and the various man-like primates.

A number of anthropological and biochemical studies have pointed to the emergence of all present-day human beings from a small group of individuals, perhaps somewhere in Africa. It is supposed that their descendants soon migrated to various continents and the different environment and climatic conditions led to the variations in the skeletal, muscular, and other details giving rise to different races.[357]

Darwin did not complete his medical education but instead went on to study Divinity at Christ's College, Cambridge, to become a clergyman. But he developed an immense interest for natural history, one of his subjects, which led him to fieldworks and finally into evolution. The evolution debate started off around Darwin's time but he was not the first to have contemplated it. Muslim scholars had already considered evolution long ago.

---

[357] Afzal, Ahmed, 1996, p. 53.

Past Muslim Thoughts on Evolution of Life

Al-Jahiz (776-869 CE), a famous scholar and author of a number of books including *Kitab al-Haywanat* (Book of Animals), was the first person to postulate evolutionary forces at work. According to him inanimate objects evolved to plants which then evolved to animal life. He hinted at the changes in animal life caused by migrations and environment.[358] He discussed existence, adaptation and animal psychology that make the centre point of Darwin's natural selection.[359] His works influenced the later scholars like al-Mas'udi, al-Damiri, al-Biruni, Ibn Tufayl and Ibn Khaldun. Other Muslim scholars like Ibn Haytham and Ibn Rushd also hinted at evolutionary processes.

Al-Mas'udi in his *Kitab al-Tanbih wa al-Ashraf* agrees with al-Jahiz on evolution.[360] Ibn Miskawayh (942-1032 CE), the author of Al-*Fawz al-Asghar* (*The Small Achievement*) believed in the aquatic origin of life,[361] and gave a clear and in many respects thoroughly modern theory of the origin of man.[362]

The theory of evolution is also contained in 'The Epistles of the Brethren of Purity' (Ikhwan al-Safa') of around the 10th century CE. These Muslim thinkers state that the ape evolved into a lower kind of a barbarian man (that is comparable to the *Australopithecines, Homo habilis, Homo erectus, Homo sapiens neanderthalenisis, etc.*). He then became a superior human being (comparable to *Homo sapiens*). After that, man becomes a saint, a prophet, and will evolve into a higher stage and become an angelic being.[363]

---

[358] Iqbal, Muhammad, 1974, p. 121.

[359] Siddiqi, Habib Ahmad, 1988, p. 276.

[360] Rathor, Iftikhar al-Din Tariq, 1985, p. 112.

[361] Hamid, Khawaja Abdul, 1946, p. 29.

[362] Iqbal, Muhammad, 1974, p. 121.

[363] Hamidullah, Dr. Muhammad, 2004, p. 180; Iqbal, Muzaffar, 2000, p. 33.

Professor John William Draper, a contemporary of Darwin, states, "Sometimes, not without surprise, we meet the ideas with which we flatter ourselves with having originated in our own times. Thus, our modern doctrine of evolution and development were taught in their (Muslim) schools. In fact, they carried them much farther than we are disposed to do, extending them even inorganic and minerals".[364] Draper calls it the 'Mohammedan theory of evolution'. The Muslim theory of evolution does not start with the first simple life form but much earlier from the very clay or mineral which first gives rise to the first life forms.

By the 13th century the evolution concept had attained popularity among the Muslims. Jalal al-Din al-Rumi wrote verses elaborating the evolution of life and man. Sir Dr. Muhammad Iqbal comments, "The formulation of the theory of evolution in the world of Islam brought into being Rumi's tremendous enthusiasm for the biological future of man. No cultured Muslim can read such passages as follows without a thrill of joy."

Low in the earth
I lived in realms of ore and stone;
And then I smiled in many-tinted flowers;
Then roving with the wild and wandering hours,
O'er earth and air and ocean's zone,
In a new birth,
I dived and flew,
And crept and ran,
And all the secret of my essence drew
Within a form that brought them all to view—
And lo, a Man!
And then my goal,
Beyond the clouds, beyond the sky,
In realms where none may change or die—

---

[364] Draper, J. W., 1875, p. 118.

In angel form; and then away
Beyond the bounds of night and day,
And Life and Death, unseen or seen,
Where all that is hath ever been,
As One and Whole.

—*Rumi*, Iqbal, Muhammad, 1974, p. 186-187

In a more distinct yet no less dramatic style Rumi also wrote:

First man appeared in the class of inorganic things,
Next he passed therefrom into that of plants,
For years he lived as one of the plants,
Remembering nought of his inorganic state so different;

And when he passed from the vegetative to the animal state,
He had no remembrance of his state as a plant,
Except the inclination he felt to the world of plants.

Especially at the time of spring and sweet flowers;
Like the inclination of infants toward their mothers,
Which knew not the cause of their inclination to the breast.

Again the great Creator, as you know,
Drew man out of the animal into the human state.

Thus man passed from one order of nature to another,
Till he became wise and knowing and strong as he is now,
Of his first soul he has no remembrance,
And he will be again changed from his present soul.

—Iqbal, Muhammad, 1974, p. 121-122

More than a century before Darwin, Shah Wali Allah al-Dihlawi (1703-1762 AD) proposed a scheme of creation in which there are two types of Divine creative activities: *alam al-*

khalq and *alam al-amr*. The *alam al-khalq* is the domain of God's general creation, in which everything that happens takes times (*e.g.* the universe took nearly 14 billion years to develop to its presents form starting from the Big Bang and a primitive gaseous state, and a fertilised ovum takes 270-280 days to grow into a fully developed baby). The *alam al-amr* is the domain of God's direct command 'Be!' There is absolutely no time factor involved in this realm and things happens instantaneously. If He wants to create something, He says, 'Be!' and it is (Qur'an, Yā Sīn 36:82). The initial act of the creation of matter out of nothing (creation *ex nihilo*) represents a direct command of God.[365]

Any time-taking evolutionary process would be part of the *alam al-khalq* and Darwin's investigation belonged to this part. The credit to Darwin is not for proposing the idea of evolution, that belongs to the Muslim scholars, but of systematically researching fossils over different regions in an attempt to prove it scientifically.

A summary of books of many Muslims scientists was translated into Latin by Abraham Eehellensis and then published under the title *De Proprietatibus et Virtutibus Medicis Animalium* in Paris, in 1617, in French. Soon after that appeared the evolutionists of Europe, precursors of Darwin, such as F. Redi (1626-1698), C. Linnneus (1707-1778), Buffon (1707-1788) and Lamarck (1744-1829). It also explains why the first evolutionists of Europe come from France.[366]

[365] Afzal, Ahmed, 1996, p. 50-51.
[366] Mieli, Aldo, 1938, p. 263-264.

Contemporary Muslim Thoughts on Evolution of Life

In medieval Europe, scientists were historically thwarted by Christian theologians. Later, when their turn came European scientists and scholar denied divinity, even prior to Darwin. Many European scholars could not agree with certain aspects of Christian theology. In the European context, the theory of evolution was used by the atheists for the study of the amazing diversity of life-forms without taking recourse to the creative power of God. "The theory of evolution soon turned into a dogma, precisely, because it rapidly replaced religious faith and came to provide what appeared to be a 'scientific' crutch for the soul to enable it to forget God".[367]

On the contrary, Islam had not denied natural sciences. Up to the end of the 19th century, orthodox Muslim scholars did not care about any evolution theory as it was not against the Islamic view *per se*. It became significant only when materialists and atheists of Europe started to use this theory as a refutation against religion. It was due to this socio-political agenda that the orthodox scholars simply refused to accept it anymore.

There are, certainly, many Muslim scholars who disagree totally with any form of evolution, such as Shihabuddin Nadvi and Wahiduddin Khan to name a couple. Wahiduddin, in his book *God Arising: Evidence of God in Nature and in Science*, writes about evolution, 'For a hundred years this theory held sway over human thought. But then further investigations revealed that it had loopholes. It did not fully fit in the framework of creation. In certain fundamental ways, it clashed with the order of the universe as a whole'.[368]

But, there also have always been Muslim scholars who were quite comfortable with a created-evolving universe. They

---

[367] Nasr, S. H., 1993, p. 94.
[368] Khan, Wahiduddin, 1999, p. 182.

considered that God created the universe along with its processes and properties. It is these created processes that progressively develops the universe and causes evolution, and it is these properties of things that are perceived in nature (like the properties of minerals, energy, mass, *etc.*). Thus, from this perspective, God created objects and also the laws, processes or forces that govern those objects.

> *He created the sun, the moon, and the stars*
> *(all) governed by laws under His command.*

> —Qur'an, Al-Aʿrāf 7:54

Abu al-Majid Muhammad Rida al-Isfahani, an Iraqi theologian of the 20th century, addressed the evolutionary theory in his book *Naqd Falsafah Darwin*, (*Critique of Darwin's Philosophy*). Al-Isfahani defends a God-initiated version of evolution and counted the proponents of evolution like Lamarck, Wallace, Huxley, Spencer and Darwin among those who believed in God. He referred to the works of Imam Jaʿfar al-Sadiq (especially to his *Kitab al-Tawhid*) and to those of *Ikhwan al-Safa'* to point out anatomical similarities in man and ape, claiming that Darwin could never provide full treatment of these similarities as compared to *Ikhwan*. In spite of the embryological similarities between man and other mammals he affirmed that the structural unity of living organisms was a result of heavenly wisdom and not a consequence of blind chance in nature.[369]

According to contemporary Muslim scholars like Dr. Afzal Ahmad and Dr. Israr Ahmad evolution is not synonymous with Darwinism and although evolution is a universal fact which can be established through the study of comparative morphology, palaeontology, embryology, anthropology and genetics—the

[369] Iqbal, Muzaffar, 2009, p. 187.

theory which is commonly propounded to explain its mechanism, *i.e.*, natural selection, is by no means a secure and scientifically proven fact.

They consider that human beings have a dual nature. There is a non-material mind or spirit or ego which exists side by side with human's corporeal body. They further argue that the real essence of a human being is the spiritual soul which has been directly inspired in humans and has nothing to do with evolution. Evolution concerns only with the physical body of man. Man's true superiority over the rest of creation, including angels, is not because of his physical body (that comes from clay), which he shares with other animals, but is actually due to his spiritual soul (which has been fashioned in God's image) which truly distinguishes him and sets him apart from all living creatures.

The Basics behind the Muslim Concept of Evolution:

In the Qur'an it is stated that God made humanity out of clay. The literalist concept of the creation of human is that God moulded clay into shape and breathed his spirit into it and Adam was thus created. But the 'moulding of clay' is a *process* that involves time. This indicates some intermediate stages in-between the starting with clay at the beginning and the final human form at the end. Some verses of the Qur'an states that God created man from clay while some says from sperm (Qur'an, Al-Kahf 18:37, Al-Ḥajj 22:5, Al-Furqān 25:11, Al-Mu'min 40:67). It is obvious that the initial sperm did not form out of clay and that there were intermediate stages. A process is involved, which is evolution in human terms. The mention of all intermediary stages of evolution has not been detailed and attention is drawn to the original source, which is clay, and the final cause, which is the sperm of man that stays in the womb of a woman.

The missing intermediary stages from the clay to human can

be defined by the progression of evolution from clay (or minerals) to plants and then to animals and finally to human beings with water playing an important role at the beginning.

We made from water every living thing.
Will they not then believe.

—Qur'an, Al-Anbiyā' 21:30

As the biological (animal) evolution reached its goal and the final human form appeared on earth, God selected a single pair, a male and female, and endowed them with their spiritual souls. After that God placed Adam and Eve in Paradise and told them that they are free to enjoy of its fruits except not to eat fruit from a certain tree (Al-Baqarah 2:35). But Satan made them slip (Al-Baqarah 2:36) and they ate of it. Adam and Eve were sent to earth, not really as a punishment but as a chance of redemption with inspiration, guidance and promises of mercy from God (Al-Baqarah 2:37-38).

It is not entirely inconceivable that all other members of the previous species from which the body of Adam and Eve were selected had died and became extinct. With the incorporation of soul, Adam and Eve became the first human pair and humankind is, therefore, their descendant as alluded to in the Qur'an (Al-Ḥujurāt 49:13).

The Qur'an, however, does not deal with the intermediate stages in any details but only gives indications.[370] According to the Qur'an (Nūḥ 71:14), 'He created you in stages' (*Wallahu khalaqakum atwaran*). This may refer to the embryonic stages before birth as in verse (Al-Mu'minūm 23:13-14). But in Arabic grammar, the word **tawr** is the root of *tatawwar*, which means 'evolution'. Thus, this can also mean the process that God

---

[370] Afzal, Ahmed, 1996, p. 53.

fashioned life from minerals (clay) in stages, first minerals developed into vegetation, which developed into animal life.[371]

Some other verses of the Holy Qur'an in which the stages of human creation are mentioned are as follows:[372]

> *Allah has caused you to grow as a growth from the earth.*

> —Qur'an, Nūḥ 71:17

> *He brought you forth from the earth and settled you therein.*

> —Qur'an, Hūd 11:61

> *He created man of fermented clay*
> *dried tinkling hard like earthenware.*

> —Qur'an, Al-Raḥmān 55:14

> *He fashioned man from fermented clay dried tinkling-hard .*

> —Qur'an, Al-Ḥijr 15:26

> *It is He who created man from water.*

> —Qur'an, Al-Furqān 25:54

> *(Allah is the one God) Who made all things He created*
> *excellent; and He began the creation of man from clay.*

> —Qur'an Al-Sajdah 32:7

Qur'an Al-Ḥashr 59:24 is also quite interesting in this respect. It states:

---

[371] Iqbal, Muzaffar, 2000, p. 42.
[372] Afzal, Ahmed, 1996, p. 51-52.

He is Allah, the Creator, the Evolver,
the Bestower (or Fashioner) of Forms.
To Him belong the Most Beautiful Names:
whatever is in the heavens and on earth,
declares His Praises and Glory:
and He is the Exalted in Might, the Wise.

Unlike the name 'Creator' that relates to the power of instantaneous creation, the qualities 'Evolver' and 'Fashioner' defines processes, and processes by nature are time reliant like the process of evolution. Thus, God does not just create but also evolves and fashions. A similar idea is found in verse Al-A'rāf 7:11, which states:

*We created you **then gave you shape** then*
We told the angels, 'Prostrate yourselves to Adam.'

Here it is clear that the initial creation of man or Adam was not in the shape of 'man'; this shape was given later after the creation.

In finalising the evolution process, modern scientific findings confirm that all human beings of today are the descendants of a single pair, 'because the Mitochondrial DNA in each living human being can be traced back to a single female, who lived in Africa or Asia some 100,000 years ago'.[373] The Qur'an declared this fact 14 centuries ago.

O mankind! Reverence your Lord,
who created you from a single soul, and
He created thereof his mate and from them twains,
He spread countless men and women.

—Qur'an, Al-Nisā' 4:1

[373] Herlihy, John, 1999, p. 49.

Influence of Islamic Law

Islamic law or Sharia preserves and protects certain rights (*Maqasid of Sharia*). There are five primary rights of Religion, Life, Intellect, Property (wealth) and Progeny (family). These rights are unalienable, provided by the Creator, and above the authority of the rulers. The Sharia, codified by the four great Imams, has been used to rule great empires and kingdoms for more than a millennium and has influenced the whole world.

Its influence on the British Common Law and the Magna Carta is significant. King Henry II enacted the Common Law in the 12th century that unified the British law. Before that the judges used to give verdicts on their own authority as there was no standard central legal system. The judges did not have any basis for scholarly training either and mostly were important and upright members of the society. The enactment of the Common Law caused revolutionary changes in the English legal system introducing such institutions like the Trial by Jury, the Action of Debt and the Assize of Novel Disseisin (Court for seizure of land or property rights). Most importantly, it caused the formation of a central legal system like the Sharia.

Professor John Makdisi in *The Islamic Origin of the Common Law* states that the above-mentioned institutions (Jury, Action of Debt, and Assize) of the Common Law can be traced back directly to Islamic Sharia. It originated from the works of Thomas Brown of England who went to Sicily and worked in the *Diwan* (fiscal department of the Sicilian government) of King Roger. He held an important position being the protégé of chancellor Robert of Selby. He returned to England on the personal invitation of King Henry II in 1158 and was given a seat at the exchequer (royal treasury). His position was of considerable importance and he enjoyed a high degree of personal and official confidence of the king.

Sicily under King Roger II was powerful and the wealthiest government in Europe. The success of Roger's administrative prowess was Islamic in origin. The area of government that Brown knew best was the Islamic Sicilian Bureau, which recovered land for the king of Sicily. He was well versed in the concepts of *istihqaq* (Islamic procedure for land recovery), and the *lafif* (Islamic Jury used to establish evidence in the procedure of istihqaq). The concepts of *Istihqaq* and *Lafif* can be found in much older classical Islamic Law. Brown became an invaluable source of such information to King Henry II. Within eight short years after Thomas Brown appeared in England, the English Assize of Novel Disseisin was decreed and the English Jury in its modern form made its appearance.[374]

In 1215, The Magna Carta Libertatum (The Great Charter of the Liberties) was agreed to by King John of England. It established the principle that everyone, including the king, was subject to the law. It upheld the rights of gentry, the right to justice and the right to a fair trial. Before that time, the king was the law and above the law. The origin of the Magna Carta is linked to the returning Crusaders who had witnessed similar Islamic laws in practice while in the Muslim domains. They had observed great Islamic rulers like Saladin being subject to a law higher than royal decrees. So, when the Crusaders returned they had developed the notion of law above the royalty. Rose Wilder Lane discusses the above topic in her book *The Discovery of Freedom* and shows that the notion of rights of the gentry within the Magna Carta was taken directly from the Muslims. The book also shows that when Spain was reconquered by the Christians from the Muslims, the Catholics refused to conform to the new Christian rulers until an overarching law like the Sharia was enacted and certain rights that

---

[374] Makdisi, John. A., 1999.

the Sharia gave to them were also provided.[375]

The Common Law and the Magna Carta are the precursors of the American Constitution which declares, "We hold these truths to be self-evident, that all men are created equal and endowed by their Creator with certain unalienable rights including Life, Liberty, and the Pursuit of Happiness." A key role was played in this statement by the famous English philosopher John Locke. He was an Oxford University alumnus and carried out his works a generation before the American Founding Fathers. In Oxford he was contemporary with and very influenced by the works of Edward Pococke, the famous orientalist. In the 17th century, Pococke had travelled to Istanbul, which was the capital of the Ottoman Caliphate. At that time, the Ottoman Empire was huge and powerful and its prevailing law was the Shariah. The Ottomans were remarkably ahead in legal matters from the rest of the world. Even in the 15th century, Ottoman Caliph Suleiman the Magnificent was also known as Suleiman the Lawgiver.

Pococke studied in Istanbul for many years and translated classical Arabic texts to English. There are significant similarities between these translations and the philosophical theories of Locke. One such example is Ibn Tufail's famous 12th century book *Hayy ibn Yaqzan*, which is a philosophical treatise on human nature set in a fictional narrative. The ideas of this treatise, including specifics, are found almost in its entirety in John Locke's works. Locke also wrote of unalienable rights of man—Life, Liberty (his primary connotation was religious freedom) and Property that has originated from the primary rights (*Maqasid*) of the Sharia. He aspired for the liberty of religion similar to the laws of Sharia. In his letters on toleration he stated that 'is it not ironic that Muslims allow Christians more freedom than Christians

---

[375] Lane, Rose Wilder, 1943.

allow other Christians?'.[376]

With regards to the philosophy of rights, the American Founding Fathers were influenced by John Locke. Thomas Jefferson wrote in the constitution about the unalienable rights to Life, Liberty and Property but changed Property to Pursuit of Happiness, thus, finalising it to Life, Liberty and Pursuit of Happiness. He did not copy it directly from the Shariah but its influence via Pococke and Locke is evident.

---

[376] WR 25.

CHAPTER 11

The European Age

Two of the main events that led to the modern era were the Industrial Revolution and the French Revolution. The industrial revolution, starting from Britain, enabled the making of machines that worked and produced goods in mass scale for human consumption. The old economy of manually crafted goods was of no match to this new mechanised mass-producing economy. The French Revolution gave a new concept of state governance that represented the general mass, in place of the hereditary monarchy. These two revolutions put together produced the model for a new state which was efficient and progressive.

These changes did not just happen by themselves. The West, over the last few centuries, had produced a profusion of brilliant academics, scholars, scientists, social scientists and innovators. They were the thinkers who had inherited the existing knowledge and progressed it to a level that shaped the new world. Their indebtedness is not to the Greeks, as is often portrayed, but to the Muslim scholars.

During the time of the Renaissance the Greek knowledge was more than a thousand years old. On the other hand, since the 8th century, the Muslims had progressed knowledge to an extent far ahead of the Greeks. They did the same to the knowledge of the

Indians, Persian or Chinese. It was this knowledge of the Muslims that the Renaissance thrived on.

The foundation of the European Age was laid when the Europeans had taken on the mantle of knowledge where the Muslims had left off. In *Making of Humanity*, Robert Briffault states:[377]

> "It is highly probable that but for the Arabs modern Europeans civilisation would never had risen at all. It is absolutely certain that but for them it would not have assumed that character which has enabled it to transcend all pervious phases of evolutions. For although there is not a single aspect of European growth in which the decisive influence of Islamic culture in not traceable, nowhere is it so clear and momentous as in genesis of that power which constitutes the permanent distinctive force of the modern world and supreme source of its victory—natural science and scientific spirit."

During the early Islamic period, the tidal wave of research that had originated from the study of the Qur'an, the promulgation of jurisprudence (*fiqh*) and the collection and systematisation of the ḥadīth ultimately led to philosophy and rational sciences. The huge mass of people reading, writing and researching came upon various branches of knowledge. Innovations started to take place while ancient knowledge was understood and improved. Soon, from this incredible mass of scholars rose a plethora of the greatest minds, scientists, social scientists, philosophers, *etc.*, of that age. The great contributions of the Muslim scientists have not escaped the notice of great scholars of recent times. George Sarton, founder of the modern discipline 'history of science', comments:

---

[377] Hasan, M., 2004, p. 595.

"The most valuable of all, the most original and the most pregnant works were written in Arabic ... From the second half of the eighth to the end of the eleventh century, Arabic was the scientific and most progressive language of mankind. During that period anyone wishing to be well informed and up-to-date had to study Arabic. It will suffice here to evoke a few glorious names without contemporary equivalents in the West: Jabir b Hayyan, Al Kindi, Al Khwarizmi, Al Farghani, Al Razi, Thabit b Qurrah, Al Battani, Husain b Ishaq, Al Farabi, Abul Qasim, Ibn Al Jazzar, Al Beruni, Ibne Sina, Ibne Yunus, Al Karkhi, Ibn Al Haytam, Ali b Isa, Al Ghazzali, Al Zarqali, Umar Khayyam —a magnificent array of names which it would not be difficult to extend. If anyone tells you that the Middle Ages were scientifically sterile, just quote these names to him. All these scientists flourished between 750 and 1100 AD."

Dawn of Industry

In the 18th century, Europe had started to surge ahead of the rest of the world. It was the dawn of the Industrial Age which had started from Britain. Healthy population growth, increased agricultural output and technological innovation were the key factors driving the Industrial Revolution. Over the ages, science had kept on advancing and in the 18th century it had developed to a point where humans could create all manner of machinery to assist in processes of mass production. Colonial expansion provided both resources for the development of the industries and infrastructure and external markets for the end products.

The technological advance started in the second half of the 18th century and gradually accelerated. By the late 19th century the effect of industrialisation was marked by major shift in socio-economic and cultural life. The manual labour based economy was slowly replaced by a machine based economy. First the textile and iron making industries were mechanised. Energy usage, from refined coal, increased. To facilitate trade, the communication infrastructure had to be developed. The road and canal networks were improved and developed, then railway and steam ships eventually took over the job of mass transportation of people and goods. In the 19th century, industrialisation spread all across Western Europe and North America.

Innovations improved textile, mining, metallurgy, steam power, chemicals, and gas and lighting industries. Improved roads, navigable rivers and artificial canals made transport far more efficient. Machine tools were improved so that newer and more efficient and better machines could be made—soon machines were making more precise machines. Cheap labour with improved diet and longevity became available for the industries. Factories leapt up and the process of urbanisation and housing developed leading to a better organisation of labour.

Research and Development (RAD), the root of the innovations that developed the machineries for the factories, became the mainstay of staying ahead in industrial competition. In continental Europe, factories started to develop in various nations. Soon these nations would start their own RAD and become self-dependent. The Ottomans set up factories but failed to setup their RAD in any significant manner. Japan, on the other hand, was able to set up a strong disciplined RAD culture.

In the United States, industrialisation started in the north-eastern region where rivers with fast currents were located and water power was used to run factories. In the 1860s, with the development of steam power, industries began to spread across the nation.

The second stage of the Industrial Revolution started in the late 19th century and included the development of chemical, petroleum, electrical industries, and in the 20th century the automotive industries. It was marked by a transition of technological leadership from Britain to the United States and later was also embraced by Japan. By the 1890s, industrialisation had created the first giant industrial corporations with burgeoning global interests, when companies like U.S. Steel, General Electric and Bayer AG joined the railroad companies on the stock markets.

The industrialisation of Japan started after a group of Japanese politicians known as the Iwakura Mission toured Europe and the United States in 1871. On the advice of this mission the Japanese government started a state-led industrialisation scheme and plans for colonisation. Modern education was expanded and Japanese students were sent to study in the West to develop skills. In the 20th century, Japanese RAD would improve until they became second only to the US. In the latter half of the 20th century, China and India joined in the industrial age. China became the second biggest economy in the early 21st century. Thus, under European enlightenment, all the empires of antiquity, Indian and Chinese, had turned into developed nations except for the Muslims.

Political and Economic Theories

Advance in the sciences gave rise to industrialisation. With industrialisation and colonisation, the Western countries accumulated more wealth at a rate faster than ever before. The consequent changes in the society required new economic processes for the management of the modern state. In 1776, Adam Smith published his work 'The Wealth of Nations' which is considered the start of classical economics. It was the time in which the modern state was emerging from the legacy of feudalism. The classical economists perceived economy in the light of a national income rather than a ruler's treasury.

The vital suggestion of Adam Smith was that the free market

that appeared chaotic was actually self-regulating. The basis of the
Smith's work was class-based and described a system in which
individuals sought to improve their own conditions in a
competitive environment. The national income was divided up
between labourers, landlords, and capitalists in the form of wages,
rent and interest. One of the main arguments in favour of
capitalism was, and still is, that it made some very rich but also
increased wealth for all, as evidenced by rising life expectancy,
reduced working hours, and no work required of children and the
elderly.

Despite those improvements, many found capitalism to be
biased towards the rich. Marxism rose essentially as a working
class response to the Industrial Revolution which had caused
inequalities in the distribution of wealth created by capitalism.
According to Karl Marx, industrialisation polarised society into
the few very rich bourgeoisie and the much larger in numbers but
much poorer proletariat. He believed that the industrialisation
process was the logical dialectical progression of the feudal
economy. And the full development of capitalism would produce
the foundation that would lead to the development of socialism
and eventually communism in the world. Socialism asserted
economic equality among people and the abolition of private
property, either wholly or partially.

After the death of Marx his ideas began to exert a major
influence on workers' movements. This influence was given an
added impetus by the victory of the Marxist Bolsheviks in the
Russian 'October Revolution'. During the 20th century many
regions of the world including the Soviet Union, Cuba, and China
inherited Marxist political system, or some form of it.

During the Industrial Revolution an intellectual and artistic
resentment had also developed towards the capitalist industrialist
processes. This was known as the Romantic Movement. Its major
exponents in England included the poets William Blake, William

Wordsworth, George Gordon Byron, Samuel Taylor Coleridge, John Keats and Percy Bysshe Shelley. The movement stressed the importance of 'nature' in art and language in contrast to 'monstrous' machines and factories. The mention of 'Dark satanic mills' in Blake's poem 'Jerusalem' and Mary Shelley's novel *Frankenstein* reflected concerns that scientific progress may also have a negative effect on humanity.

Europe's First Colonial Expansion

The Iberians (Spain and Portugal) were the first European colonial powers. European colonial expansion is synonymous with its intellectual and rational development on the one hand and sea faring and naval development on the other. It was not by luck or pure chance that the Iberians became the first Europeans to take to the seas and establish colonies on other continents. It was the knowledge they inherited from Spanish Muslims that had enabled them to do so.

The only land connection that the Iberian Peninsula has to the rest of Europe is through the Pyrenees bordering France, the other three sides being bordered by the sea. The Muslims of Spain and Portugal, being barricaded by the Franks on the north, did not have any land connection to rest of the world. The only way to survive was via the seas, and survive they did in an enlightened and grand manner.

They developed enterprising naval and commercial connections with distant lands. With the sometimes-not-so-friendly Abbasids on the east, the sea faring was also directed towards North West Africa. They improved cartography, maps, naval instruments and ship design. They had become experts in the geography of the great seas and used mathematics and astronomy to guide them across. The shape of the earth, the African coast and some Atlantic Islands became known to the

Muslims. The Muslims had highly refined the use of the astrolabe by the 9th century and introduced it to Spain. It would remain the most popular astronomical device in Europe till the mid-17th century.

All this seafaring knowledge of the Spanish Muslims was automatically inherited by the later Portuguese and the Spaniards. This enabled them to make the first major European naval expeditions. Ceuta, the small but strategically placed North African port across the southern coast of the Strait of Gibraltar, was occupied by the Portuguese Prince Henry the Navigator in 1415. This capture opened up the door of Saharan trade routes. It was the first little step that was to start the process of colonisation.

In Europe, the translated tales of Muslim travellers, from al-Mas'udi (9th century) to Ibn Batuta (14th century), were read with great interest. Along with these travelogues the translated geography books also whetted the taste for exploration of the Western intelligentsia. The geographer al-Idrisi had produced maps in the court of Roger of Sicily in the 12th century that would be used in various regions of Europe without alterations for three centuries. Such factors, ultimately, led to the epoch-changing voyages and journeys of Vasco da Gama, Ferdinand Magellan, Marco Polo, Christopher Columbus, and James Cook. The initial explorers were Portuguese and Italians, who were also among the first to be influenced by the Muslim knowledge.

As the Spanish Muslims had been land-locked by the Franks, so the Europeans were also hedged in by the Ottomans. During hostilities between Byzantium and the Ottomans, Europe would become almost completely landlocked. The journey via Russia-Siberia was challenging due to the climate, geography and undeveloped roadways and paths. Land travel and carrying of merchandise to India and China would become difficult and long, so an alternate sea route was always sought after.

When Constantinople fell to the Ottomans the Portuguese

discovered the sea route to India around Africa. At about the same time the Italian Christopher Columbus decided to investigate another route to India across the Atlantic. The world was unaware of the existence of the Americas that lay between India and Europe. Al-Idrisi's maps and the *Elements of Astronomy on the Celestial Motions* by al-Farghani, the famous Muslim astronomer of the 9th century, were contributory in working out the circumference of the world at that time. Spain was the most advanced country in Europe, so it was only fitting that they, not Italy, sponsored the Italian Columbus' journey to discover the Americas.

Christopher Columbus had discovered America in 1492. In this voyage he led three small ships named Santa Maria, Pinta and Nina. Santa Maria, nicknamed Gallega, was the flagship commanded by Columbus. Two brothers Martin Alonso Pinzon and Vincente Yanez Pinzon captained the Pinta and Nina. Mauricio Obregon (writer, diplomat, and 'Columbus' expert of the 20th century who had lectured in Universities from Harvard to Dubrovnik) states that these two brothers were Muslims and related to Abuzayan Muhammad III, the Moroccan sultan of the Marinid Dynasty (1196-1465).[378]

Politics and Prejudice Against Muslims

Muslims have always shown respect towards other religions, especially towards Christianity and Judaism. During the time of the Prophet, when there was war between the two superpowers of the time, Roman Byzantium and Zoroastrian Persia, Muslims had morally sided with the Christian Byzantium. This is evident in the Qur'an (Al-Rūm 30:1-4). Later, under the Rashidun Caliphs, the Muslims had fought the Byzantines but their armies had been put

---

[378] Dame, Frederic William, 2013, p. 74.

under special instructions not to harm the Christian clerics, monks and their monasteries. The battle was not against Christianity but against imperialism and for freeing the lands that the Romans had occupied.

The Christians and Jews living in Muslim domains were considered *dhimmi*s or people to be protected, allowing them freedom of religious practice. They had to pay a *jizyah* tax but that was in place of the zakat that Muslims had to pay. Besides, by paying *jizyah* they need not be conscripted to the army. There was no *jizyah* for women, children or old people.

The latter battles, after Muslim empires had developed, were also between empires rather than religions. There had been healthy debates between the different religions as seen in the times of the Prophet or in the court of Caliph al-Ma'mun. In the early 11th century, feuding Muslim Berbers and Arab armies of Spain had Christian allies. Over the thousand years, obviously, there had been some exceptions but the general case was a definite goodwill towards the 'people of the book'.

But in the 11th century things were going to change. The problem that Europe faced was of political as well as intellectual nature. Europe was divided into kingdoms and realms incessantly in conflict with each other. The church did not have much control and the Muslims had driven the Byzantines from the Syriac Arab lands. In addition, the European scholars were all being attracted by the advanced Muslim knowledge and rationalism. The whole of Europe was opening up to the Muslim entity politically and intellectually. The authorities felt an existential threat.

European leaders like Gregory VII and Urban II decided to act and turned the politico -intellectual conflict to a religious one. The aim was to take the battle to the Muslim lands in the name of reconquering Holy Jerusalem. They started the Crusade with a frenzied propaganda against the Muslims to justify the invasion. The core message of this propaganda comprised four central themes:

1. Islam distorts the word of God,

2. it is spread solely by violence,

3. it perverts human sexuality, either by encouraging the practice of polygamy, as in the harems of the sultans, or through repressive or excessively prudish attitudes, and

4. its prophet, Muhammad (ṣ), was a charlatan, a tool of the devil, or even the Antichrist.[379]

This demonising was to sustain all through the centuries when the Crusades were fought. A few centuries later, the Ottomans ruled the biggest empire of their time which included a significant part of Europe. The battles against the Ottomans definitely did not help in assuaging the anti-Muslim feeling that had been raised since the Crusade propaganda. The Renaissance was contemporary with the Ottoman reign. So, removal of the credit due to the Muslim scholars became politically acceptable, even expedient. In order to claim a direct succession from the idealised Greeks, a time came when the Western thinkers overlooked the contributions of the 'inimical' Muslim scholars. At best they were projected as neutral caretakers of Greek knowledge who had just passed it along. During the Ottoman period, unfortunately, the Muslims did not much care what the European intellectuals thought because the Muslims and their empires were again at the top of the world. What the Europeans did or thought did not matter to them. So, they made no attempt to rectify the fact that Europe was harbouring Muslim knowledge.

The West's wilful forgetting of the Muslim legacy in the development of their knowledge began at that time. Anti-Muslim propaganda crafted in the shadows of the Crusades and the wars

---

[379] Lyons, Jonathon, 2009, p. 3.

with the Ottomans, over the many centuries, began to obscure any recognition of the profound role Muslim knowledge had played in the development of modern sciences.

After that came the colonial period. During this period the Muslims truly regressed. They even forgot their own heritage. They no longer had any scholars who could understand what their own predecessors had written five centuries earlier. The indebtedness to the original Muslim scientists were thus erased, put in the backburner, and forgotten. By mid-19th century, it appeared as if all the philosophy and natural science were from the Greeks, and all the scientific discoveries and inventions were modern European. The in-between centuries of academic and intellectual history was lost, not completely by accident. If the attempt to blot out almost a thousand years of human progress is tragic, the ignorance of the Muslims of their own heritage is pathetic.

There still remains subtle fallouts from the past. What the Muslim scholars were, what kind of scholars they were, what did they represent are being defined by modern scholars as they feel like. Many contemporary Western scholars tend to call Muslim scholars of the past as Arabs, not Muslims, because the initial Muslim generations of scholars included Christians and Jews. Before Islam came, all scholars were obviously non-Muslims as Muslims did not exist. Thus, when Islam came the majority of scholars with the knowledge of the ancients were, obviously, non-Muslims. Initially, the knowledge of these scholars, a majority of Christians, Persians and some Jews, were sought after. A few Indians also arrived during intervals.

But the environment was Muslim and, soon, in a few generations the vast number of scholars were Muslims. By then, there were many non-Arab Muslim scholars from Africa, Persia, Anatolia and Central Asia. All these scholars wrote in Arabic but were from different ethnic background and different places, all in a Muslim environment. So, calling them Arab scholars is inappropriate due to the large number of them being non-Arabs. They should be called Muslim scholars, of course, with special mention to those who were not Muslims. The names and religion of the non-Muslim scholars have been retained in Muslim annals.

Besides their important and serious works the early Muslim scholars had also written books on 'popular literature' like astrology, dreams, magic, talisman and omens, purely for public consummation and pecuniary return. Sometimes, undue attention is given to such popular literature instead of paying proper attention to the genuinely great works. This makes the Muslim scholars appear rationally unsound.

In some recent books and in the internet as well whenever mentions are made of exceptional Muslim scholars or Muslim rulers, it is often appended with some negative information about the person. If such a person had achieved a hundred good things but done one thing that may be negative, that one negative aspect is somehow highlighted. Even fiction shows great Muslim rulers as villains. All such biased preconceptions ultimately instigate the misguided belief that Islam was somehow not congenial towards scholarship, or those who did indulge in some great work were basically perverted beings. Even in the 21st century, many find it difficult to give due credit to the early Muslims.

There is also the issue of prejudice among a minority of 'lesser' scholars in the West—they would prefer not to give any credit to Muslims for Europe's enlightenment. Nevertheless, the early Muslim scholars did contribute to European knowledge development.

Long ago, Adelard had just the opposite view about Muslim scholars and rulers. In a section of his *On the Use of the Astrolabe*, he proposed a radical mode of rule for the kingdom to Henry Plantagenet. He proposed that the rulers should be philosopher-kings who speak the truth and are guided by natural justice and reason. They should be tolerant to all religions and beliefs. And they should recognise the authority of the Arabs (Muslims)—that is, of the scientist and thinkers—and not that of the rigid Church fathers.[380] Adelard had lived during the First Crusade and, at that time, due to political exigency, some of the Church figures were highly prejudiced against the Muslims.

Today, unlike some fringe political-evangelists, the Catholic Church has forgone this prejudice. The Vatican, in 1970, had tried to rectify it. A 150 page document, *Orientations pour un Dialogue entre Chretiens et Musulmans* (*Orientations for a Dialogue between Christians and Muslims*) by Father Maurice Borrman, produced by the Vatican Office of Non-Christian Affairs, stated that they must stay away from the outdated image of Muslims that has been inherited from the past, or distorted by prejudice and slander.

The document notes with regret that far too many Christians, brought up in an atmosphere of open hostility, are against any reflection on Islam. The text under the title of *Nous Liberer de nos Prejuges les Plus Notables* (Emancipating ourselves from our worst prejudices) asserts that there is a need for deep purification of attitude, particularly, from certain 'set judgement' that are all too often and too lightly made about Islam. It says that such views that are too easily or arbitrarily arrived at, which the sincere Muslim finds confusing, should not be cultivated in the heart.[381]

---

[380] Burnett, Charles, 1997, p. 46.
[381] WR11.

SECTION THREE
Muslim Intellectual Regression

CHAPTER 12

Causes of Muslim
Intellectual Regression

Since the dawn of civilisation, for thousands of years, the progress of science in human society has been markedly slow. But since the 8th century the interest and progress in science has moved relatively rapidly. Science took off from the scholarly fountainhead that was established by the passion for knowledge of the early Muslims. This passion was taken over by Europe leading to the Renaissance and in the last two centuries, technology has grown phenomenally. A very interesting question is, why, then, did the Muslims, who started this incredible scientific quest, suddenly give it up sometime around the 13th century?!

For a long time now, reformers among Muslims have been wondering what had gone wrong with their society that they have fallen from the top of world to an ignoble almost contemptible status internationally. The misconception was that most of the reformers have been searching for *the* cause of regression. But there has not been just one event causing this fall to ignominy. The regression was spread over historical time and there have been different causes at different juncture of history.

Before dealing with the causes, there are two disputes

relevant to Muslim intellectualism that need to be understood
first. It gives some context to the intellectual movements during
the early Muslim period.

Two Intellectual Disputes of the Past

The Mihnah of al-Ma'mun

During early Islam, there was a theological dispute on the
'createdness' of the Qur'an. One group, the traditionalist, claimed
that the Qur'an as the 'word' of God was eternal and uncreated.
Another group, the rationalist, contented that even though the
Qur'an was the 'word' of God, it was not eternal. According to
them, since God is transcendent, human beings do not 'hear' him.
What they hear is what God creates for them to hear.

Imam Abu Hanifah, in the 8th century, took a middle stance
in this debate, probably, meaning to diffuse the dispute. In *Al-
Fiqh al-Akbar* he wrote that 'the Qur'an is the Word of God
Almighty, written on collections of leaves [*masahif* or manuscript
made of papyri], preserved in men's hearts [memorised], recited
on men's tongues, and sent down to the Prophet, upon whom be
God's peace and blessing. Our uttering of the Qur'an is created,
and our recitation of the Qur'an is created, but the Qur'an itself is
uncreated'.[382]

But the debate persisted. In 827 CE the Abbasid Caliph al-
Ma'mun sponsored Islamic rationalist thought in the politics of
his realm. The Mu'tazilis, Islamic rationalist scholars, held
important positions in his court and bureaucracy. Al-Ma'mun
wanted all the scholars, officials and bureaucrats to accept his
position on rationalism. Six years later, the Mihnah (a trail or test)
was initiated based on this debate. A system was established for
open declaration and acceptance of rationalism by all. Muslim

---

[382] Koelliker, Lee A., 2011.

scholars were compelled to come to the court (or the governor's office) and openly accept the principle that 'the Qur'an, though the word of God, was created'. But just a few months later, Caliph al-Ma'mun died. Nevertheless, the Mihnah lasted for 15 years under subsequent caliphs.

Almost all the scholars gave their acceptance. But two legal (*fiqh*) scholars, Ahmad ibn Nasr ibn Malik, who died protesting in prison, and Imam Ahmad ibn Hanbal, defied the doctrine of al-Ma'mun.[383] Under threat and even after being tortured Imam Hanbal stood resolute for two years in prison till he was finally released. Ultimately, the Mihnah was ended after Caliph al-Mutawakkil came to power in 850 CE.

Though the Mihnah is historically known and has been studied by a number of scholars the actual reason and context of the Mihnah is still somewhat ambiguous. The question that is being raised by contemporary scholars is: Why did al-Ma'mun actually initiate the Mihnah? The two main hypotheses are that he initiated the Mihnah either to centralise religious authority to the caliphate or to control all the many local jurists and theologians.[384] But al-Ma'mun was a supremely powerful ruler of the most powerful empire of his time. Acquisition of power, if at all, was probably the secondary aim of the Mihnah. His primary aim, probably, was to establish a unique stable guiding principal or system of governance for the empire that would be acceptable to all the various groups and sects within the empire.

By the time of al-Ma'mun there were many competing 'thoughts', ideologies, groups and sects in the empire. These ideologies had started to form a few centuries ago from the very start of the caliphate system. The four Rashidun Caliphs were both temporal and spiritual heads of the caliphate. Towards the

---

[383] Lapidus, Ira, 1975, p. 380.
[384] Zaman, 1997, p. 2; Patton, 1897, p. 2.

end of the Rashidun period, there arose different schools of thoughts such as the Khawarij and Murji'ah. There also had developed different types of scholars, like the *mufassir* (Qur'an exegete), *muhaddith* (ḥadīth and *Sunnah* scholar), *faqih* (legal scholar), *mutakallim* (theologian) and *faylasuf* (philosopher), who did not always see eye to eye.

The Shi'ah-Sunni divide was also starting to solidify. Up to the time of Imam Ja'far al-Sadiq, great grandson of Caliph Ali, Shi'ism was a political movement of a group who believed that Ali ibn Abi Talib, son in law of the Prophet, should have been the first caliph after the death of the Prophet. But the caliphate went to Abu Bakr and then to Umar ibn al-Khattab. Ali contested for the caliphate after the death of Caliph Umar. But the selection was in favour of Uthman, who became the third caliph. When, finally, Ali became the fourth caliph, a civil conflict (*fitnah*) had already started. The Umayyad faction refused to accept him as their leader. After his death, the Umayyad Mu'awiyah became the caliph and established the Umayyad dynastic rule. The pro-Ali movement continued against the Umayyads rule. Over the years, there were several revolts against the post-Mu'awiyah Umayyads by the Alids, some put done with considerable force and cruelty.

Imam Ja'far al-Sadiq, descendent of Ali, had found the political movements to be considerably distressful as revolts against the ruling entity led to retributions, becoming a constant source of conflict and pain. Probably that was the reason that he refused to take part in any political movements and rather endeavoured in scholarly and legal work. After him Shi'ism transformed to a legal-sectarian movement with a distinct theology. He died about 20 years before al-Ma'mun was born.

All empires have latent disintegrational forces and the best emperors control such forces with justice and equity. The Abbasid Empire already had different religious, including Non-Muslims, and ethnic groups. By the time of al-Ma'mun there had also developed different political, theological and sectarian groups. These were disintegrational forces trying to surface.

Al-Ma'mun was a visionary and had anticipated that other such groups would rise in the future as well. The conflicts between them would be perennial leading to turmoil. So, he decided to impose a neutral all-inclusive ideology that would be the governing political system and acceptable by all. His great passion for Islamic rationalism and the sciences is well known. So, he made Islamic rationalism the main political ideology and asserted that all others abide by it. To ensure its public acceptance al-Ma'mun initiated the Mihnah along a theological line.

But, his mistake was that of framing the motion on a highly contentious theological issue—the createdness of the Qur'an. Imam Hanbal maintained that the legal schools and jurisprudence (*fiqh*) could not accept such a theological innovation or bow to any authority—caliphal, rational, *etc.* And thus, the conflict commenced. But al-Ma'mun died before any resolution was reached and ultimately jurisprudence won. It remained free of any political overlord.

That was, though, not the end of Islamic rationalism. It maintained its sway in academic circles and institutions. The Muslim academic institutions kept on producing large number of brilliant scientist, and fashioned great scientific achievements, and rational advancement continued even after the lifting of the Mihnah. What it did do, though, was make a rigid demarcation between the orthodox and the rational scholars. That, at later stages in the history of knowledge, would irk some of the orthodox against rationalism.

The Theology of al-Ghazali

The other important phenomenon was al-Ghazali. He was one of the all-time greatest intellectuals. He studied all the knowledge spheres of his time—philosophical, theological, rational, mystical, *etc.* Then he decided to cleanse knowledge from what was speculative in it. In rational science, for example, he declared astrology, dream interpretation, talismanic arts, the arts of magic, alchemy and physiognomy to be blameworthy,[385] but declared subjects like astronomy and mathematics to be praiseworthy. Al-Ghazali also criticised some metaphysical speculation in philosophy but found logic satisfactory.

Scholars like 19th century orientalist Eduard Sachau have put the blame of Muslim scientific regression on the Ash'ari theology in general and on al-Ghazali in particular.[386] According to them, because al-Ghazali attacked philosophy, Muslims gave up philosophy and that resulted in an end to the pursuit of the sciences. There are many logical reasons, some shown below, that actually nullify such arguments:

- There is a lack of understanding of Ash'ari theology. The Ash'aris believed in the objective and systematic study of nature. Some of the greatest scientists in Islam, such as Ibn al-Haytham, who discovered the basic laws of optics, and al-Biruni, who measured the circumference of the earth and discussed the rotation of the earth on its axis, were supporters of Ash'ari theology.[387] What is further interesting is that the Ash'ari school also believed in the atomic theory that the world (matter) is made up of minute particles.

- Sufficient information about al-Ghazali was not available to the orientalists to arrive at any correct conclusion about him. Al-Ghazali did not attack all of philosophy but some of the speculative conjectures in metaphysics.

---

[385] WR7.
[386] Iqbal, Muzaffar, 2007, p. 120.
[387] WR19.

Today, in fact, those speculative metaphysics are likewise rejected.

- After al-Ghazali there was no decline in the advancement of the sciences. The rational environment kept on producing brilliant scientists. That actually proves that al-Ghazali's views did not negatively affect science.

- At a later stage, the study of science did decline among the Muslims for other reasons. It is not that Muslim stopped studying science because they stopped studying philosophy. They stopped studying philosophy and science at the same time. The quality of study in both science and philosophy deteriorated together.

It may be true, though, that some anti-rationalism orthodox scholars probably had used the huge influence of al-Ghazali's *Tahafut* to create an indiscriminate blanket aversion towards philosophy and the sciences from their own bias. After the Tri-Military Events, as people became less educated and unable to understand the high erudition of al-Ghazali, this altered notion may have influenced general consensus. But philosophers did continue to persist after al-Ghazali. Spain produced Ibn Rushd who in fact countered al-Ghazali. Only after the Muslims were forced out by the *Reconquista* and Spanish Inquisition did Spain stop producing philosophers of note.

Philosophical activities persisted in the eastern Muslim World, especially in the Persian-Indian region. Some of the philosopher-scholars of the 13th to the 20th centuries are: Ibn Tufayl, Fakhr al-Din al-Razi, Nasir al-Din al-Tusi, Qutb al-Din Shirazi, Ibn Sabin, Ibn Khaldun, Mir Damad, Mir Fendereski, Mulla Sadr, Muhammad Iqbal, Sayyid Muhammad Husayn Tabataba'i and Abd al-Rahman Badawi.

Thus, Ghazalian theology, in itself, was not detrimental in the study of science. In fact, it had put the philosophers on the right track. The real causes, from past and present, which have damaged the progress of sciences among Muslims are discussed below.

Past Causes of Intellectual Regression

The quest for knowledge, being a major religious dictate, became an ingrained culture among the Muslims. To change that kind of mentality some serious events had to take place. A spirited and resilient nation does not collapse suddenly, it follows a protracted path to ruin.

For instance, negative socio-political factors—like injustice, iniquity, prejudice, greed, fear, *etc.*—increase self-interest among the ethnic or sectarian subgroups causing a kind of self-centredness or micro-nationalistic feelings to surface. The escalation of such feelings, ultimately, results in infighting leading to disintegration. The weakness caused due to the infighting and disintegration opens up the nation to external invasive forces. These external forces take the opportunity to take control of the nation. In the past, there was a complex of such factors, catalytic to each other, which ultimately had a negative effect on intellectualism among the Muslims.

The dynastic infighting among the Muslim royalties for succession is seemingly one of the main palpable causes. Such has been the case of all dynastic rule in history. But there was a complex of other abstruse factors that had been at the root of increasing the divisiveness and infighting within the empires. Those factors are discussed below.

The Factors Causing Disintegration

Conflict between Scholars

Scholars were always held in high esteem among the Muslims

with the ulema holding the apex. So, if there is disagreement among the scholars it affects the general people to a considerable extent.

One glowing example of agreeing to disagree among the ulema is the formulation of the *Ahl al-Sunnah Wa al-Jama'ah* or, in short, the Sunni group of Muslims. The four Imams—Abu Hanifah, Malik, al-Shāfi'ī and Hanbal—established four schools of jurisprudence. There were some differences in the jurisprudence of the four *madhhabs* but the followers of these schools agreed to disagree and still remain within the same Sunni group. Unfortunately, there are not many such examples of unifying attitude among the Muslims.

Ikhtilaf or scholarly difference of opinion is held to be positive by Muslim scholars. It leads to dialectical debates which helps to arrive at the correct inferences. But when a consensus cannot be reached there should be a process to agree to disagree. The inherent inability to 'agree to disagree' can turn into political conflicts. Unfortunately, such conflicts are historically replete among Muslims. Political sponsorship had given such differences permanence. Many a times chaotic *fitnahs* have arisen in the name of *ikhtilaf*.

Among the early Muslims, the scholars were the most respected of all. Over time this respect for the scholars has eroded considerably. With respect gone, the proper sponsorship for scholars has failed as well.

Luxury and Indolence

Islam is not an ascetic religion. Creation of wealth is not prohibited as long as it is legal (*halal*). Some of the Prophet's Companions, for example Abd al-Rahman ibn Awf, were rich. Luxury in life is not a sin as long as it is *halal*. But a luxurious life, on the long run, can make one lax and indolent and open to temptations. Most susceptible to such temptations are the people with political authority leading a luxurious life. Thus, when the Prophet and his righteous caliphs became rulers, they gave their wealth to the poor and led austere lives.

There were times when the Prophet is known to have given appropriate attention to self-image. He has taken care of his hair, dyed his beard with henna, applied perfume and used kohl, a traditional eyeliner for men, women and children. But when needed he also gave it all up.

In Madinah, the Prophet was the 'ruler' of Arabia. Umar ibn al-Khattab once went to his house. Inside all he found was just a raw mat on the floor, on which the Prophet was resting, along with a blanket and a pitcher of water and nothing else. As the Prophet got up, there were puffy red streaks on his back from the raw mat. Umar's eyes filled with tears and he said to the Prophet that the emperors of Rome and Persia live a luxurious life. If the Prophet allowed, the Companions could arrange for some comfort for him. But the Prophet declined. Whatever he would receive he gave to the poor.

Abu Bakr and Uthman ibn Affan had been merchants and were quite well to do. But by the time they became caliphs they had given up their wealth as well. As caliphs they lived their life on bare essentials. Umar was the most austere and egalitarian amongst them. The way he lived and the way he advised his governors and generals to live is exemplary. Ali ibn Abi Talib was a scholar and a warrior with no interest in luxury.

They all lived an austere life not because they were poor but as rulers they chose austerity. They had been rich and they had full control over the state treasury but they gave up their personal wealth and considered the treasury to be the wealth of the people —its ultimate owner being God. The salary that they accepted for subsistence was bare minimal. When they died they left nothing significant for their heirs.

While wealth accumulation is of primary importance for the development of a nation, wealth and luxury among the rulers and political leaders have always exposed them to indolence, greed, temptation and, ultimately, wrong doings. To the general mass such leaders had appeared questionable giving rise to dissension leading to instability.

Some latter caliphs and royalties did indulge in a luxurious life. Most of them were not wrongdoers but being models for the society they opened up the doors of temptation for others. Different regional governors and military generals and thus the people in authority all wanted a piece of that same luxury in their life as well. Intellectuals aspired and competed for the high offices for the wrong reasons and once they acquired such an office they, obviously, paid undue attention to personal acquisitions rather than work ethics. Ostentation became more important than efficacy.

There were many ethnic groups among the Muslims like Arabs, Turks, Persian, *etc.*, along with different theological and legal factions and sects. All of them also wanted a piece of that same luxurious and comfortable life. In the historical process, ostentation led the groups to crave and compete in earthly things which led to the development of earthly feelings like envy towards one another. Thus, luxury was catalytic in strengthening the negative factional feelings more and more over time.

Both good and bad influences flow very easily from the top to the lower rungs of the society. Thus, the best rulers were those who gave importance to affairs of the state, not to luxuries. Under them corrupt or greedy people did not aspire for offices as there were not sufficient paybacks. Only those whose motive was to serve the people aspired for the important offices. That was the case with the Rashiduns and caliphs like Umar ibn Abd al-Aziz.

The Effect of Chauvinism and Corruption

Chauvinism leads to nepotism, and as merit is no longer primary it leads to a lowering of intellectual standards in all national fields. The lowering of intellectualism had produced visionless and myopic people of authority. Some of the Umayyads were Arab chauvinists which caused divisive feelings to rise among their non-Arab subjects, especially the Persians.

Corruption also affected the offices of a few of the latter Umayyads, latter Abbasids and latter Ottomans. A combination of seemingly mild corruption and luxury led to the mismanagement of the affairs of state. Deserving people did not get their due positions and administration came to be manned by incompetent people. The rulers of such an administration lacked vision, information and ability to unite people of different ethnicities and groups that was needed to maintain powerful empires. In 750, the Umayyads had lost their empire to the Abbasids due to factors which included a chauvinistic attitude and a life of indolence and luxury.

Tribalism, Sectarianism and Ethnicity

During the time of the Rashidun Caliphs there was no tribal or racial superiority. Black Africans and slaves, like Bilal, were equal to and had the rights of any other Companions of the Prophet. In his last sermon, the Prophet had said that people—white, black, Arab, non-Arab—were all equal. And this dictate was put into practice. During this period a large number of people entered the folds of Islam—Persians, Turks, *etc*. Towards the end of the Rashidun reign there were revolts as to who would succeed to the office of the caliph. The Umayyads seized power. They set up a hereditary monarchy to resolve the succession issue. The son of the caliph would become the next caliph.

In the long run, though, the succession issue was not truly

resolved only contained among the contending royal family. It still led to revolts. But it added another element into the tussle. Dynastic succession meant that there was no chance for the non-Arabs to ever aspire for the caliphal office. Only those born in the royal family, who were Arabs, would hold true imperial power and the office of the caliph. Besides, the Umayyads to some extent were chauvinists. With time, this would lead to some degree of discontent among the non-Arab Muslims who constituted a large part of the populace.

Unlike the Umayyads, the Abbasids were not chauvinist but they pitted one ethnic group against another. First, the Persians of Khorasan were used against the Umayyads. The chauvinist nature of the Umayyads had made it easier for the Abbasids to 'recruit' the Persians against the Umayyads. When the Persians, at a latter historical stage, were deemed a political threat then the Turks were introduced into the fray as the main component of the army to counter them. While the Umayyads were defeated and Persians were controlled by this strategy, the Turk army became very powerful within the empire.

Caliph al-Mutawakkil had to contend with disintegrational forces and his method was to be stern towards internal groups like the rationalist scholars, the Shi'ah, the Khawarij, the Christians and the Jews. But the disintegrational forces also afflicted the royal family. In a palace coup carried out by the army he was killed and al-Muntasir became the caliph. This was the first time the Abbasid Turk army had tasted caliphal blood and unshackled command.

From then onwards, the army kept on acquiring more and more power till they virtually took over all the executive powers of the caliphs who remained in charge all but in name. During the period from 862 to 870 five successive caliphs were removed or killed by the Turk generals. This led to anarchy throughout the Empire. There were also a number of revolts by the Shi'ah, the

Qaramatian and the Khawarij.[388]

Previously, whenever the frontiers had been attacked by external forces, the Abbasids had repulsed those attacks vehemently and carried out counter attacks into the invader's land. However, in 926, when the Byzantines invaded and captured the city of Maltiyah defeating the Abbasid force stationed there, no action was taken. In the following year the emboldened Byzantines captured Damietta in Egypt and the next year Khalat in Armenia. The Abbasid army had become too engrossed in palatial politics and a royal way of life to really take effective measures against revolts and invasions.

This self-serving attitude began to permeate into all the ethnic components of the caliphate. The Persians and Turks, among others, who had represented universality in the earlier stages of the caliphate, now became a motley of self-interested groups. They acquired separate nationalistic characters within the empire. Facing raised taxes, corruption and hardships the general masses became unhappy. That caused the people to support dissenting forces leading towards revolts and disintegration.

These were all preambles to the political fragmentation of the empire that followed. The latter Abbasids were unable to deal with the rising disintegrational forces. As ethnic conflicts increased, the empire disintegrated into a number of ethnic, sectarian or clan based monarchies—mainly a variety of Arab, Berber, Persian or Turk subgroups. The caliphate lost lands to these 'independent' states. As disintegration intensified a time came when the authority of the caliph became restricted to just Baghdad and the immediate area around it. They were no longer a political force of a mighty empire rather a principality with token spiritual authority.

One by one many new states formed as the empire became

---

[388] Hasan, Masudul, 2004, p. 229-230.

smaller and weaker. Besides the already established Spanish Umayyads, the new sovereignties included the independent Shi'ah state established in Morocco, the Aglabids in Tunisia, the Tahirids in Khorasan, the Tulunids in Egypt, Samanids in Transoxiana, the Qarmatians in Bahrain, Saffarids in Sistan, Kirman, Fars and others. Some paid token allegiance to the caliphate, the more powerful ones while paying spiritual allegiance overtly, controlled it furtively.

Religious sectarianism has also caused considerable disintegration in Muslim history. The intrigue and rivalry between the political entities and distrust and hatred between sects, like the Shi'ah and Sunni, was very convenient for external invaders. When the Crusaders had first attacked the Sunni Seljuks, the Shi'ah Fatimids had done nothing to help them. When the Mongols had attacked Khwarizm or the Nizari Shi'ah of Alamaut, the other Muslim entities were silent. When the Abbasid caliphate was destroyed Muslims did not come forward to protect it. Similar events would be re-enacted many times in history.

Like ethnicity, tribes are a historical reality. But tribal affiliations, under insular leadership, had sometimes proven to be a great divisive force. Islam is universal and the Prophet had cautioned against any divisiveness based on racial or tribal affiliations. In his last sermon he had made human equality one of the most important points. But in spite of the Prophet's admonition tribalism and ethnicity did become fervent in certain Muslim communities leading to inter-tribal conflicts.

Divisive tribal forces had played an important part in the disintegration of the Andalusian (Muslim Spain) Caliphate and the latter North African domains. In 1031, the Umayyad Caliphate of Spain was fragmented into a number of minor states and principalities. Attacks from the relatively more united Christians kingdoms intensified. To counter the Christians the Almoravid and Almohad, Berber empires based in Morocco, invaded and ruled Spain for about two more centuries. But the same tribal divisiveness caused civil wars again leading to disintegration into small principalities known as *ta'ifah*s. These newly independent small political entities were quickly taken over by the united Christian kingdoms.

The Weakening of Universalism

With the Umayyad's Arab-chauvinism, the different ethnic groups among Muslims always felt segregated. As long as the royal family and the empire were strong and just, they could hold the ethnic feeling at bay. But whenever the rulers became weak and incompetent, these feelings would surface. People never like to be considered second-class.

Non-discrimination was at the root of running the multi-ethnic multi-sectarian Muslim empires. But whenever there had been nepotism or iniquity it had had a catalytic effect on the divisive factors mentioned earlier—tribalism, ethnic discord, sectarianism, indolence and luxury. Sometimes meritless people got appointed to authority and led the community to flawed governance. Grudges arose among people who had been marginalised. Divisiveness led to conflicts and conflicts led to enmity and hatred. Self-serving feelings became more powerful than the universal forces of Islam that had bonded together the different ethnic and sectarian groups into empires. Thus, local entities arose leading to the breakup of the empires into smaller contending units—sultanates, kingdoms, principalities and emirates.

But even the political disintegration had not ended the pursuance of Total Knowledge including natural sciences in the Muslim world. The scholarly culture was still retained. All the big and small domains sponsored their own scholars like Omar Khayyam, al-Biruni, *etc.* The disintegration was just the first stage of the regression process in which the Muslims' defensive capability weakened. The next stage when Muslims would give away their 'passion for knowledge' was yet to come.

As long as they had been powerful empires they had vast resources and power. Becoming smaller emirates and sultanates limited their resources and they became weak and unable to defend themselves. Powerful external forces took advantage of the weakness and invaded the Muslim empires. While the Muslims disintegrated, other forces unified. In Spain, Christian alliances attacked the Andalusian Muslims. During the Crusades, alliances of European powers attacked the Muslims of Levant. The Mongols tribes unified under Chengiz Khan before they started their conquest. These invasions destroyed the Muslim way of life including their academia and intellectualism.

Effect of the Tri-Military Events

The disintegration of the early Muslim empires had left them weakened. So, they became prey to all kinds of predatory and imperial designs. Taking advantage of this weakness the Spanish *Reconquista* and Inquisition, the Crusades, and the Mongol invasion took place.

The Spanish *Reconquista* and the Spanish Inquisition thoroughly eradicated the Muslim from Spain and Portugal. Next, the Crusades further dented the Muslim from the west. The Levant, the region along the Eastern Mediterranean shore, was devastated by the First Crusade. Places of learning in Jerusalem, Aleppo and Damascus were destroyed and countless people including scholars were killed. The third and the most devastating event was the calamitous Mongol scourge that destroyed the Muslims from the east of Persia near China to the west of Syria nearly up to the Mediterranean.

The Tri-Military Events were conflicts between united

Europeans and united Mongols against divided Muslims. After these three major destructions the world of the Muslims was changed. All the major institutions were demolished, all their books and works destroyed, and all their scholars massacred. The sophisticated academic network of institutions and scholars that had been built up over the centuries crumbled and disappeared. The whole scholarly environment vanished.

People were left to ponder more mundane thoughts of existence rather than indulge in the scholarly. Scientists like Ibn Haytham and al-Khwarizmi ceased to be produced. The Muslims of North Africa and India though spared from massacre were still affected by the general regression. The academia of these two regions had a different structure in which pure science was yet to be introduced. With the science network destroyed it was not to be so.

This was the time *ijtihad* (research) did not seem important anymore. The Muslims were the most advanced people of the world, central in geographic position, and the most scholarly, with knowledge being their main aspiration in the world. But that concept was shattered due to the Tri-Military Events. To them science did not seem to have done anything to protect them. Science was deemed not a necessity but a luxury in life. It felt like not scientists but men of war were needed to protect the general populace. The Muslims retained their praying but left the thinking to God. A civilisation came to an intellectual end. The Muslims would never be able to reclaim their past scientific brilliance.

Destruction of Academic Institutions

Academic institutions are not merely buildings but comprises scholars, students, books, research resources, research libraries, and research works—consisting of a whole environment, a whole networked culture. All these were destroyed by the Tri-Military

Events.

Scientific studies needed institutions and sponsors to effectively provide intellectual and financial support to students studying science. Due to the Tri-Military Events Muslims had become significantly poorer as their wealth was taken over by conquering forces and their trading prowess vastly reduced. They no longer had sufficient wealth to sponsor intellectualism. Without sponsors and without institutions the surviving scholars found themselves unable to support their researches and investigations.

The academic centre in cities like Baghdad, Balkh, Damascus, Nishapur, Aleppo, Jerusalem, Cordoba, Toledo and others were all gone, never to be restored. Those cities that still persisted starved for sponsorship and finance. There remained old buildings rather than academic institutions.

Some scholars, who had run away from destruction, went to still standing cities. The medical great Ibn an-Nafis went to Egypt. Philosopher, poet and sage Ibn Arabi went from Spain to Konya. The family of the great poet Jalal al-Din al-Rumi went there as well from Balkh, escaping the Mongols.

The 'arts' scholars were able to set themselves up in the new regions. Poets and similar scholars depend more on personal skills. But the uprooted scientist with their network, academies, and libraries gone were left in the lurch. Ascetic Sufis tried their best to fill the intellectual vacuum giving people spiritual hope and cultural relief.

Closing the Gates of Ijtihad

Ijtihad is a term that is used by Muslim jurists for personal investigation and reasoning employing thorough exertion of one's mental faculty in finding a solution to a legal question. Some of the Prophet's governors and representative residing far from

Madinah were not in touch with him for advice on administrative and other matters over significant periods. He told them in order to resolve general, administrative and legal issues they should research the Qur'an and the ḥadīth tradition to see whether they could find any precedents. If any precedent was found then the governors were to apply it to resolve the issue.

But if no precedent was found then they were to use their own analysis, intellect and reason to resolve such issues. This methodology of using the intellect led the Muslims into critical thinking. As time went by they applied this faculty of reasoning and critical thinking to all kinds of other disciplines, which became comparable to 'research and development'.

The Qur'an as well as the Prophet's tradition strongly advocate 'thinking and contemplation' and the pursuit of knowledge. The early Muslims, thus, endeavoured to a quest for all types of knowledge and became critical thinkers—a nation of scholars. The first few centuries of this quest led to the golden age of knowledge acquisition and development in the world. All the branches of knowledge including religious studies, jurisprudence, science, arts, literature, philosophy and cultural disciplines developed with vigour and vitality. Brilliant scholars—jurists, scientists, philosophers, theologians, poets and others—were produced.

But sometime in the 10th century, there was some socio-structural change hindering this pursuit. It appears to have started off with a banning of any further development of jurisprudence. There had developed a number of vast systems of jurisprudence and legislation which was considered sufficient to support the empires and kingdoms.

An *ijma* (consensus) of the ulema is supposed to have been held which had 'closed the gates of *ijtihad*'.[389] The *ijma* is a legal

---

[389] Ahmed, Moinuddin, 1992, p. 49.

instrument in Islamic jurisprudence and binding on all. The process of *taqlid* replaced *ijtihad* where *taqlid* represents emulation or following of past precedents only. Over time, this closure of *ijtihad* appears to have spread from jurisprudence to other disciplines like philosophy and the sciences. People only needed to follow the already established works of past scholars which meant there were no more innovations and no need for critical thinking. *Taqlid*, over a few centuries, stagnated the academic environment producing scholars with lower innovative skills.

Recent researches indicate that the information about the 'closure of the gates of *ijtihad*' is vague.[390] First of all, the date of the *ijma* that took this momentous resolution is not known. The authorities who took the resolution are also not known. Why precisely the *ijma* was called is not known. There isn't any significant historical documentation available about it but only words of mouth that has reached the recent generation of ulema orally. These ulema also can't seem to justify why there was an *ijma* against *ijtihad* in favour of *taqlid*.

Islamic history has recorded all important events of the past. Much older events like development of jurisprudence are recorded in significant details. But there appears to be no record of such an important event like the banning of *ijtihad* which the Prophet himself had initiated. Scholars who have tried to fathom the 'closure' did not find any historical detail of this momentous event. Emeritus Professor W. Montgomery Watt delved deep into history but could not find anything about this closure.[391] Dr. Sir Muhammad Iqbal considered the whole issue as an elaborate hoax.[392]

---

[390] Ahmed, Moinuddin, 1992, p. 56-58.
[391] Montgomery, Watt, W., 1961, p. 243.
[392] Ahmed, Moinuddin, 1992, p. 62.

There are a number of reasons why *ijtihad* could have been banned by a group of local scholars and then the notion had just spread over time. Historically, around the 10th century, multifarious ideas were being discussed and debated in the academic and socio-political circles. A few of those are listed below:

- In jurisprudence and law, the schools had already produced huge legal systems and adequate laws to run the empires. At that time, the impression was that no further new laws were needed, and thus no further need for *ijtihad*.

- Sectarian influences had caused the development of different diverse jurisprudences. No further division was encouraged, so a ban on *ijtihad* would be expected to stop further divisive jurisprudence.

- Intellectual conflicts like the Mihnah and speculative notions like those of metaphysics could have been looked at with wariness. Such thoughts were not deemed sound and the orthodox ulema may have decided to do something about it, *i.e.* stopping innovations by banning *ijtihad*.

This was followed by a period of great political instability. The Muslim domains were disintegrating. The Muslims in Spain and Portugal came under protracted attack from the Christian North. The Crusades started towards the end of the 11th century. The huge Abbasid Empire had fractured into kingdoms and emirates with the caliph only controlling Baghdad and surrounding area. There remained no central political authority that could take the responsibility for changing laws for all Muslims or to whom all Muslims would pay allegiance. So, instead of letting each political entity keep on developing their own diverse shariah, the ulema would have wanted to ban *ijtihad*.

After the Mongol invasion in the 13th century, this closure appears to have been reaffirmed. Many of the scholars had died and institutions destroyed. The remaining scholars would be apprehensive that the new political overlords, non-Muslim barbaric Mongols, may try to influence Islamic jurisprudence and social concepts. So they again ensured that changes in jurisprudence was no longer possible. Throughout these periods *taqlid, i.e.* emulation, instead of reasoning was advocated. For similar reasons, *taqlid* would continue through the much later colonial period as well.

So, in summation, the view was that as all the laws needed had been developed and there was so much political, sectarian and military uncertainty all around that there was no further need or scope for *ijtihad*. Thus, the scholars decided to 'close the gate of *ijtihad*' by *ijma*. With apprehension due to political disintegration and invasions, metaphysical speculations, foreign and pagan views abound in the society and a possible decline in morality, it probably seemed appropriate at the time.

Although authorities like al-Ghazali and Ibn Taymiyyah, who lived in the period of the ban, show no awareness or adherence to *taqlid* for they were involved in very high quality *ijtihad*. Al-Ghazali, in fact, revitalised the spirit of *ijtihad*. Ibn Taymiyyah also raised a strong voice against rigid conformity and undertook *ijtihad*. This indicates the 'closure' to be a local phenomenon.

The most likelihood is that the *ijma* was not held by any authoritative body but by a local group. Once a local group had called an *ijma*, it probably gained acceptance over time by ulema of different regions over subsequent times. As one after another disastrous military events devastated the Muslim domains, the anxious ulema hung on to the 'closure' even more rigidly. The 'closure' thus permeated to modern times.

In the course of history, there has been intellectual conflicts, and thus antipathy, between the ulema, philosophers, rationalists and Sufis. Such antipathy may also have led some local ulema to extend what has started as a ban on changes in jurisprudence to all of philosophy and sciences as a measure of control over other scholars. This is similar to the extension of al-Ghazali's refutation of speculative metaphysics to the entire range of philosophy.

This closure led to a move away from the concept of Total Knowledge. A time came when some ulema decided that the study of knowledge that is encouraged in the Qur'an was the study of religious knowledge *only* and not the sciences. This was, obviously, against what the early Muslim scholars had believed or practised for centuries. But, as an effect, the definition of knowledge in the Muslim society changed. Whereas the early Muslims considered knowledge to be 'Total Knowledge', the latter Muslims came to understand it as just religious knowledge.

As the society stabilised during the period of latter empires— Ottoman, Moghul, Safavid—there was an opportunity to lift the ban on *ijtihad*. But there appears not much information about this *ijma* even then. When Ottoman Sultan Abd al-Hamid showed interest on the subject, a Turk scholar Shaykh Husayn Afandi prepared and published the journal *Al-Hamidiyyah fi Haqiqah al-Diyanah al-Islamiyyah wa Haqiqah al-Shari'ah al-Muhammadiyyah* in which he mentioned that the Hanafi ulema had accepted the 'closure' since around 328-329 Hijri (941-942 CE).[393] Again, there was no mention of any details about the *ijma* or its participants in the journal.

The suggested date supports the idea that the *ijma* was initiated in the 10th century. But science had continued to develop in Muslim societies after that period. It, thus, also supports that notion that, initially, the 'closure' was for jurisprudence and not for science but at a latter period the

---

[393] Ahmed, Moinuddin, 1992, p. 60.

'closure' became generalised to other disciplines. This may also be the reason that caused the discouragement from some Ottoman ulema towards research in pure sciences.

Whatever the original causes of the 'closure', the attitude of discouraging Muslims from seeking and improving knowledge affected their society causing regression in development of science and technology, ultimately, leading to much ignorance. The Europeans were able to colonise the Muslim domains because they had become industrialised and technologically advanced. After colonisation, the Europeans were, obviously, viewed as invaders by the Muslims. The Muslims, the main aggrieved party during the colonial period, remained aloof from all European scholarship mistrusting the cultural baggage that the Europeans brought along with them. Any overture that may have been made by the Europeans was suspect and the Muslims hung on to the 'closure' even more strictly. This led to the further distancing from the sciences, which was now, ironically, considered to be European.

There have been calls to reverse the *ijma* decision over ages by many scholars, such as by Dr. Muhammad Iqbal and Sayyid Jamal al-Din al-Afghani.[394] The question that now arises is – was there a valid *ijma* that needs to be reversed? If there was an *ijma* at all it appears to be not against science but against changing of jurisprudence. Further investigation may or may not lead to an answer. But irrespective of whether the *ijma* was genuine, imaginary or non-authoritative, the effect of it, specially generalising it to other disciplines, has been negative. The fact of the matter is that Muslims did stop studying the sciences.

[394] Hanifi, M. Jamil, 1974, p. 38.

The Rise of Popular Religion

There is a tendency by some to blame Sufism for the regression of rational intellectualism. But Sufism is a universe of its own and had coexisted with rationalism and orthodoxy in the past. It actually filled in the intellectual gap after Muslim intellectualism was ruined by the Tri-Military Events. While science had needed institutions, sponsors and intellectual network, which the Muslims no longer had or could no longer afford, Sufism progressed under individual effort and talent as can be seen in the activities of Ibn Arabi and Jalal al-Din al-Rumi.

Sufism influenced the poetical, psychological and cultural side of society which, in reality, did not conflict with rationalism being a separate domain. Such oeuvres needed individual talent not academic institutes. It could thrive on dedication alone where funding was not available. The literary products of Sufism led to a rich Muslim culture that influenced the entire world. It was an art which required intellect and skills. The poems of Rumi, Nizami, Jami and Hafiz are of truly great literary value.

But soon, charlatan pretenders and fraudsters started to claim religious pretences which led to a 'popular religion' that started to influence the society. They could be very charismatic and in cases masses followed them.[395] Sufism became a problem when this 'popular religion' became the dominant influence on society while at the same time the ulema were pushed to the social fringe and rationalism and pure sciences became non-existent. Thus, the society transformed from a knowledge seeking one to an emotive-recreation seeking one and, at many instances, tended towards innovative spiritualism.

Soon, like in the rest of the intellectual fields, the Muslim society stopped producing high quality poets and writers leading to a decline in Muslim culture as well. Even if there were talented

---

[395] Ahmed, Moinuddin, 1992, p. 160.

writers their works never received the patronage needed and, thus, never reached the general masses. At the same time European culture improved dramatically and by the 20th century dominated the world arena. With development of mass media and mass communication this influence increased exponentially. The Muslim societies came under this influence as they did not have anything or anyone to counter or complement such cultural influence.

Colonisation

The latter Muslim empires—Ottoman, Moghul and Safavid— were the biggest empires of their time in the world. For centuries they were the dominant powers. They sponsored knowledge of all kinds. They produced superb administrators, military leaders, marvellous builders, and were fair lawgivers to all in their domain. They were at the foremost in marine and naval sciences and had the best military, engineers, poets and architects. But they had lost the pure sciences. The technological importance of science was not yet realised and, in some quarters, there remained a certain antipathy towards it. And when they did start to care about science it was too late. Europe had moved on far ahead and any competitors were soon to be swept aside.

Thus, the latter empires did not have the same passion for the sciences like the early Muslims. The scholars were not as innovative or fervent about pure science and sponsors were hard to find. In fact, the general mass became engrossed in the popular religious culture. Consequently, they did not advance into the phase of industrialisation. Europe became an industrial-technological power and through it an economic superpower. Gradually, they colonised the world which provided them resources they needed.

When the Europeans colonised Asia and Africa, they had

occupied the lands from mainly the Muslims. The Muslims have been rulers everywhere and thus the biggest losers. A good example is India. When the British occupied India, the rulers were mostly Muslims. They were the most solvent and literate group in Indian society. They also fought back the British most bitterly. The British, thus, considered them the biggest hindrance to the continuation of their colony. The Muslims were hit the hardest by the British and, consequently, regressed the most.

Whatever minimum education and infrastructure the colonisers developed was for the administration of these colonies. Many times, the colonisers wanted to 'modernise' the Muslims. Their offer of education always came with some cultural strings attached. Instead of adding more knowledge to the Muslim society, they were mostly attempting to change the social side of the Muslim society. Thus, the ulema reactively considered any education from the colonisers as double faced and advised the general mass to stay away from it. The scientifically regressed Muslims tried to hang on to their 'way of life' by clutching to their fundamentals and rejecting everything that the colonial masters would associate with. In the process they also rejected European sciences.

Within a few generations, the Muslims changed from the most solvent and literate to the poorest and most illiterate people of the civilised world. It was during this period that all that they had studied, researched and upheld, over centuries was completely given up and forgotten. They had not only lost the passion for knowledge but, over generations, forgotten their own intellectual heritage. Only the ulema, under cultural attack, were passionately trying to preserve their religion, religious texts and scholarly traditions.

Finally, the Muslims realised that they needed to catch up with the rest of the world in other disciplines. But they had become extremely poor unable to afford any decent education.

Under the prevailing conditions, for many Muslims, even basic study had become a luxury, higher study was not even conceivable. This situation still exists in many Muslims societies.

With intellectualism depleted and its history erased from most of the collective Muslim mind, they arrived at an ignorant state that had been harboured in the pre-Islamic days. A group of Muslims, now ignorant of their own past traditions and intellectualism, frustrated by their prevailing pitiable condition, became radically opposed to their own heritage. They started to question everything—like 'What good is ḥadīth?' 'Why does one need to accept those vague imams of the past?'—completely oblivious of the great contributions of such scholars and the enlightened way of life they had provided to humanity.

Many such supposedly 'new' questions had already been asked a thousand years ago and answered brilliantly by scholars of the past ages. But in contemporary times, such scholars who could properly answer are largely absent due to a lack of intellectualism and historical knowledge. There also developed many equally ignorant pseudo-scholars among the masses who took up their own misguided stand, making their own Islam and their own history of it.

During the colonial period, the European scholars did not really understand or cared about the true reasons of Muslim regression. Much of the information about the contributions of the Muslims were forgotten. The Europeans did not actually lend a hand to the Muslims to support the Islamic Total Knowledge paradigm so that the Muslims could evolve again to a high quality society. Instead, ironically, they accused Islam of being irrational. Islam was defined as a part of the oriental unreason and eastern backwardness by orientalist missionaries and philosophers such as Joseph Ernest Renan.

Renan in his lecture 'Islam and Science' given at Sorbonne (published in the *Journal des Débats*, March 29, 1883) attacked

Islam and Arabs as innately incapable of practicing philosophy and science. But, surprisingly, he was also aware of the historical contribution the Muslims had made in science and philosophy for in his *Averroes et l'Averroism* he states, 'The taste for science and literature had, by the tenth century, established, in this privileged corner of the world (Cordoba, Spain), a toleration of which modern times hardly offer us an example. Christian, Jews, and Muslims spoke the same tongue ... participated in the same literary and scientific studies. All the barriers which separated the various peoples were effected; all worked with one accord in the work of common civilisation. The mosques of Cordoba, where the students could be counted by thousands, became the active centres of philosophical and scientific studies.'

So, in his lecture he was either criticising the *condition of Muslims of his time* when the Muslim intellectual regression had taken place or he was trying to discredit the Muslims out of pure prejudice. Muslim scholars like Rashid Rida and Jamal al-Din al-Afghani had countered portraying the aspects of reason and rationalism inherent in Islam.

The views like those of Renan is no longer tenable in the mainstream Western intellectualism but remains in the fringes with the extremist evangelists. Non-Muslim scholars are now becoming aware of the reason and critical thinking that Islamic theology has always pursued. Islam is now accepted to be the 'reasonable' religion *par excellence* not just by the Muslim scholars but by many non-Muslim scholars as well. Professor Oliver Leaman states, 'Whereas Judaism is strongly linked with ethnicity and Christianity with a leap of faith, Islam has successfully grown by a contrast with these religions by stressing its rationality and evidentiality'.[396] Professor Joseph Van Ess of Tubingen, Germany, who had written an enormous four-volume history of early

---

[396] WR8.

Islamic theology states similar views, "Christianity speaks of the 'mysteries' of faith; Islam has nothing like that. For Saint Paul, reason belongs to the realm of the 'flesh', for Muslims, reason or *aql*, has always been the chief faculty granted human beings by God".[397]

The Secularising of Knowledge

Medieval Christian Europe had failed to accept philosophical and scientific knowledge. Thus, Renaissance Europe had to opt for the separation of religion from statecraft to progress their nations. But that is a European paradigm not an Islamic one. Early Muslims had, in fact, sponsored philosophy and scientific knowledge. As such there was no need to separate religion and statecraft.

It was only at a later period, due to various crises, that science regressed among the Muslims. In fact, reintroducing the Early Muslim paradigm would make the Muslims more progressive than their current mind-set.

The Muslim concept of creation is that the universe and all its processes is under the will of an all pervasive and omnipotent God. God has not only created the universe of matter and energy but has also put in place the processes and properties that matter and energy follow and He is in full control of all such processes. So even the concept of evolution was not really an issue with the Muslims, it was considered as just another process.

But in Europe science could express itself only after fighting theology. The scholars had to go against religion to establish scientific knowledge. So, they developed their sciences in a secular manner. In the modern era, philosophy expunged the need for God in their metaphysics. The likes of Nietzche preferred that man become a 'Superman' with no need for God. Late in the 19th

---

[397] *Ibid.*

century, social scientist like Marx and Comte developed social sciences in an overall godless system.

Muslim scholars refrained from these 'secular' subjects that denied the spiritual dimension. Thus, secularisation placed a psychological barrier between many Muslims and sciences, especially, the social sciences. Ironically, they were unaware that at the very core of development of the social disciplines—sociology, anthropology, economics—were the works of Muslims like Ibn Khaldun and al-Biruni.

The other thing that happened during this period was the removal of Muslim names from the text books. While the names like Kepler, Galileo or Newton were retained in all books of science, the contributions of the Muslim scientist, based on whose works the European had built their works, just vanished from the texts. Even the mention of the likes of Newton and Galileo, who believed in God, somehow appeared as if they were atheists. Great Muslim scholars, Islamic academies, and Muslim rulers who had sponsored knowledge were forgotten. The great Islamic heritage was removed from history and school texts made no mention of it. Generations grew who did not have any idea of Muslim contributions.

By the modern age, the Muslims, by and large, had also lost their intellectual capacity. Most did not know their own heritage in the history of the sciences. Gradually, all, including Muslims themselves, started to think that there never was any Muslim contribution. It was as if that the Greeks gave philosophy after which there was a general decline in global intellectualism till Europe 'invented' the sciences.

Secularisation denied religion and brought science to the forefront to an extent that science itself became the religion. In the contemporary world it has become so dominant that it has displaced religion and placed the liberal arts to a distant second. No doubt that science is of prime importance, a splendid tool that can change life but it remains a tool and it is not a way of life. Science as a code of life, ultimately, can become emotionless that can only support self-gratification denying even love and humanity.

The term 'secularisation' of knowledge is not the proper one to apply in this case. True secularisation is supposed to be neutral to religion not biased against any one religion. A better term to explain what has happened is 'atheistification' and 'de-Islamisation' of knowledge.

Rise and Decline of Female Scholars

In the past, Muslim women attained high rank as scholars of ḥadīth, jurisprudence (*fiqh*), and exegesis (*tafsīr*).[398] These three subjects had played a vital role during all ages of Islamic history. The names and biodata of female scholars who studied and taught all these subjects have been recorded over centuries. They were treated with respect and dignity by their male peers. Ḥadīth scholars did not discriminate between men and women as being more or less worthy.[399] It is quite interesting to note that many of the female scholars were daughters of *qadi*s (judges), imams and members of the *huffaz* (Qur'an memorisers). It is evident that men who were most committed to the education of females, respecting and treating them as peers, were the ulema.[400]

Mohammad Akram Nadwi, after a key in-depth research produced a book *Al-Muhaddithat: The Women Scholars in Islam*. It provides significant details about thousands of such female scholars. He listed four major historical periods[401] indicating both the growth and decline of female scholars.

---

[398] Naqwi, M. A., 2013, p. 3.

[399] *Ibid.*, p. 227.

[400] *Ibid.*, p. xii.

[401] *Ibid.*, p. 246.

The First Period, 7th-8th century CE (1st–2nd AH): This was a period of growth of female scholars. It starts from the time of the Prophet and includes the period of the first three generations of Muslims known as the *Salaf*. These three generations included the *Sahabah* (Companions of the Prophet), the *Tabi'un* (generation after the *Sahabah*) and the *Tabi'u al-Tabi'in* (the third generation following the *Tabi'un*).

There is a vast encouragement for knowledge in the Qur'an and the Prophet made knowledge acquisition mandatory for all. This resulted in both men and women to read, study and acquire knowledge. Women scholars were abundant and conspicuous during this period. They were teachers of both men and women and their examples starts from the very wives of the Prophet. This was also the time when female poets like al-Khansa and Rabi'ah Basri wrote their verses. From the time of the third generation (*Tabi'u al-Tabi'in*) there started a slow decline of female scholars.

The Second Period, 9th-11th CE (3rd-5th AH): This was a period of dramatic decline in the number of female scholars but a high period for men. The six authentic ḥadīth compilations (*Al-ṣaḥīḥ al-Sittah*) were written during this period and all were authored by men. The years of the 9th and 10th centuries CE were the leanest for female scholars.

Specialised learning centres for ḥadīth had developed in different towns. The distance between such towns were quite extensive. Nadwi considers that to study and compile ḥadīth from these far apart centres men were more adapt to taking the arduous journeys required[402] and thus the female scholars started to drop out from this vocation. While distance may have played a part, it is likely that there were other reasons for the decline of female scholars.

---

[402] Nadwi, M. A., 2013, p. 252.

This period corresponds with the Abbasid era. Just before this period renowned scholars like Shu'bah ibn al-Hajjaj (d. 722), Imam Abu Hanifah (d. 772), Imam Malik (d. 795) and Sufyan al-Thawri (d. 778) all had female teachers at one time or another.[403] Imam Malik's daughter Fatimah studied ḥadīth and memorised the whole of the *Muwatta* and became a teacher and transmitter while his son did not. But none of the six *Sittah* ḥadīth writers had any female tutors on record. Though they have referred to female scholars in the *isnad* of the ḥadīth they had compiled.

One more thing to note is that the female scholars not only gave up the ulemaic disciplines, they also did not progress into the study of science as was done by the male scholars. So, something must have happened between the end of the 8th century and early 9th century that led to this dramatic decline in female scholars. This was the time when the schools of *fiqh* (jurisprudence) were finalised. There may have been some correlation between these two events.

The 9th century was also a period of political turmoil, revolts and start of disintegration of the Abbasid Empire. All these political instabilities would have caused women to give up travelling to the famous centres of knowledge thus harming their vocation. There remained some female *shaykhah*s in Baghdad, Nishapur and Jurjan and in some cities of Transoxiana (Central Asia). One such famous *shaykhah* of Baghdad was Amah al-Wahid who, according to al-Daraqutni, besides being a *muhaddithah* was also a *faqih* (jurist) and *hafizah* of the Qur'an.[404]

The Third Period, 12th-15th centuries CE (6th-9th AH): The next period was another high for female scholars with an increase in the number of female scholars. The Tri-Military invasions were

---

[403] *Ibid.*, p. 250.
[404] Nadwi, M. A., 2013, p. 253-254.

the main events of this period. The Spanish *Reconquista* and Inquisition, the Crusade and the Mongol invasion took place during this period. Many major centres of knowledge were destroyed, for example, Jerusalem by the Crusaders and Nishapur, Jurjan and others by the Mongols. Huge numbers of Muslims were killed and displaced and were on the run as refugees. While men were out fighting or negotiating the hostile environment the women took up the scholarship to protect the religion. The shocking catastrophes awakened Muslims both individually and collectively. Men and women all fervently strove to save their way of life, personal safety became secondary. Besides, this time women scholars did not have to travel for ḥadīth collection from various centres as the compilation had already been completed in the previous period. Women could settle in one place with all the ḥadīth books required and teach the locals.

During the Tri-Military Events many scholars fled to the few remaining knowledge centres. Some of the Sufis converged in Konya while some ḥadīth scholars went to Egypt. As all the scientific centres were destroyed or had gone under non-Muslim rule the scientists had no place to go and the last remaining few worked under the Mongols and in Christian Spain as long as they were allowed.

The reinvigoration of the religious disciplines started with the scholars who had fled from Jerusalem when it was occupied by the crusaders in 1099 CE.[405] Ibn Asakir al-Dimashqi and the family of Ibn Qudamah settled in Damascus. They and their women revived the ḥadīth discipline and they were joined by other local people in the process. By the 13th century a number of ḥadīth institutions had developed in that region. These institutes always had female students and teachers.[406]

---

[405] Nadwi, M. A.,2013, p. 257.
[406] *Ibid.*, p. 259.

Up to that time, some of the main centres for ḥadīth were in Baghdad and Isfahan. In Baghdad the most famous of the female ḥadīth scholars were Shuhdah bint al-Ibri (d. 1178) and Tajanni bint Abdullah al-Wahbaniyyah (d.1179). In Isfahan, Fatimah bint Abdullah al-Juzdaniyyah (d. 1129) was considered one of the most outstanding figures in the history of ḥadīth. Her student Fatimah ibn Sa'd al-Khayr went to Syria (Damascus) and Egypt and taught ḥadīth there. Thus, both Syria and Egypt started to further strengthen as an important centre of knowledge.

At this time male scholars like Ibn al-Jawzi, Hafiz Ibn Asakir, Abu Sa'd al-Samani had multiple female teachers. Ibn al-Najjar speaks of coming under the purview of four hundred female scholars.[407] Aisha bint 'Abd al-Hadi (d. 816 AH) was appointed to the position of Principle Teacher in the Grand Mosque in Damascus that had been originally established centuries ago by the Umayyad. This mosque had a great tradition of female scholars, as Umm al-Darda (d. 81 AH) had taught ḥadīth and jurisprudence at the same mosque about 8 centuries ago.[408]

After the crusades came the Mongol invasion. As a consequence of the Mongol attacks, the academic centres including ḥadīth schools in Baghdad, Samarqand, Bukhara and Nishapur were utterly devastated. Fortunately, by then Syria and Egypt had developed as knowledge centres with ḥadīth being one of their specialisations. About 90 percent of female *muhaddithat* were from Egypt, Syria and the Haramayn (Makkah, Madinah) region. The *muhaddithat* reached their peak in Egypt during the 14th–15th century.[409] Female scholars continued through to the early Ottoman age. While ulemaic disciplines were revived due to the great efforts of both men and women, the sciences remained

---

[407] Nadwi, M. A., 2013, p. 258.

[408] *Ibid.*, p. x.

[409] *Ibid.*, p. 269.

regressive.

The Fourth Period, 16th-21st Century (10th-15th AH):
Throughout all the previous periods, despite the fluctuating numbers of female schlars, Muslim women were the most educated women in the world. Even during their low periods their learning was higher than the women of the rest of the world. A woman in 'hijab' was viewed to be a progressive, literate and modern person. But the fourth period witnessed the most dramatic decline. The sweeping deterioration in learning and education was indiscriminate between men and women.

During the colonial period the quest for knowledge had reached its lowest ebb among the Muslims. A very few female ḥadīth scholars persisted up to the 20th century like Amatullah bint al-Imam Abd al-Ghani al-Dihlawi.[410] At the start of this century, women like Rokeya Begum of Calcutta (Kolkata, India) struggled for female education and emancipation at a time when females were still considered unequal all over the world. Rokeya was a literary figure writing both poetry and prose and was an educationist who opened a school for Muslim girls in Kolkata.[411]

But such women were very few and women of these latter generations, by and large, had to give up literacy mainly due to financial constraints and social priorities. The average Muslim families had become so poor that they could not afford proper education for all the offspring. If some degree of education could at all be afforded, the males were preferred over females as they were expected to be the bread earners for the family. The 'image' of the Muslims changed. As a general case, women in 'hijab' came to be considered illiterate and backward as were the men in beard.

---

[410] Nadwi, M. A., 2013, p. 263.
[411] Bhowmik, Rita, 2002, p. 18.

Current Issues in the Muslim Domains

The most important resource of a country is its human resource. Infrastructure, edifices and industries are all very important but without properly educated and skilled human resource all these are useless and redundant. A country is what its people are. So, the main aim of any country's authority should be the proper development of its human resource. In contemporary times, China and India are good examples of how human resources can be developed suitably in adverse economic situations.

All Muslim countries need better educated and skilled people. To efficiently develop human resource, as well as the country as a whole, there are two imperative conditions: political stability and a war free zone.

Political instability can make the national environment chaotic that causes all development works including human resource development to slow down or come to a grinding halt. This lack of development is not always immediately perceptible as economic downturn may take some time to manifest. Nevertheless, political instability is very harmful to the country and when its negative effects does eventuate, it is generally too late to do anything about it.

War, the other calamity, destroys whatever infrastructure and industry that the country may have developed. The war efforts also eat up all the scarce resources that the country may possess as more and more weapons are bought. Many Muslim countries, unfortunately, are beset with political instability or war.

To avoid such calamities, it is best to look at countries which are free from them. There is no perennial internal political instability within the the Western countries. The reason is because the West abides by two of its fundamental institutions—Electoral bodies and Courts of Justice.

The elections in the West are fair and no matter what the

result both the government and opposition abide by it. This leads to stability and there is no rejection of elections and no consequent fight in the street to force the formation of the next government. The new government brings new ideas of governance which gives dynamism. The judiciary in the West is powerful and independent. Politicians do not have much influence on it. That also gives stability as offenders are duly punished no matter who they are, thus, inhibiting corruption.

In the Muslim countries, many a times, elections are not fair. Judiciary is controlled directly or furtively by the ruling powers. Militia, gangsters or even the army are used by politicians for power struggle and suppression that obviously causes instability. These all breed contempt, unhappiness, and frustration among those who are victims leading to retaliation and conflicts. This kind of governance ultimately leads to hatred among the political parties. National policies and election agendas become dominated by hatred and emotive issues rather than pragmatic socio-economic issues.

To avoid war, the best would be to follow the European model. There has been no war in Europe since the Second World War (aside for the Bosnia and Kosovo hostilities). The European Union (EU) is an economic zone with free movement of people and goods among the member states. Such economic and human resource integration leads to a goal of common good. From the economic benefits and group-strength that is reaped from such an integration it becomes quite clear that the alternate isolation, let alone war, is harmful.

Certainly, there are times of stress and concern like Brexit, when Britain elected to leave the EU, or supporting one of the member countries whose economy has fallen. But, the benefits from such a union are so high that the issues of concern can be weathered jointly. The main thing is that due to integration the European countries decide on conflicts and issues across conference tables rather than on the battlefields.

Such institutions like electoral body, judiciary, economic union, *etc.*, all are possible due to the existence of another important institution—the higher education institution, namely, the universities. The universities produce excellent intellectuals who efficiently run all the above mentioned institutions and organisations, making policies and carrying out cutting-edge research for the government and private enterprises. This complex of high class interacting institutions form the basis of a developed nation. The institutions of many Muslim nations are not mature or advanced sufficiently to be considered developed.

It is important to restate that the West upholds the value of two institutions in their countries as utmost—the courts of justice and the universities. These two institutions of the West are the best in the world which gives them the power and moral authority to do what they deem to be right. These two institutional practices are needed to be emulated by the Muslims. If the Muslims can provide courts of justice better than the West and produce universities more advanced than the West, their nations will also be accepted as the best. But let alone emulation, many Muslims do not even understand the fundamental values of the West. In their myopic vision becoming westernised only means drinking alcohol or wearing skimpy clothes.

In Europe, monarchies have been an important and age-old institution. They too have altered and adapted themselves for political stability. Over time, they have educated their masses, built institutions and converted themselves to parliamentary monarchies. That is the most stable form of monarchy in the contemporary world. It took a long time, but some historical incidents give an understanding of the challenges they had to face. A quick study of the French Revolution and its aftermaths as well as the dynamic changes the royal families underwent during the world wars should make clear why such actions became necessary.

It stabilised the royal families and their countries.

All the above may sound as praising the West and, indeed, these are praiseworthy achievements. It is due to such institutions and such human resources that the Western countries are the most advanced of all. Many may be concerned about the foreign affairs and defence policies of some Western politicians, their at-times support for corrupt Muslim politicians, their anti-Islamic political rhetoric in the name of free speech, and the concern of such people are fair. But that is a discussion for another time and another forum.

In the present Muslim countries and societies, there are countless issues and problems—political, economic, social, legal, academic and military. But at the root of it all are two fundamental problems, intellectual backwardness and moral degeneration. Contrastingly, the search for knowledge and moral fortitude were the main strengths of the early Muslims.

Intellectual backwardness

The current academic institutions in most Muslim countries are of low grade. These institutions mostly produce 'workers' for government or private enterprises. They are not really involved in any ground-breaking 'research and development' nor do they support technological entrepreneurship. Many of these institutions may as well be considered as somewhat advanced vocational centres rather than research universities. Most of the scholars in the Muslim world have no standing or contribution in the international level.

The contemporary Muslims can be categorised into three types based on their pursuit of knowledge.

1. Those who seek rational knowledge—like university students.

2. Those who seek religious knowledge—like madrasah students.

3. Those who seek basically no significant knowledge—the illiterates.

The third group, unfortunately, consists of a very significant proportion among the Muslims today. The other two groups are the rational modernists and religious traditionalists between whom there is considerable antipathy. Many modernists encourage the sciences but consider the ulemaic disciplines as ancient. Many traditionalists encourage only the ulemaic disciplines and are implicitly against the pure sciences and social sciences. The pursuit of the Total Knowledge advocated by the Qur'an and practised by the early Muslims is no longer cognised.

There are some Islamic universities which are 'geared' for Total Knowledge but, unfortunately, they are not of a high standard and do not receive sufficient sponsorship. In fact, most lie behind the standard universities in academic quality and ranking. Similarly, the madrasahs generally attract students of lesser intellect than the regular schools. In the madrasahs of the early Muslims, intellectual elites debated on various subjects and topics including new ideas in philosophy and syllogism. There was a richness that has been abandoned in the name of modernity by both the madrasahs and general education system in Muslim countries.[412]

The existing state school model in the Muslim countries has not inculcated compassion, aesthetics, wisdom, deep dialectics or philosophical wisdom required for adherence to the Total Knowledge paradigm. The sponsoring of secular universities that do not have such higher values and, contrariwise, the existence of a madrasah system that does not incorporate critical thinking

---

[412] WR8.

have caused a cognitive dissonance within the Muslim society. These institutes produce two very different streams of scholars that have no understanding of each other. They cannot reconcile between what has now become two completely different worlds. There is chaos and confusion, causing the young to seek an escape into total rejection of either reason or religion. Thus, giving rise to the two opposing forces of atheistic materialism and fundamentalism.

Muslim countries have to set aim to achieve much higher intellectual levels. It won't happen overnight but if directions are not set it won't happen ever. Maybe the rich Muslim countries can start by making contributions to top-level universities and to institutions like NASA and CERN. That may be the first step towards a cooperation with such elite organisations and universities with local institutions in Muslim countries.

While setting up high intellectual levels, there is another aspect that needs to be taken care of. As the Muslims of the recent past distanced themselves from Total Knowledge by ignoring pure science, now some are again making the same mistake by over-compensating and moving away from Total Knowledge in the opposite directions. They are moving away from the ulemaic and liberal academe to a form of secularised 'scientism'.

In 1962, Bayard Dodge, president of the Protestant University in Beirut, in his book on medieval Muslim education, warned, 'The Muslim education of the Middle Ages is rapidly being superseded by schools and universities, which are both modern and secular. This widespread movement is so recent that it is impossible to tell how it will affect the cultural and social life of Islam. It is clear, however, that in this age of chaotic change, when members of the rising generation are confused by bewildering doubts, the reformer must not neglect that basic principles of medieval education which were a search of spiritual truth and faith in the reality of Allah'.[413]

Moral Degradation

In the present, some of the Muslim countries are the most corrupt ones in the world. Some are systematically corrupt from top executives to the lowest levels—including politician, judges, law enforcing agencies, businessmen, bureaucrats, *etc.*

Corruption is unacceptable at any levels, but if it happens among the elite level then it becomes more harmful. This allows corruption to flow down the administration and spread to the root levels very easily. At the same time, it should be noted, that corruption at the lower rungs can also go upwards, for example, when corrupt officials are 'promoted' to higher positions they take their corrupt baggage along with them, but that is a slower process. There is a vicious cyclical effect between corruption and mismanagement of the affairs of state. Mismanagement increases corruption which, in turn, increases mismanagement which further increases corruption and so on.

The vicious cycle is also evident when economy is taken under consideration. Sometimes, a country may start to develop slowly. But before it can truly develop it falls victim to another round of unrest, internal instability or war, which destroys all the past developments and the cycle to develop starts again. This complex cycle seems to be unceasing with the only beneficiary being international arms manufacturers, infrastructure builders and corrupt politicians.

The lack of intellectualism combined with corruption causes rational incapacity in nations. It is due to the deficiency of these two primary qualities that there have cropped up all the multifarious problems in the Muslim world. The price the

---

[413] WR8.

Muslims have paid for all these substandard governances is perpetual disgrace, dishonour, poverty and ignorance.

The Total Knowledge Paradigm

In the greater accumulative history of knowledge, the Muslims were the first heir of *global* knowledge. Before them the Greeks were heir to the *regional* knowledge of the Egyptian and Persian-Babylonians. But the Muslims, inspired by knowledge seeking dictates of their religion, sought out and inherited the ancient works of the Greeks, Indians, Chinese, Persians and Babylonians, *i.e.*, all the existing knowledge of the world. The rulers sent out scholars to various lands to search and bring back all the knowledge they could gather. They correlated and corrected these ancient works of their deficiencies and mistakes and, at the same time, they produced vast novel knowledge becoming the best in all disciplines.

The Qur'an advocates the pursuit of knowledge and the Prophet made knowledge mandatory for all Muslims. The early Muslims followed those guidance and became a nation of scholars. Their rulers and 'governments' sponsored every kind of knowledge. A true scholar just had to walk into any of the courts in a Muslim domain and they would get sponsorship and assistance. They established a large number of educational institutes and knowledge kept on developing progressively. Thus, Muslims became very erudite scholars of every manner. And they were all the best in the world.

The ulema scholars wrote massive works of exegesis and jurisprudence. The philosophers became the best in the world in their critical discussion and rational arguments. The theologians were masters of their craft defending and upholding the balance between rationalism and spiritualism. The Sufis of past were among the most erudite and deep thinking scholars. The scientist carved out the domain of empiricism. They introduced the sciences and social sciences as distinct and discrete subjects, giving rise to the scientific spirit and the scientific method. Those marvellous Muslims built an amazing intellectual environment of Total Knowledge.

Muslim scholars approached knowledge from a variety of perspectives. They never limited their quest for knowledge to any particular type. For them knowledge was multifarious, comprehensive and complete. The early Muslim scholars had graded knowledge into different categories.[414]

Imam al-Maturidi classified knowledge into three types:	▪ Knowledge from sensory perceptions which include experience and experiment. ▪ Divine revelation from the prophets and messengers. ▪ Knowledge through reason.
Al-Farabi categorised knowledge into two types:	▪ Practical knowledge that deduces what needs to be done. ▪ Theoretical knowledge which helps the soul to attain perfection.
According to **Ibn Khaldun** knowledge is of three kinds:	▪ Knowledge by inference. ▪ Knowledge by perception. ▪ Knowledge by personal experience.
Al-Ghazali, further widened knowledge into two more types:	▪ Acquired knowledge. ▪ Innate knowledge.

Acquired knowledge is simple to understand that which is

---

[414] Hossain, M. A., 2013, p. 228-229.

learned. Innate intellect can be compared, in a mundane sort of way, of being something akin to genetic memory. Humans appear to have *a priori* knowledge of ethics and axioms. Even arithmetic truths appear to be innate—one agrees to simple arithmetic notions as being true instinctively, it is not actually learned. The senses are inadequate to explain how individuals come to have such innate knowledge or understanding.

There were critical but positive interactions between all the branches of knowledge. The ulemaic disciplines guided the Muslims and theology defended them. Philosophy, sciences, and social sciences progressed them. The scholars positively debated the mistakes of one another and critiqued the mistakes of the existing institutions. Imam Abu Hanifah fought the political system itself with his legal system. Al-Ghazali attacked the speculative mistakes of the philosophers but accepted the rational aspects of philosophy. Imam Hanbal fought the rationalist dominance but never said rational or scientific studies were not needed. Ibn Taymiyyah contradicted the fallacies of 'popular religion', charlatans, and the pretences of false Sufis but also had good words for genuine *tasawwuf*. All of them understood and maintained the healthy balance of knowledge.

Then due to a series of political, military and socio-structural changes the balance was disrupted and the Muslim society regressed. The progress and spread of knowledge came to an end. During this time of degeneration and internal political conflict led to disintegration of the Muslim empires and subsequent invasion by foreign powers. A putative ban on further development of jurisprudence somehow spread to scientific research and philosophy as well. It led to a decline in critical thinking. The influence of the ulema was also marginalised due to the 'popular religion' which led to moral deterioration.

In all, there was a shift from a knowledge seeking society to a pleasure, ease and comfort seeking one. It was not that the

Muslims gave up any special discipline, they gave up thinking critically in all disciplines. Fortunately, Europe inherited all these knowledge from the Muslims. As the regression set in among the Muslims, the Europeans translated their works and took it to their lands. They became the heirs of Muslim knowledge and continued from where the Muslims had left off.

Today's Muslim academia and knowledge cannot be compared with those of the marvellous Muslims who followed the quest for Total Knowledge. Today, there exist two contradicting types of thinking in the Muslim world—the modernists and the traditionalists. Both are afflicted by a barren and stifling mediocrity. Students just strive for a piece of paper that will permit them to get some type of salary. And the teachers provide them exactly that. Those who try to strive for higher goals, give it up on the face of governmental apathy.

Sufficient incentive or sponsorship for scholars is missing and the treatment meted out to them is as shabby as the environment that produces them. The political leaders spend more money to remain in power, live a luxury filled life and to win elections then educating their populace. Some are even ready to entice the people to an indolent and ignorant life, if that helps to retain their power, rather than really educate them.

Muslim scholars of any worth have to go off to the West to get the intellectual sustenance they require. While, at the same time, corrupt tycoons, bureaucrats and political cronies live luxurious lives in Muslim countries. Muslims have become the importers of knowledge not producers of knowledge. And only the producers can contribute to humanity and have a 'say' in this world.

It is not just in science that they lag behind, they do not have sufficient understanding of social sciences and behavioural sciences in which the world has advanced so much. Most do not understand their own religion. The Qur'an praises the people of understanding. The Muslims no longer belong to that group.

The early Muslims scoured the world for all the knowledge that they could access and developed it so successfully. Today, all the knowledge of the world is available and accessible to the Muslims. But they appear to be heedless of it.

They have hearts with which they do not understand,
they have eyes with which they do not see, and
they have ears with which they do not hear.
Those are like cattle; rather, they are more astray; those!
It is they who are the heedless.

—Qur'an, Al-A'rāf 7:179

Epilogue

Human progress requires both morality and knowledge. The standard bearer of morality is the judiciary or justice system. It is justice that makes the foundation of a nation, society or civilisation stable. Thus, it is the lofty ideals and freedom of the judiciary from any overlord that keeps the nation safe from chaos, instability and hostile conflicts.

Knowledge or, its derivative, technology by itself is not an indication of human progress. Without morality, technology can be used to commit all kinds of inhuman atrocities like war and pillage. On the other hand, morality on its own is not worldly-wise. Morality needs worldly knowledge to build up a truly progressive society that can help humanity and also fend for itself. So, a combination of knowledge and morality is imperative for true human progress. This combination has been missing among Muslim societies for some time.

There was a time when the world viewed all scholarly disciplines—science, social science, philosophy—as belonging to the Muslims. It is no longer so. This regression has changed the Muslim society fundamentally. So now, it is up to the Muslims to once again reclaim their great literary and scholarly heritage. A Total Knowledge paradigm needs to be reintroduced and prevail as it had done from the time of the Prophet through to the early Islamic centuries. The traditional Islamic teaching method also needs to continue as it produces scholars who are dedicated to knowledge for life.

Through all the historical obstacles and disasters—invasions, occupations, internal instabilities, lack of funding, lack of education, challenges of mediocrity, external and internal criticism, threat to life itself—only one group of scholars has been able to maintain their original responsibility. They are the ulema and they have maintained the pristine purity of the *integrated intellect*—the Qur'an and *Sunnah*. The religion remains absolute. The ulema have been pushed and probed and penalised causing extreme pain at times but they have never budged. They have done their part of the job, it is now up to the other scholars— scientist and social scientists—to take responsibility of progressing, sponsoring and facilitating knowledge.

It is the study of sciences and social sciences that need to be re-invigorated without any consideration. *Ijtihad* and knowledge quest in all these areas need to be encouraged as is encouraged by the Qur'an and *Sunnah*. The social sciences and philosophy has to be freed from its atheistic shell and improved on a larger framework—a reality that is boundless, perpetual and universal. It is not a necessity that all the disciplines be taught in the same institute because institutes specialise in its own sphere, but some understanding of each other is necessary. All types of education should be available in the society and, importantly, all should be of high quality with really dedicated teachers and devoted students. Spiritual compassion and rational dialectics must learn to coexist with one another.

On the other hand, reversing the closure of *ijtihad* for Islamic jurisprudence without a well laid plan may be unsafe. There is no central authority among the Sunni now, thus *ijtihad* on jurisprudence will lead to multifarious changes of jurisprudence at different regions by a variety of local authorities. That will cause further divisiveness and sectarianism. Such considerations need to be placed in front of a central authority like a universal *fiqh* council. This is where the ulema can contribute.

To achieve the high intellectual dynamics that was present in the past and to re-initiate the quest for knowledge some social-political factors need to be overhauled as well. The root fix can be stated quite simply: restrict corruption and immorality from the society and encourage and sponsor knowledge acquisition. From within a corrupt society this task may look daunting. But there are nations where corruption is under control and knowledge is being diligently pursued. If they can do it why can't the Muslims?

While the situation appears very complex and difficult, it should be realised that Muslims are now much more prevalent and resourceful than they were in the days of the Rashidun Caliphs. At that time, under innumerable odds, they prevailed and became the most scholarly society in the world because they wanted to uplift humanity. This unselfish motive and attitude is of prime importance. The aim should be to seek out knowledge to contribute to all of humanity that will make the whole world a better place. A nation without knowledge and morality is not truly an Islamic nation and an individual without knowledge and morality is not a complete Muslim.

Every mosque needs a school and a library to be attached to it turning it into a centre of high learning as they were in the early days of Islamic civilisation, and every Muslim needs to be reminded of the first command of the Qur'an—'*Read!*' and made to understand that first and foremost they are a nation of scholars and that this passion for knowledge is their salvation.

Knowledge in Pre-Islamic Civilisations

Introduction: Knowledge and Civilisations

There are three factors that play crucial roles in the rise and fall of empires—knowledge, morality and enterprise. In the context of a nation, these factors are represented by institutions or systems. Knowledge can be represented by universities and schools, morality by the legal system and courts, and enterprise by entrepreneurship and industry. These factors are interactive, *i.e.* the condition of any one of the factors affects the others. As long as these remain positive the civilisation progresses. If any of these become negative the civilisation regresses.

Knowledge is thus one of the critical components in the rise and fall of civilisations and nations. Knowledge that the human world possesses today has been accumulated over the past ten thousand years. Every civilisation had searched and accumulated knowledge. Even in their fall, they have passed on their knowledge to subsequent civilisations. The new civilisations have improved on the knowledge that was inherited by them. Thus, as time has progressed the subsequent civilisations had accumulated more and more knowledge.

There have been continuous rise and fall of civilisations

throughout historical time. The first civilisations were the
Mesopotamians and Egyptians closely followed by the Chinese
and the Indian Indus Valley civilisations (2600 BC to 1900 BCE).
These were followed by the Median-Persian, Greek and the
consequent Roman civilisations (678 BCE to approximately the
Muslim civilisation). Then came the Muslim civilisation (7th
century CE to 19th century CE) followed by the European
civilisation (CE to present). Two or more 'civilisations' may have
coexisted during the same time period. At its own peak every
civilisation was the 'modern' civilisation of the world for that time
period. Due to globalisation the civilisations are becoming more
integrated.

Historically, the fall of civilisations have not necessarily been
the end of those civilisations. Resurgences of civilisations are
common. One such resurgence is the Italian Renaissance in
Europe. Currently, the Chinese and Indian resurgences are also
evident though the Western Civilisation (extension of the
European civilisation) remain dominant.

Though each civilisation is associated with some form of
knowledge quest, the motivation for the quest have changed over
time. In the ancient past, knowledge has been the by-product of
religious enterprise. The Pharaohs had huge pyramids built to
provision for their 'journey' to the after-life. But for building the
pyramids they tackled and accumulated geometric and
engineering knowledge. The ancient Indians set up standard
measure and shape for the funeral pyres that led them to the
understanding of geometric concepts. The Babylonians pursuit for
astrology, the imagined effect of stars on human beings, led
towards astronomy.

At other times knowledge was searched through a
philosophical frame of mind as did the Greeks in their quest for
disciplines like logic, ethics, medicine, and mathematics. Then
there was the search for all or Total Knowledge using scientific

empirical methods as was set up by the early Muslims and then followed by the Europeans since the renaissance. This remains the pre-dominant method of knowledge acquisition.

Chronological Development of Civilisation

Civilisations can be divided into five phases chronologically with increasing intellectual development:

Phase 1 (Pre-6th century BCE)

The Mesopotamians and Egyptians were the first civilisations to develop during this phase. They were closely followed by the Chinese and the Indian Indus Valley civilisations. Most of intellectual works from this period have been lost and can only be surmised from archaeological and structural remnants of the period like the Ziggurats and Pyramids. Such civilisations must have understood engineering, mathematics, labour organisation and management to build such huge structures. Literature of that period, for example, the Mesopotamian *Epic of Gilgamesh* and Egyptian *The Story of Sinuhe*, unearthed by archaeologists, also gives insight into that period. Pantheons of gods and goddesses were widespread and appear to have overshadowed monotheism. But the concept of one God did exist in old scriptures.[415]

Phase 2 (6th to 1st century BCE)

In the second phase of intellectual development came the Persian, Greek and Roman civilisations. Knowledge from Egypt, Babylon and India was assimilated by the Persians and Greeks. The Greek intellectualism eventually overtook others contemporary civilisations. This phase was also the period of rise of philosophy.

---

[415] Rig Veda 6:45:16.

There are many archaeological records that reflect developments of this phase. A variety of texts that originated in this period are also known. During this period the Hebrew tribes struggled to retain monotheism in a polytheism dominated world.

Phase 3 (1st century BCE to 500 CE)

During this phase a high degree of morality was established in a large region of the world with Christianity spreading in the west and Buddhism in the east. It was not that morality did not exist previously. The Jews with laws for their tribes, the Darius inscriptions of Mount Behistan, the codes of Hamurabi and the Roman Law, attest to great civilisations with law and order. But this phase brought in a uniformity based specifically on religious morality over large stretches of the world. In the previous phases, law was dispensed to a large extent at the whim of the ruler. In this phase established norms started to play a more important role.

Phase 4 (600 CE to 1500 CE)

This was the period of further affirmation of morality and monotheism with the rise of Islam. Law became entrenched and even the rulers were subject to it. The phase was also, importantly, the start of the scientific age. This age was initiated by the early Muslim scholars as part of a Total Knowledge paradigm. In the latter part of this period, as the Muslims disintegrated, books of knowledge were translated and transferred to Europe.

Phase 5 (1600 to recent)

This phase represents the consolidation and further development of the scientific age that resulted in the Renaissance and the consequent rise of industrialisation in Europe. This was followed by the modern era when along with tremendous technological advances, economics and social sciences also took on a whole new world-shaping meaning.

Similarities Between the Ancient Civilisations

There are many similarities among the ancient civilisations in many different aspects—mythology, academic disciplines, development of oral and written literature, development of writing, megastructures and edifices, *etc.*

Similarities in Philosophy and Cosmology

Different disciplines that have been studied by the ancient civilisations (first three phases) include mathematics, medicine, astrology, astronomy, philosophy, and the subject of authority (how to rule by monarchs). But in all those civilisations most of these disciplines were not separate 'subjects' but just scattered concepts within religion or philosophy. For example, some concepts of astronomy were present within religious astrology and a few concepts of sciences were still notions within philosophy. Some rudimentary ideas about economics and social or political sciences have been present within the subject of 'authority'—the 'how to rule' category. All these notions would emerge as independent, separate and distinct subjects only after the 8th century CE in the works of early Muslim scholars.

There has also been a sharing or inheriting of knowledge between civilisations. This has resulted in the commonality of knowledge. For example, there are many common elements in the 'philosophical' thoughts of different civilisation of the past.

Duality is a common feature found in different cultures. It means two opposing or complementary forces working concurrently. Duality can be interpreted in two ways, cosmically or morally. Cosmic duality defines opposing forces within the

THE FIRST COMMAND

universe and moral duality represents opposing forces that affect the individual's mind and actions.

A duality in Chinese philosophy is represented by Yin and Yang that states that all things exist as inseparable and contradictory opposites, for example, dark-light, female-male and old-young. These two concepts of Yin and Yang are very similar to the Tamas and Rajas Gunas of the Samkhya system of Indian philosophy. Dualism in Persian Zoroastrianism is the existence of and constant battle between good and evil force. The good is represented by the 'god' Ahura Mazda while the evil by Angra Mainyu.

In Plato's *Timaeus,* the Demiurge is the divine creator of the universe similar to the Semitic concept of God the Creator. But Plato's cosmogony differs from the Semitic one in the sense that the Demiurge is not omnipotent and cannot create out of nothing. The 'first being' is, in fact, the Monad that emanated the Demiurge. The Monad and Demiurge is a cosmic duality.

There is a secondary duality in the Platonic theory. He mentions another eternal being or 'necessity' and named it Ananke. This duality, Demiurge-Ananke represents 'intelligence and necessity' unlike the moral 'good versus evil' of the Zoroastrian duality. The two platonic dualities can be combined to form a trinity—Monad, Demiurge and Ananke. In the Pheado, Plato presents another duality of the soul and the body. Plato also believes in two different universes of existence, one of perfect Forms and another of imperfect Matter which are imperfect copies of the Forms. The imperfect universe being the one inhabited by human beings.

There are also similarities in the cosmologies of all ancient mythologies. Mythologies of ancient civilisations state that the cosmos was created from the remains or parts of some enormous entity variably mentioned as a huge cosmic Ocean or cosmic Chaos or cosmic Night. In some myths, for example the Egyptian, these huge entities or beings gave birth to the gods who become a 'family' creating and ruling the world of human kind.

In the mythologies, the world was believed to comprise a rectangular or circular plane resting on a water body or with water bodies around it. There is also a mention of mountains in most mythologies (like the Greek Olympus) which were the abode of the mythical gods.

While most ancient philosophies of the world have mythic cosmogony as one of the central aspect of thought, ancient Chinese philosophy pays less heed to it. It is involved more with pragmatic political thinking of state governance and authority. The Indian cosmology differs due to its concept of reincarnation, *i.e.*, the universe is recreated and destroyed in a cyclic manner. It passes through the same four ages (*Yuga*) which comprises one cycle (*Kalpa*) over and over again.

There is an 'atomic' theory concept in philosophy. This is not the concept of modern atoms, as understood in physics. The philosophical 'atomic' theory refers to the basic unit of matter of which the physical universe was supposed to be made of. In the Chinese 'Five Elements' concept the universe was considered to consist of five basic elements—earth, wood, metal, fire and water.

The Vaiseshika School of India also consists of a similar cosmological theory where the universe is made of five basic elements—air, fire, water, earth and *akasha* (sky or ether).[416] This atomic theory known as *Paramanus* is found in the *Abhidharma Hridaya* which is a doctrinal text translated into Chinese in the late 3rd century CE.[417]

The Greek philosophers considered the physical universe to constitute of the four elements earth, water, air and fire. In addition, Plato, in his Timaeus, linked these elements to different

---

[416] Das Gupta, S. N., 1975, p. 118.

[417] *Ibid.*, p. 144-145.

geometric shapes. The consideration of actual atoms as 'particles' associated with motion instead of basic matters was first conceived by Muslim scholars like Abu al-Ash'ari in the 10th century CE.

The improvement of health, or the 'vital' energy of the self, through some form of meditative exercises is also quite common in different philosophies. Basically, Chinese Taoist and Indian Yoga exercise have three similar regulations—'Regulation of Posture', 'Regulation of Breath' and 'Regulation of Heart and Mind'. The followers of such schools have generally been associated with an austere life and control of desire. The disciples of Chinese thinker Mo-tzu (480-390 BCE) lived in penury.[418] The Indian sages also practised penury, and the followers of Pythagoras also led a very strict code of life.

The Chinese Taoist, to whom individual salvation is important as opposed to collective salvation, believed that the self was not separate from others or other 'selves'. According to them, such *misunderstanding* of the 'self' as being completely separate individual leads to a troublesome ego and illusions which leads to unhappiness and loneliness. In a similar way, the Indian Samkhya-Yoga philosophers believed all miseries were caused due to *avidya* (superlative ignorance).

Logic developed in ancient Greece, China, and India. The *Organon* is the most famous work on logic by Aristotle consisting of six parts. The Indian *Nyaya* system was a school of logic similar to the Aristotelian school but more cumbrous.[419] The Chinese logic was started by the Mohist School which gave rise to the logicians known as the 'School of Names'. One of the few surviving texts from the Mohist School narrates, 'From a one-foot stick, every day take away half of it, in a myriad of ages it will not

---

[418] Gernet, Jacques, 1996, p. 67-68.
[419] Das Gupta, S. N., 1975, p. 117.

be exhausted.' This is similar to one of the narratives of the Greek Zeno. But it is obviously a formulation independent of Zeno's paradoxes.[420] The 'arrow' paradox of Zeno is also present in Chinese rhetoric.

Ethics has been part of all ancient civilisations. Most of it fostered within a religious form like in Hinduism and Judaism. The Greeks and Chinese stand out as having studied ethics as a subject on its own. Aristotle's best work on Ethics is known as the Nicomachean Ethics. Important works on ethics can be found in ancient Chinese text on Confucianism, Mohism, Daoism and Legalism.

Similarities in Other Disciplines

The discipline of 'political and legal authority' (governance) of the rulers have received much attention in the past in different civilisations. There have been different views on how the ruler should rule. The ancient *Shang-chun Shu,* a Chinese text of the 3rd century BCE, states that politics is not a matter of morality but is essentially the means and stratagems which ensure and maintain the power of the state.[421] Machiavelli, in the 16th century CE, shows similar political opinion.

On the other hand, morality played a more important part in the teachings of the Chinese Legalist school. Han Fei, founder of the legalist school in the 3rd century BCE, believed that human morality and ethical values are to be established by the head of the state. Mencius, a 4th century Confucian philosopher, on the other hand believed the establishment of morality was through the virtue of holy men. Hsun-tzu was more of a 'realist' and believed society had an important role to play in the establishment of morality.

---

[420] Needham, Joseph, 1956, p. 185.
[421] Gernet, Jacques, 1996, p. 90.

In Babylon, city-state of Mesopotamia, the famous 'Code of Hamurabi' (1787 BC) was the first constitution to give rights to the state by curtailing the power of the king. Along with other laws, it also contained legal aspects of everyday life. Darius the Great of Persia promulgated a 'code of rule' over his vast empire. Plato in the Republic wrote about the character of a just city and just man around 380 BCE. It depicts a good 'city' being governed by philosopher-kings who have knowledge and rule for the good of the city-state but are disinterested in personal wealth or enjoyment. The Indian *Arthasastra* of Kautilya (293-235 BCE) have aspects similar to the Legalist and Taoists but diverges somewhat from the 'holy men morality' of Mencius.

Ancient Mathematics has much in common among civilisations. For example, the Pythagorean Theorem, which states that in a right-angled triangle if the lengths of any two sides are known then the length of the third side can be worked out, is expected to be from about 600 BCE. The Berlin Papyrus, an ancient Egypt papyrus-document from before 1200 BCE, contains mathematical and medical knowledge including pregnancy test procedures. This document also contains a mathematical problem which is almost the same as the right-angled triangle theorem. The Indian Baudhayana Sulbasutra of approximately 800 century BCE also states the same theorem.[422] Arithmetic and Geometry were the main components of ancient mathematics.

Medicine follows a similar trend of development in different civilisations. In the ancient times diseases were considered to occur due to curses and magic. Then people decided to look for some rational causes of diseases. This lead them to believe that all illnesses were the result of an imbalance in the bodily fluids known as 'humours' such as blood, phlegm, yellow bile and black bile.

---

[422] Kak, Subhash, 2010, WR9.

This 'medical' concept first started in ancient Egypt[423] or Mesopotamia[424]. From there the concept went to Greece, so this same humour-fluid concept can be seen in Galen's work. The same concept then appears in Indian Ayurvedic[425] and Chinese traditional medical works.

In medical careers, the selfless sincerity of physicians towards the patient has been emphasised in different civilisations. In China, it is known as 'Absolute sincerity of great physicians',[426] while the one from Greece came to be known as the 'Hippocratic Oath'.

Development of 'Writing' and Literature

There are similarities in the development of writing methods and literatures of different civilisation as well. The art of 'writing' has developed, over time, is a similar fashion in vastly different regions. First writing was pictographic, *i.e.*, pictures and symbols were drawn that represented things and actions.

The Mesopotamians had a pictographic writing system but later developed a cuneiform wedge-shaped writing.[427] The old Egyptian writing was hieroglyphics consisting of symbolic characters which were similar, not in design but in principle, to the Chinese writing. Both the writings were symbolic and thus needed a vast number of symbolic characters to represent the real world.

The complex writing system forced the Egyptians and the Chinese to develop a cursive writing form for practical purposes. These were a sort of shorthand writing which could be used to

---

[423] Van Sertima, Ivan,1992, p. 17.

[424] Sudhoff, Karl, 1961, p. 67, 87, 104.

[425] Das Gupta, S. N., 1975, p. 149.

[426] Sass, Hans-Martin, 2005.

[427] Koutsoukis, A. J., 1990, p. 2.

take notes quickly. While the Egyptians gave up their 'symbolic' writing about a 1000 years ago, the Chinese continues to write with symbolic character to this day. The 'symbolic' or pictographic writing was also the initial writing method in the Greek region.

A great development in writing was the introduction of phonetic alphabets. The words composed of phonetic alphabets (such as A, B, C, *etc.*) as is known today, were first used by the Phoenicians (people of an ancient Lebanese region) who were a sea faring people. They introduced the alphabet to different regions including what was to become Greece.

Initially, ancient poetry developed orally, passed on through generations, and being written down at a later stage. The hymns of priestess Enheduanna of ancient Semuria was written down at a very early ancient time (c. 2260 BCE) and is an exception. The first poems that are known were mostly hymns. Poems were also used for remembering oral history, genealogy, and law. The literature of the past was initially poetical with prose being a much later addition. Poetry appears among the earliest records of most literate civilisations, with fragments of poems discovered on ancient monoliths, runestones and stelae.

One of the most favourite genres in ancient epics of all ancient civilisations is the travel-adventure fiction. The oldest surviving such fiction poems are:

- The **Epic of Gilgamesh**—Mesopotamian: This is the tale of a mighty king named Gilgamesh. There are five episodes in the epic and second one 'The living one's mountain' is an adventurous journey tale.

- **Tale of the Shipwrecked Sailor**—Egyptian: The original Robinson Crusoe tale with a bit of magic in it.

- **Adventures of Sinuhe**—Egyptian: The story depicts the flight of Sinuhe from Egypt in the wake of a murder plot of the Pharaoh. His adventure leads him to what is now Syria and then to Lebanon. Nearly dead in a desert he is rescued by Bedouins. Courage and determination enables him to progress in life and marry a princess and finally become a king. But after many years he becomes nostalgic for his homeland and returns to Egypt welcomed by the Pharaoh.

- **Mu-tien-tzuchuan**—Ancient Chinese: This story recounts the legendary travels of King Mu.

- **Story of Wenamun**—Egyptian: Wenamun is robbed on his way to buy cedar from Lebanon. Left helpless he struggles to return to Egypt.

- **Ramayana**—Indian: Journey to Sri Lanka by Lord Rama to free his abducted wife Lady Sita.

- **Iliad, Odyssey and Aeneid**—Greek: The Iliad is the story of battle between the Greeks and Trojans. In it the Achaeans Greeks travel by water to fight the Trojans over the elopement of Queen Helen. The Achaeans ultimately win after 10 years.

  The Odyssey, a sequel of the Iliad, narrates the adventurous return home journey of King Odysseus, a member of the winning alliance, from Troy to his island kingdom in Ithaca.

  The Aeneid is another sequel to the Iliad but this one is not about the Achaeans but of Aeneas, a prince of Troy. As the Trojans lose the war he flees Troy and embarks on an adventurous journey to Rome to become the ancestor of the Romans.

The tales of adventurous journey have continued through time up to the present. Two of the famous such tales are the journeys of **Sindbad the Sailor** of around the 8th century and the travel of Frodo in the **Lord of the Rings** written in the 20th century.

Development of Structures and Edifices

The ancient civilisations have built a number of megastructure in the past: pyramids, ziggurats, the Great Wall, the Colosseum, *etc.* The pyramid shaped megastructures of the ancient past are quite common and can be found in different regions of the world such as the Egyptian pyramids, Mesopotamian ziggurats and South America pyramids of a much later age.

Etcmanaki was the famous ziggurat of Babylon which is associated with the biblical Tower of Babel. It is supposed to have a similar towering shape. In South America, there are quite a few Mayan step pyramids mostly from around the 9th century CE and the later (15th century CE). One of the factors for this similarity in shape was that it was easier to build a tiered conical structure as building materials could be carried up the tiers as the edifice rose high. The technological support to build very high straight walls was not available.

This type of towering shape has even influenced the cosmology of India (Sumeru Mount), China (Kunlun Mount) and Greece (Mount Olympus). These mythical structures appear to be the much exaggerated accounts of the same tiered 'pyramid' shape.

Mount Kunlun was the fabled abode of immortal gods and goddesses of ancient China. It has been described as being of a tiered form surrounded by water in some descriptions. In Indian philosophy the world itself is considered to be a huge tiered pyramid form, Mount Sumeru, with concentric water bodies. These structures have a temple at the top similar to the zigurrats. In the Greek mythology Mount Olympus, like Mount Kunlun, is the abode of the gods and goddesses. The more recent Machu Picchu of the Incas in Peru also consisted of a terraced abode on top of a mountain.

Knowledge Syncretisation

The knowledge of the world has not been developed by any one civilisation. Starting from the oldest civilisations—Mesopotamians (Semurian, Assyrian and Akkadian civilisations of Iraqi region), Egyptians, Chinese, Indians and Babylonians—world knowledge has been progressively built up. Then followed the Persian, Greek and Roman civilisations. After the initial development there have been two great nexuses of knowledge in history. The first was the regional syncretisation of knowledge by the ancient Greeks. The second was the global syncretisation by the Muslim Umayyads and Abbasids.

The Greeks syncretised the knowledge of the Egyptians, Babylonians, and Persians. Located on the fringe of these empires for centuries, the Greco-Roman region had seen a continuous import of ideas and religious doctrines. The Egyptians, being the first to discover the sail, were also the first to influence the Mediterranean Greeks as they sailed to the Island of Crete.

Mathematics came from Egypt when the likes of Pythagoras and Democritus journeyed to Egypt and became acquainted with Egyptian knowledge. The observations of Egyptian physicians were included in the works of Hippocrates of Cos. Around 270 BCE the school established by the Babylonian Berosso (Bel-reusu) on the island of Cos played a large part in translating the Persian-Babylonian astronomical knowledge to Greek.

The Egyptian influence on the Greeks is evident in the works of Plato. In some of his important dialogues he operated from a world-perspective in which Egypt was omnipresent and ubiquitous. *Timaeus* is the dialogue which is famous for presenting the Forms of Plato. It also portrays the extensive and prolonged relationship between Greece and Egypt. This dialogue depicts Egyptians priests teaching history to the Greeks and also that Athena is the Greek version of an Egyptian goddess. It also shows that the Egyptians were cordial towards the Greeks – an Egyptian priest stating that Greeks are all children under the ancient eyes of Egypt.

Laws, which is Plato's last work, portrays desirable political and social conducts. It also presents the excellence in the Egyptian forms of music, arts and education. The *Republic* is not entirely free of the Egyptian influence, in which Socrates twice swears 'by the dog of Egypt', referring to Anubis, the Egyptian god of funerary and judgment. By thus swearing Socrates was asserting the veracity of his proposition.

The west Asian empires—Babylonian, Persian, Hittite—influenced the Ionian and Dorian Greeks of Asia Minor. Due to their proximity to these empires the Ionians and Dorians became enlightened first among the Greek tribes. The initial west Asian influence was greatest in Miletus a city of Ionia (now western Turkey) and the birthplace of Greek philosophy and mathematics. Miletus was located near the Persian border and was first influenced due to proximity.

Starting from the Persian borders, this influence gradually moved inwards towards central Greece. Before approximately 600 BCE, Miletus was the greatest Greek city. After Miletus, as the influence moved inwards into Greece, Athens gradually became the centre of philosophy and mathematics in the classical period between 600 and 300 BCE.

Later, when Alexander conquered Persia all the books from the Persian palace library were taken and became the kernel of latter Greek learning.[428] Ibn Khaldun elaborates on this issue, saying, "Among the Persians, intellectual sciences played a large and important role, since the Persian dynasties were powerful and ruled without interruptions. The intellectual sciences are said to have come to the Greeks from the Persian when Alexander killed Darius and gained control of the Achaemenid Empire. At that time, he appropriated the books and sciences of the Persians".[429]

The progressive influence of one civilisation on another, over time, can also be observed in the artefacts recovered through archaeological excavations. One such artefact discovered is of the mythical creature Griffin, which has the body of a lion and head and wings of an eagle. The Griffin is first known from the arts of Babylon and next, around 6th century BCE, depicted in the artwork of ancient Persia such as the sculptor in Persepolis and Bronze Griffin in Susa. Griffin-headed gold rhytons (drinking containers) have been excavated from Achaemenid sites of ancient Persia.[430] Finally, this artwork became popular in other parts of the ancient world including Scythia, Macedonia and Greece.

There has been a sharing of literary-mythical ideas as well among the civilisations. The Phoenix is an interesting mythical bird in Greek mythology. When it dies it bursts into flames and turns into ashes. But it cyclically regenerates rising from the ashes of its dead predecessor. This bird was adopted by the Greeks from the Bennu bird of Egyptian mythology.

---

[428] Gutas, Dmitri, 1998, p. 33-46.
[429] Rosenthal, Franz, 1967, p. 113-114.
[430] Curtis and Tallis, 2005.

List of Early Sufi Scholars and Orders

9th Century   Al-Fudayl, Shafiq Falkhi, Ma'ruf al-Karkhi, Bashr ibn al-Harith, Abu Bakr al-Shibli, Ahmad ibn Harb, al-Harith ibn Asad al-Muhasibi, Hatim al-Asamm, Dhu al-Nun al-Misri, Ahmad ibn Khudriyyah, Abu Yazid al-Bastami, Sahl ibn Abdullah al-Tustari, Abu Abdullah al-Tirmidhi

10th Century   Ibrahim al-Khawwas, Abu Hasan al-Nuri, Abu al-Qasim al-Junayd, Amr ibn Uthman, al-Hallaj, Samnun, al-Rudhbari, Ibn Khafif, Abu Nasr al-Sarraj, Abu Bakr al-Kalabadhi, Abu Talib al-Makki

11th Century   Abu Abd al-Rahman al-Sulami, Abu al-Hasan al-Kharqani, Abu Nu'aym al-Isfahani, Abu Sa'id ibn Abi al-Khayr, Abu al-Qasim al-Qushayri, Abu al-Qasim al-Gurgani, Abu al-Ali al-Farmadhi al-Tusi, Abdullah al-Ansari, Ali al-Hujwiri, Abu Bakr al-Nassaj.

12th Century   Abd al-Qadir al-Jilani, Yusuf al-Hamdani, Ahmad al-Yasawi, Abu Madyan Shu'ayb, Ibn al-Kizani, Abu Najib al-Suhrawardi, Ahmad al-Rifa'i

13th Century   Ibn al-Farabi, Ibn al-Farid, Jalal al-Din al-Rumi, Hafiz

The 12th century saw the establishment of the following Sufi orders:

Sufi Order	Founder
Naqshabandi	Yusuf al-Hamdani
Qadiriyyah	Abd al-Qadir al-Jilani
Yasawiyyah	Ahmad al-Yasawi
Kinziyyah	Ibn al-Kizani
Suhrawardi	Abu Najib al-Suhrawardi
Rifa'iyyah	Ahmad al-Rifa'i
Shadhiliyyah	Abu Madyan Shu'ayb

Farabian Metaphysics

In Farabian metaphysical theory, the Neoplatonic Plotinus emanation postulation that the world and the universe were created in a step by step emanation from God replaces the *ex nihilo* (out of nothing) creation by God. These emanations originating from God can be considered as similar to the light that emanates from the sun. The following are the stages of emanation in the Farabian Model:

- At the top of this hierarchy is the, apparently remote, Divine Being (God) whom al-Farabi characterises as 'the First'.

- From It emanates a second being which is the First Intellect. (This is termed, logically, 'the Second', that is, the second being.) Like God, this being is of an immaterial substance.

- This second being comprehends God and, in consequence of that comprehension, produces a third being, which is the Second Intellect. The second being also comprehends its own essence, and the result of this comprehension is the production of the body and soul of *al-sama al-ula*, the First Heaven.

A total of ten such intellects emanate in stages. Of particular significance in the emanation hierarchy is the last or the Tenth Intellect. This is the 'intellect' which constitutes the real bridge between the heavenly and terrestrial worlds. This Tenth Intellect (called the *nous poiétikos* in Greek, the *aql al-fa'al* in Arabic, the *dator formarum* in Latin and the 'active or agent intellect' in English) was responsible for both emanating the sublunary world including the 'form' of the man and for actualising the potentiality for thought in man's intellect.

Ibn Sina's Elaboration of the Farabian Prophet Model

Al-Farabi believed that the ideal state is ruled by a prophet-imam. He considered Madinah of the Prophet Muhammad as the best example of an ideal state. Ibn Sina elaborates the Farabian model of prophethood and postulates a four level model: the intellectual, the inspired-cognitive, the miraculous-revelatory and the socio-political-legal levels.[431] These are the level or qualities that a man needs to possess to be a prophet.

Intellectual Level: In the intellectual level Ibn Sina states that people differ vastly with regard to their intuitive powers both in quality and quantity, and while some men are almost devoid of it, others possess it in a high degree. So, there must be a rare exceptionally endowed man who has a total contact with reality. Such a man by his very nature can become the repository of truth.

Inspired-Cognitive Level: By his quality of exceptionally strong intuitive cognisance such a man transforms the purely intellectual truths and concepts into lifelike images and symbols so potent that anyone who hears or reads these images not only comes to believe in them but is impelled to action.

The Miraculous-Revelatory Level: People are impelled to

---

[431] Sharif, M. M., 2016, p. 500-501.

action not just by the purely intellectual insight and inspiration but also by revelations of the prophet, which may be technically symbolic. The revelations for the most part can be interpreted as required to elicit the higher spiritual truth.

The Socio-Political or Legal Levels: The prophet's revelations to be of use to people need laws and social structures. The prophet, therefore, has to be a lawgiver and a statesman par excellence.[432]

Al-Ghazali refutes many of these metaphysical postulations and considers them conjectures.

---

[432] Sharif, M. M., 2016, p. 500-501.

The Twenty Points of Refutation
in *Tahafut al-Falasifah*

Al-Ghazali refuted the Ibn Sinan metaphysical model. Ibn Sina was the most evolved philosopher of his age and thus the principal representative of philosophy. The twenty points that al-Ghazali refuted in his *Tahafut al-Falasifah* are as follows:

1. On refuting their (philosophers) doctrine of the world's pre-eternity.

2. On refuting their doctrine of post-eternity of the world, time and motion.

3. On showing their obfuscation in saying that God is the world's enactor and maker.

4. On showing the inability of philosophers to prove the existence of the Maker of the world.

5. On showing the inability of philosophers to prove that God is one.

6. The philosopher's doctrine of denying the existence of God's attributes.

7. On refutation of their statement 'The essence of the First is not divisible into genus and species'.

8. On refutation of their statement 'The First is simple existent without quiddity'.

9. Their inability to demonstrate that the First is not a body.

10. Discussing their materialist doctrine necessitates a denial of the maker.

11. Their inability to show that the First knows others.

12. Their inability to show that the First knows Himself.

13. On refuting that the First does not know the particulars.

14. On refuting their doctrine that states 'the heavens are an animal that moves on its own volition'.

15. On refuting what they say regarding the reason that the heavens move.

16. On refuting their doctrine that the souls of heavens that know the particulars.

17. On refuting their doctrine that disruption of causality is impossible.

18. On their inability to sustain a rational demonstration (proving) that the human soul is a self-subsistent spiritual substance.

19. On refuting their statement that it is impossible for human souls to undergo annihilation.

20. On refuting their denial of bodily resurrection and the accompanying pleasures of Paradise or the pains of Hellfire.

Latter Muslim Empires

After the Tri-Military devastations, the Muslims again rebuilt huge empires—The Ottoman, the Moghul and the Safavid. These empires flourished parallel in time with the rise of Europe. These were great empires and well advanced relative to other regions of their time period. But unlike Europe they never quite took to science and social science disciplines. As they stagnated in these disciplines, Europe caught up and surpassed them.

The Ottomans

In 1288, Othman, the founder of the Ottoman dynasty, became the chief of a fiefdom in Asia Minor. This fiefdom showed exponential growth. By 15th and 16th centuries they ruled over the greatest empire in the world stretching from Persia on the east to North Africa on the west as well as a sizable part of Eastern Europe. Their European conquests included Bulgaria in 1396, Byzantium (Constantinople) in 1453 and Greece in 1456. Serbia in 1459, Bosnia in 1462, Albania in 1468 and Herzegovina in 1481. With the fall of Constantinople came the end of the last vestige of the Roman Empire. The Ottomans accomplished everything in a grand manner, be it building palaces and roads or be it going to war. They were the first in Europe to have a permanent military band music-corp called the *Mehterhane*.

In the history of empires, the Ottomans were one of the greatest. They are the longest ruling dynastic family in the history of the world. All through the centuries their successes, their domains, their cities all appeared otherworldly which dumbfounded both friends and foes. Their ceremonies were more lavish than the Romans, their dignity higher than the Persians, and wealth greater then all. More than thirty nations were incorporated into this empire. As in other Muslim empires there was no great missionary impulse and administration was collaborative. Their dignitaries, officers and troops to a significant extent were Balkan Slavs. Many of their merchants were Armenian and sailors Greek.

Ottoman Education

The education system of the Ottomans can be divided into three stages based on three periods:

1. Stage one, during the early Ottoman period in which multi-discipline education thrived.

2. Stage two, during the middle Ottoman period in which education regressed.

3. Stage three, during the late Ottoman period in which reformations were made to re-introduce the sciences.

In **stage one**, a large number of madrasahs were established. They developed into the *kulliyyah* which constituted of a mosque surrounded by complex of madrasahs and other amenities. The Fatih *kulliyyah*, for example, consisted of the Fatih Mosque surrounded by eight high madrasahs, followed by eight small madrasahs along with a primary *kuttab*, hospital, library and kitchen for students and staff.[433]

The majority of Ottoman scholars from the 14th to the 16th century developed under the al-Ghazali and al-Razi schools of thought. The subjects taught besides the ulemaic disciplines included grammar, syntax, logic, rhetoric, geometry, astronomy, philosophy and mathematics.[434] The syllabus for madrasah drawn by the great Ottoman scholar Tashkopruluzade Ahmad (1495-1561) included the following:[435]

1. The calligraphic disciplines: writing implements, styles of writing, *etc.*

2. The oral disciplines: the Arabic language and phonetics, lexicography, etymology, grammar and syntax, rhetoric, prosody, poetry, composition, history and other literary subjects

3. The intellectual subjects: logic and dialectic

4. The spiritual sciences:

    a. The theoretical rational sciences: general theology, natural sciences, mathematics

    b. The practical rational sciences: ethics, political science

        i. The theoretical religious disciplines

        ii. The practical religious disciplines

In the 14th century, the *Sharh al-Aqa'id* by al-Taftazani was one of the standard theological texts of the madrasahs. Three quarters of it was dedicated to systematic metaphysics and the rest dedicated to prophethood, revelations, *etc.* In addition, algebra, geometry, astronomy and classical physics, study of astrolabe,

---

[433] Hossain, M. Amjad, 2013, p. 190.
[434] *Ibid.*, p. 191.
[435] *Ibid.*, p. 194.

mechanics were also taught.[436] Thus, there was more or less a balance in the Total Knowledge and the Ottomans started off correctly and had the best centralised education system of their time. Both Ibn Taymiyyah and Sufi discourses were absent in the general curriculum. Sufis were generally present in khanqah lodges. The khanqah and madrasah had different forms of education.[437]

There was, however, a sense of overconfidence in the intellectual sphere. The Muslims had overcome the Mongol debacle mainly by plain intellectual superiority. Where the sword had failed, the pen had prevailed. Europe had still not scientifically progressed beyond the Muslims and significant part of their lands was under the rule of the Ottomans. This overconfidence caused some indolence in the intellectual fields.

In the **second stage** of Ottoman education, from the 16th century onwards, the academic environment faced a crisis due to socio-political reasons. While the Ottomans remained the political superpower, Europe became an investigative power. They had inherited the passion for science from the early Muslims. They investigated the sciences, their explorers investigated the world, their business people started to investigate trade the world over.

The Ottomans were connected by land to the major continents and so, even though they did develop a formidable navy, the age old pattern of doing business by land was adequate for them. Europe, on the other hand, was hemmed in by the Ottomans and did not have appropriate land connection to Asia or Africa. They had to investigate and develop alternate sea routes to reach their business destinations. All their investigations kept improving their knowledge and especially their sciences and technology. When industrialisation came to Europe, they mass

---

[436] Hossain, M. Amjad, 2013, p. 200-201.
[437] WR8.

produced commodity and advanced weaponry like never before. The Ottomans from that period onwards were no match for other European powers.

In this stage, science and social sciences stagnated and, in fact, regressed among the Muslims. The passion for knowledge was gone and had been replaced by scholars and students whose only aim of education was to be able to earn sufficiently. Consequently, there was a lowering of intellectual standards. The issue of falling education was realised among the Ottomans quite early. Tashkopruluzade had criticised the declining popularity of mathematics and the falling standards of scholastic theology.[438] The scholars considered themselves as learned after reading a few 'handbooks'. Their interest in the ulemaic disciplines, theology and the sciences dwindled while poetry, composition, anecdotes and acquisition of quick fame became paramount.[439]

Another 16th century scholar, Gelibolulu Mustafa Ali Efendi stated that there was a lack of interest in scholarly studies, a decline in the writing of scholarly works, nepotism amongst senior scholars, bribes in the educational profession and there was no real differentiation between real scholars and charlatans masquerading as scholars.[440] While the Ottomans had spent considerably in setting up a network of schools throughout their empire, the sponsorship and incentive for high level or tertiary sciences at this point of history was negligible.

Scientists faced hindrance from another quarter. These were conservative religious circles who were against science. Their view was based on no Islamic principles and, in fact, against the principles of the early Muslims. There was a ban on research of jurisprudence known as 'closing the gates of *ijtihad*' from the time

---

[438] Robinson, Francis, 1997, p. 151-159.
[439] Inalcik, Halil, 1973, p. 179.
[440] Hossain, M. Amjad, 2013, p. 204.

of the latter Abbasids. It seems to have continued to this period and more so because the ban apparently was extended across to other disciplines.

There developed a superstitious ill-will towards the sciences. The 16th century scholar Takiyyuddin Mehmed (Taqi al-Din Muhammad ibn Ma'ruf, d. 1578) built an astronomical clock and observatory which matched the most advanced observatory in Europe that of Tycho Brahe. The local 'scholars' decided it was blasphemous. When there was an outbreak of plague, they considered that a bad omen and used it as an excuse to destroy the observatory. In the vacuum created by the absence of intellectualism, superstition gathered strength.

Seventeenth-century scholars Katib Chelebi and Koci Bey wrote that the rational and physical sciences were being taught but were losing prominence.[441] Katib Chelebi wrote, 'But many intelligent people remained as inert as rocks, frozen in blind imitation of the ancients. Without deliberation, they rejected and repudiated the new sciences. They passed for learned men, while all the time they were ignoramuses, fond of disparaging what they called the "philosophical sciences" and knowing nothing of earth or sky. The admonition (in the Qur'an) "*Have they not contemplated the kingdom of heaven and Earth?*" made no impression on them; they thought "*contemplating the world and the firmament*" meant staring at them like cows.'

In the early 18th century, the Shayk al-Islam declared in a fatwah that it was illegal to keep books on astronomy, history or philosophy and such books were confiscated.[442] Possibly, in the confused aftermath of the Tri-Military Events, al-Ghazali's previous critique on some of the speculative metaphysical concepts was extended to all of sciences and philosophy

---

[441] Hossain, M. Amjad, 2013, p. 203.
[442] Inalcik, Halil, 1973, p. 179-181.

irrespective of the fact that he had actually supported the sciences. Such attitude not only stopped the advancement of rational sciences but also blocked it from coming from Europe.

Around the 10th century, the conservative scholars of Europe had unsuccessfully tried to block the sciences of the Muslim world from entering Europe. But they had failed and the sciences made its way to Europe. In the 17th and 18th century the conservative Muslim scholars were more successfully in blocking the rise of the sciences again in the Muslim domains.

The development of paper by the early Abbasid had led the Muslim to mass produce books. Similarly, the printing press enabled Europe to mass produce at an even greater rate. Ironically, printing technology was available in Istanbul from 1493 but the printing industry only got started in 1726.[443] Whereas, Europeans had inherited the paper industry from the Muslims, the Muslims, for a considerable period, failed to accept the printing industry.

Comparatively, in the 18th century, Europe had advanced and become remarkably imposing. Mass produced industrial goods from France and Britain were much cheaper than the traditional handcrafted goods of the Ottomans. These European goods flooded the Ottoman markets. As the Ottoman business failed their economy also failed. They had to take loans from Europe and, ultimately, they became indebted to Europe. The Europeans started to produce very advanced weapons which left the Ottomans vulnerable. The Ottomans were gradually losing lands, in fact countries after countries, to the European expansion.

In the **third stage** of Ottoman rule, starting from the early 19th century, technological and social regression became very apparent in the empire. Several sultans attempted important reforms. Selim III (1761-1808), for instance, initiated reforms in

---

[443] Hossain, M. Amjad, 2013, p. 205.

taxation, commerce and the military. But internal resistance, including that from the now-decadent Janissary military, made administrative changes almost impossible. He was finally assassinated.

The biggest of these attempted reformations was the *Tanzimat* meaning 'Regulation' that started in 1839 following the accession of the reformist Sultan Abd al-Mazid (Abdul Mecid). It was aimed at remodelling the economy, administration, armed forces, and the legal and educational systems so that the Ottomans could be at par with the Europeans. But opposition to the reformation cropped up from within the sultanate by the laidback segments whose personal interests would be affected by the changes to the *status quo*.

The reformers tried to adapt the state model more along the European line. Turkish students were sent to London, Paris and Vienna to receive higher education. A medical school with French doctors was set up in Istanbul. But the root issue—scientific research and development that would have given the Ottomans themselves the ability to progressively improve their agriculture, industry and military, instead of depending on Europe—was not sufficiently incorporated.

Industries set up by borrowing or buying European technology would eventually lag behind due to the absence of local scientific 'research and development' that was required to progressively improve technology and retain competitive advantage. Every time such an institution was set up, in a short time it would become outdated compared to the constantly progressing European ones. Lagging behind in industry had a negative effect on the economy. To meet their budget deficit the Sultans had to further borrow money from Europe. But they had to pay huge interest that further drained their economy. The Muslim economy opened up to the economic exploitation of interest and that would be another major factor to its ruin and downfall.

In 1861, Abd al-Mazid abdicated and his successor, Abu al-Aziz, was less interested in or incapable of carrying out the reformations. The laidback agricultural system was unable to feed the huge Ottoman population. The European economic and financial penetration into the Ottoman system began on a massive scale. The Ottoman industry was mainly of a pre-mechanised craft-based age. Unable to compete with machine industry many of these local craft-based industries were ruined.

In 1874, the Ottoman's state debt, largely to foreign banks, increased to an extent that there was a financial collapse. In 1876, Sultan Abd al-Aziz ended the *Tanzimat* with the cancellation of the Ottoman constitution. The reformation mostly failed to achieve its goals. The main beneficiary of the reformation was the military, which was modernised not by local development of military wares but mostly by buying from Europe at huge expense.

The end of the Ottomans and the Caliphate came after the First World War at the start of the 20th century. The final disintegration of the empire took place at the hands of European imperialism. But that was just the surgical tool that took the Ottomans apart. The real cause was the lack of academic, technological and industrial modernisation.

Safavids

The 16th century also saw the rise of two other great empires, the Safavids of Persia and the Moghuls of India. The rise and fall of these two empires were amazingly interwoven in time and space.

The Safavids were very cultural minded. Shah Tahmasp was a painter and Shah Isma'il was a great poet using themes and images in original lyric and didactic religious poetry. They were builders of exquisite palaces, mosques and other edifices with fine workmanship on beautiful tiles. If the Ottomans had a streak of grandiose, the Safavid creations had the sense of intricate beauty. They were great patrons of the arts and culture. Artists, poets, commerce and religion flourished.

But by their time the scientific spirit of the Muslims had been destroyed and deserted. Thus, they had never really embarked on advanced science and technology. After losses to Ottomans in the 16th century they started making rifles and later on ships, but this was with European help.[444] The Safavid dynasty ruled up to 1730 when a Persian military genius named Nadir Shah declared himself the king of Persia usurping the crown.

Moghuls

Many historical edifices of India, most of them grand in global scale, are of Moghul origin. The Moghuls established the greatest empire that India had ever seen. They were great builders of cities, palaces of unique architecture, and beautiful artistic gardens with fountains and flowing streams which still survive today. The most famous of their edifices is one of the wonders of the world—the Taj Mahal. Besides India, some of their edifices can also be found in Pakistan, Bangladesh and Afghanistan. The Moghuls were very literate and cultured, and patrons of fine arts delving deep in poetry, painting, perfumery, classical songs and choreography.

Besides enduring architecture, arts and culinary delights, the Moghuls have left behind a unified 'Indian' political identity. Before them the subcontinent was a milieu of culturally and religiously diverse kingdoms. It was the Moghuls, starting with Akbar, who had consolidated the concept of an Indian political entity representing the whole of India. They also did try to establish science. Humayun, the second emperor, after stabilising the empire the first thing he did was to establish an observatory in

---

[444] WR6.

his capital—Delhi. They were the most scientifically advanced people of India at their time. Humayun died as he fell while climbing down the stairs of the observatory.

Akbar the Great, the third Moghul emperor, collected a group of remarkable scholars and talents in his court. They are known as the *nau ratan* or the Nine Jewels and are famous as nine intellectually and artistically endowed personalities. This group included economists and astronomers as well as literary and cultural talents. The calendar developed at Akbar's behest is still in use in India and Bangladesh. Such court patronisation of talents in social science, astronomy, music, poetry and fine arts continued throughout the dynasty.

But, like the Safavids, by the time they were established as an empire the scientific age of the Muslims was over. The scientific network of all the Muslim domains had been destroyed. Without any science the same 'popular religion' of other regions dominated the intellectual sphere. There was a massive imbalance in the Total Knowledge paradigm. So, the Moghuls too remained behind the European powers in science and technology.

Nadir Shah, who carved a huge empire extending from what is now Armenia to Pakistan, would also attack Moghul India, sack its capital Delhi and break the economic backbone of the Moghuls. The weakened Moghuls would never recover and ultimately would be conquered by the British Empire in the 18th century.

Note on Books

Note 1: *The House of Wisdom—How the Arabs Transformed Western Civilisation* by Jonathan Lyons: Editor and foreign correspondent for Reuters for more than twenty years. Researcher at the Global Research Center and PhD candidate in the sociology of religion, Monash University in Melbourne, Australia.

Note 2: The *Medieval Muslim Thinkers and Scientist* by Hakim Mohammed Said is one of the first books in modern times about early Muslim scholars based on original research. It comprises very informative biographies and achievements of 26 Muslim scholars. The board of editors for the book consists of:

Dr M.A. Kazi	Adviser to the President of Pakistan on Science and Technology
Hakim Mohammed Said	President Hamdard Foundation, Pakistan
Dr Z.Z. Hashmi	Senior Scientist, National Science Council of Pakistan
Dr Raziuddin Siddique	Secretary General, Pakistan Academy of Sciences

385

Dr S.M.A. Shah   National Science Council of
                                        Pakistan

Hakim Naimuddin Zubairi   Director of Research
                                        (Academic)Hamdard Foundation
                                        Pakistan.

Note 3: *A History of Muslim Philosophy* is not only a masterpiece but an essential classic masterpiece. It also has short accounts of other disciplines and efforts at modern renaissance in Muslims lands. Edited by M. M. Sharif, a large number of scholars contributed to this masterpiece on pre-Islamic and Islamic philosophy. The committee of Directors include:

Serajul Haque   Professor and Chairman, Department of
                                        Arabic and Islamic Studies, University of
                                        Dhaka.

M. Abdul Hye   Vice-Principal, Government College,
                                        Rajshahi.

M. Ahmed   Vice Chancellor, Rajshahi University

Mumtaj Hasan   Secretary Finance, Government of
                                        Pakistan.

Chairman: I. I. Kazi   Vice Chancellor, University of Sind.

The multi-volume book was first published in 1963 by the Pakistan Philosophical Congress, and the latest edition was published in 2016 by Islamic Book Trust, Malaysia.

Note 4: *Al-Fihrist* written in 987 by Abu al-Faraj Muhammad ibn Ishaq al-Nadim, a scholar and book dealer, was an index of the sciences that was in the curricula of Islamic institutions. It contained sixty thousand topics on all the subjects found across the bookshops and libraries of the caliphate.

Note 5: *A Social History of Education in the Muslim World: From the Prophetic Era to Ottoman Times* by Amjad M. Hussain, a senior lecturer of Islamic Studies and Religious Studies at the University of Wales, Trinity Saint David. It provides a comprehensive view of education and society of the past Muslim world.

Note 6: *History of Islam, Vol 1 & 2* by Professor Masudul Hasan contains a wealth of information on topics relevant to Islamic history. He has also written other extensive works about the four Rashidun Caliphs.

References

Afzal, Ahmed, 1996. "Qur'an and Human Evolution" in the *Qur'anic Horizons*, 1:3, The Qur'an Academy, Lahore.

Agoston, Gábor and Masters, Bruce Alan, 2009. *Encyclopaedia of the Ottoman Empire*, Infobase Publishing, New York.

Ahmad, K. Jamil, 1984. *Hundred Great Muslims*, Ferojsons Limited, Lahore.

Ahmed, Absar, 1996 Religion and Science (editorial), *The Qur'anic Horizons* 1:3, The Qur'an Academy, Lahore.

Ahmed, Moinuddin, 1992. *The Urgency of Ijtihad*, Kitab Bhavan, New Delhi.

Al Mubarakpuri, Shaykh Saifur Rahman, 2003. Tafsīr Ibn Kathir. Abridged (by Al Mubarakpuri et.al), Second Edition, Vol. 2, p.411, Darrusalam, Riyadh.

Al Hassani, Salim T.S., 2007. *1001 Inventions Muslim Heritage in Our World*, Foundation for Science Technology and Civilisation. UK.

Ali, Jamil, 1967. *Al-Biruni the Determination of the Coordinates of Cities: Al-Biruni's Tahid Al-Amakin* trans. and ed. Jamil Ali, Centennial Publications, Beirut.

Arabi, Oussama, 2001. *Studies in Modern Islamic Law and Jurisprudence,* Springer, Netherlands.

Atiya, Aziz S., 1962. *Crusade, Commerce and Culture,* Indiana University Press, Bloomington.

Bennett, Clinton, 2012. *The Bloomsbury Companion to Islamic Studies,* Bloomsbury Academic.

Berggren, J.J., 2003. *Episodes in the Mathematics of Medieval Islam,* Springer-Verlag, New York.

Berkey, Jonathan P. 2001, *Popular Preaching and Religious Authority in Medieval Islamic Near East,* University of Washington Press, Seattle.

Bhowmik, Rita, 2002: *Chotoder Begum Rokeya,* Meera Prokason (Publications), Dhaka, Bangladesh.

Bucaille, Maurice, 1995. *The Bible, the Qur'an and Science.* Translated from French *'La Bilble, le Coran et la Science'* by A. D. Pannell and author, Millat Book Centre, New Delhi.

Burnett, Charles, 2001. "The Coherence of the Arabic-Latin Translation Program in Toledo in the Twelfth Century," *Science in Context,* 14 (2001): at 249-288.

_____, 1998. *Adelard of Bath, Conversations with His Nephew: On the Same and Different, Questions on Natural Science and on Birds,* trans. and ed. Charles Burnett, Cambridge University Press, Cambridge.

_____, 1997. *The Introduction of Arabic Learning into England,* British Library, London.

Casulleras, Josep, 2007. "Banu Musa". In: Thomas Hockey et al. *The Biographical Encyclopedia of Astronomers,* Springer, New York.

Cooperson, Michael, 2005. *Al Mamun,* OneWorld, Oxford.

Cosma, Sorinel, 2009. *Ibn Khaldun's Economic Thinking*-Ovidius University Annals of Economics (Ovidius University Press) XIV: 52-57, Ovidius University Press, Romania.

Coulson, N.J., 2011. *A History of Islam.* Transaction Publishers, New Jersey.

Curtis, J. and Tallis, N., 2005. *Forgotten Empire—The World of Ancient Persians,* University of California Press with the British Museum. USA.

D'Alverny, Marie-Therese, 1982. Translations and Translators: *In Renaissance and Renewal in the Twelfth Century,* ed. Robert L. Benson and Giles Constable, Harvard University Press, Cambridge, Massachusetts.

Dame, Frederic William, 2013. *The Muslim Discovery of America,* BoD Book in Demand.

Danner, Victor, 1985. *Islamic Spirituality.* Ed. Seyyed Hossein Nasr, SCM Press, London.

Das Gupta, S.N., 1975, "Philosophy", in: *A Cultural History of India,* Editor A. L. Basham, Clarendon Press, Oxford.

Dodge, Bayard, 1970. *The Fihrist of Al-Nadim,* translated and ed. Bayard Dodge, Columbia University Press, New York.

Draper, John William, 1875. *History of the Conflict Between Religion and Science,* Henry S. King & Co., London.

————, 1864. *The Intellectual Development of Europe,* Vol. II, p. 42., Harper Brothers Publishers, New York .

Dunlop D.M., 1971. *Arab Civilisation 800-1500 A.D.,* Longman Group Ltd., UK.

Eidelberg, Shlomo, 1977. "The Chronicle of Solomon Bar Simson". In: *The Jews and the Crusaders: Chronicle of the First and Second Crusades.* Trans and ed. Shlomo Eidelberg, University of Wisconsin Press, Madison.

Enan, Mohammad Abdullah, 2007. *Ibn Khaldun His Life and Works,* The Other Press, Kuala Lumpur.

Fakhry, Majid, 1983. *A History of Islamic Philosophy* (second edition), Columbia University Press, New York.

Farmer, Henry George, 1932. "The Influence of Al-Farabi's 'Ihsa al-ulum' ("De scientiis") on the Writers on Music in Western Europe". In: *The Journal of the Royal Asiatic Society of Great Britain and Ireland* No. 3 (Jul., 1932). pp. 561-592. Cambridge University Press.

Field, Claude, 1909. *The Confessions of Al-Ghazzali* (English translation of Al Munqidh), London.

Gernet, Jacques, 1996. *A History of Chinese Civilisation,* The Press Syndicate of the University of Cambridge, Cambridge, UK.

Gingerich, Owen, 1986. *Islamic Astronomy, Scientific American,* v.254, April 1986, p.74.

Goldstein, Bernard R., 1967. *Ibn Al-Muthanna's Commentary on the Astronomical Tables of Al-Khwarizmi,* trans. and ed. Bernard R. Goldstein, Yale University Press, New Haven.

Grant, Edward, 1974. *A Source Book in Medieval Science,* Harvard University Press, Cambridge.

Grohmann, A., 1952. *From the World of Arabic Papyri,* Royal Society of Historical Studies, Al Maaref Press, Cairo.

Gutas, Dimitri, 1998. *Greek Thought, Arabic Culture: The Graeco-Arabic Translation Movement in Baghdad and Early Abbasid Society,* Routledge, London.

Hamid, Khawaja Abdul, 1946. *Ibn Maskawaih—A Study of his al-Fauz al-Asghar,* Shaikh Muhammad Ashraf Publisher, Lahore.

Hamidullah, Dr. Muhammad, 2004. *The Emergence of Islam,* Translated into English by Afzal Iqbal, Islamic Research

Institute, Islamabad.

_____, 1997. *Khutbat-e-Bahawalpur* (*Essays of Bahawalpur*). Idara Tahqeeqat-e-Islami, Lahore.

_____, 1993. *The Emergence of Islam, Lectures on the Development of Islamic world-view, Intellectual Tradition and Polity* (Islamabad: Islamic Research Institute, 1993), quoted in Dr. Muzaffar Iqbal's paper, op.cit, pp.39-42.

Hanifi, M. Jamil, 1974. *Islam and Transformation of Culture,* Asia Publishing House, New Delhi.

Harding, Karen, 1993. *Causality Then and Now: Al-Ghazali and Quantum Theory,* American Journal of Islamic Social Sciences 1 (2): 165-177.

Hasan, Masudul, 2004. *History of Islam, Vol. I,* Revised edition. Adam Publishers, New Delhi.

Hasan, Masudul, 1998. *History of Islam, Vol. 2,* Islamic Publications, Lahore.

Herlihy, John, 1999. *Modern Man at the Crossroads: The search for the knowledge of first origins and final ends,* Suhail Academy, Lahore.

Hillenbrand, Carole, 1999. *The Crusades: Islamic Perspective,* Fitzroy Dearborn, Chicago.

Holt, P. M. et al., 1970. *The Cambridge History of Islam*: Volume 2B, Islamic Society and Civilisation, (Edited by P. M. Holt, Peter Malcolm Holt, Ann K. S. Lambton, Bernard Lewis), Cambridge University Press.

Hossain, M. Amjad, 2013. *A Social History of Education in the Muslim World,* Ta Ha Publishers Ltd, London, UK.

Ibn Al-Qalanisi, 1998. *The Damascus Chronicle of the Crusades,* Cambridge University Press, Cambridge.

Inalcik, Halil, 1973. *The Ottoman Empire, the classical age 1300-1600,* Weidenfeld and Nicholson, London.

Iqbal, M., 1974. *The Reconstruction of Religious Thought in Islam,* Kitab Bhavan, Darya Ganj, New Delhi.

Iqbal, Muzaffar, 2009. *The Making of Islamic Sciences,* Islamic Book Trust, Kuala Lumpur.

_____, 2007. *Science and Islam* (The Greenwood Guides to Science and Religion Series), Greenwood Publishing Group, Westport.

_____, 2000. *Biological Origins: Traditional and Contemporary Perspectives,* Paper presented at the International conference on God, Life and Cosmos: Theistic Perspectives, November 6-9, 2000, Islamabad, p.33.

Izutsu, Toshihiko, 2001. *The Concept of Belief in Islamic Theology,* Islamic Book Trust, Kuala Lumpur.

Jafri, Maqsood, 2003. *The Gleam of Wisdom,* Sigma Press, Islamabad.

Kadri, Sadakat, 2012. *Heaven on Earth: A Journey through Shari'a Law from the Deserts of Ancient Arabia to the Streets of the Modern Muslim World,* Farrar, Straus and Giroux, New York.

Khan, Mohammad Muhsin, 1984. *Ṣaḥīḥ Al-Bukhari—The Translation and Meaning of Ṣaḥīḥ Al-Bukhari* (Kitab al Ilm), Chpt 36, No. 101, Vol 1., Kitab Bhavan, New Delhi.

Khan, Wahiduddin, 1999. *God Arising, Evidence of God in Nature and in Science,* Goodword Books, New Delhi.

King, Charles, 1994. Leonardo Fibonacci. In: *From Five Fingers to Infinity: A Journey Through the History of Mathematics,* ed. Frank J. Swetz, Open Court, Chicago.

Khawaja, A.A., 2002. *Maulana Ashraf Ali Thanvi—His views on Moral Philosophy and Tasawwuf,* Adam Publishers and

Distributors, Delhi.

Khudabakhsh, S and Margoliouth, D.S., 1996. *The Renaissance of Islam*. (Translation of *Renaissance des Islam*, 1922, by Adam Nez), Bangladesh co-operative Book Society, Chittagong.

Koelliker, Lee A., 2011. *History Research*, December 2011, Vol. 1, No. 1, p.40, David Publishing Company, NY.

Koutsoukis, A.J., 1990. *Ancient Egypt Mesopotamia and Persia*, Longman Cheshire, Melbourne.

Lane, Rose Wilder, 1943. *The Discovery of Freedom—Man's Struggle Against Authority*, John Day Company, New York.

Lapidus, Ira M., 2002. *A History of Islamic Societies*, Cambridge University Press, Cambridge, UK.

————, 1975. The Separation of State and Religion in the Development of Early Islamic Society, *International Journal of Middle East Studies*, 6 (4), pp.363-385.

Lee, A. Koelliker, 2011. *The Mihna: Ma'mun's Inquisition for Supremacy*, History Research, ISSN 2159-550X, December 2011, Vol. 1, No. 1, pp.35-46.

Lunde, Paul & Caroline, Stone, 1989. *The Meadows of Gold*, by Al-Masudi. (Trans. and ed. Lunde and Stone), Kegan Paul, London.

Lyons, Jonathan, 2009. *The House of Wisdom—How the Arabs Transformed Western Civilisation*, Bloomsbury, London.

Makdisi, George, 1990. *The Rise of Humanism in Classical Islam and the Christian West*, Edinburg University Press, Edinburgh.

————, 1981. *The Rise of Colleges: Instituions of Learning in Islam and The West*, Edinburgh University Press, Edinburgh.

Macdonald, Duncan Black, 2008. *Development of Muslim Theology, Jurisprudence, and Constitutional Theory*, Chapter III, The

Lawbook Exchange Ltd., New Jersey.

Makdisi, John. A., 1999. *The Islamic Origin of the Common Law*, North Carolina Law Review, Vol. 77, No. 5, Article 2, pp. 1637-1738, University of North Carolina.

Marenbon, John, 1987. *Later Medieval Philosophy (1150-1350)*, Routledge and Kegan Paul, London.

Marmura, Michael E., 2007. *Al Ghazali—The Incoherence of the Philosophers*, Brigham Young University, Utah.

Menasce, P. J. de., 1948. *Arabische Philosophie*, A. Francke Verlag, Bern.

Meyerhof, Max, 1926. *New Light on Hunain ibn Ishaq and His Period*, ISIS 8, no. 4, p 690.

Mieli, Aldo, 1938. *La Science Arabe et son rôle dans L'evolution Scientifique Mondiale*, E.J. Brill, Leiden.

Montgomery, Watt W., 1961. *Islam and the Integration of Society*, Routledge and Kegan Paul, London.

Murray, H.J.R, 1985. *A History of Chess*, Benjamin Press. Northampton, Massachusetts.

Nadwi, Mohammad Akram, 2013. *Al-Muhaddithat: The Women Scholars in Islam*, Interface Publications, Oxford, UK.

Nasr, Seyyed Hossein, 1993. *The Need for a Sacred Science*, Suny Press, Albany, New York. p.156. In: John Herlihy's book *Modern Man at the Cross*roads (Lahore: Suhail Academy, 1999)

_____, (ed). 1987. *Traditional Islam in the Modern World*, KPI, Lahore.

Needham, Joseph, 1956. *Science and Civilisation in China*, Vol. 2, History of Scientific Thought, Cambridge University Press, 1956, p. 185.

Patton, W. M., 1897. *Ahmed Ibn Hanbal and the Mihna,* Ruprecht Karls Universitat of Heidelberg: Librairie et Imprimerie.

Pedersen, Johannes, 1984. *The Arabic Book.* Trans. Geoffrey French, Princeton University Press, New Jersey.

Rathor, Iftikhar Al-Din Tariq, 1985. *Islam aur Sains,* Ilmi Kitab Khana, Lahore.

Robinson, Francis, 1997. Ottoman-Safavid-Mughals, *Journal of Islamic Studies,* Vol.3, April 2009, pp.151-159.

Rosenthal, Franz, 1967. *Ibn Khaldun, The Muqaddimah: An Introduction to History* (Trans. and ed. by Rosenthal, Franz), Princeton Univeristy Press, New Jersey v. 3: pp. 113-114.

Russel, Bertrand, 1984. *Human Knowledge,* London.

Said, Hakim Mohammad, 1991. *Medieval Muslim Thinkers and Scientists,* Renaissance Publishing House, Delhi.

Salem, Semaan I. & Kumar, Alok, 1991. *Science in the Medieval World: Book of the Categories of Nations'* by Said Al Andalusi. (Trans. and ed. Salem, Semaan I. & Kumar, Alok), University of Texas Press, Austin.

Sass, Hans-Martin, 2005. Emergency Management in Public Health Ethics: Triage, Epidemics, Biomedical Terror and Warfare, *Eubios Journal of Asian and International Bioethics* 15, (September 2005).

Savage-Smith, Emilie, 1987. Celestial Mapping. In: *The History of Cartography,* vol. 2, bk. 1, Cartography in the Traditional Islamic and South Asian Societies, ed. J.B. Harley and David Woodward, University of Chicago Press, Chicago.

Sayili, Aydin, 1960. *The Observatory in Islam.* Turk Tarih Kurumu Basimevi, Ankara.

Scott, S.P., 1904. *History of the Moorish Empire in Europe,* London: J.B. Lippincott Company, vol. 3, p.598.

Sertima, Ivan Van, 1992. *The Golden Age of the Moor*, Transaction Publishers, New Jersey.

Sharif, M.M., 2016. *A History of Muslim Philosophy*. Vol 1. (Ed. Sharif, M.M.) Islamic Book Trust, Kuala Lumpur.

Sheed, F.J., 1942. *The Confession of St. Augustine* (Trans. Sheed, F.J.), Sheed and Ward, New York.

Shirazi, Imam Muhammad, 2013. *The Prophet Muhammad—A Mercy to the World*, Createspace Independent Pub.

Siddiqi, Habib Ahmad, 1988. *Musalman aur Sa'ins ki Tehqiq*, Mo'tamar al-Alam al-Islami, Karachi.

Siddiqi, Muhammad Zubayr, 1993. *Ḥadīth Literature*, The Islamic Texts Society, Cambridge.

Smith, Margaret, 1944. *Al-Ghazali: The Mystic*, Luzac & Company, London.

Stanton, Charles Michael, 1990. *Higher Learning in Islam*, Rowman and Little field, Maryland.

Sudhoff, Karl, 1926. *Essays in the History of Medicine*, Medical Life Press, New York.

Swanson, Mark N., 2003. The Christian Al-Mamun traditions. In: *Christians at the Heart of Islamic Rule*, (Ed. David Thomas), E.J. Brill, Leiden, Netherlands.

Tester, S.J., 1987. *A History of Western Astrology*, Boydell Press, Woodbridge, UK.

Thorndike, Lynn, 1955. *The True Place of Astrology in the History of Sciences*, Isis 46, no. 135, p. 277.

Verger, Jacques, 2003. Patterns. In: Ridder-Symoens, Hilde de (ed.): *A History of the University in Europe*. Vol. I: Universities in the Middle Ages, Cambridge University Press, pp.35 -76.

Walzer, Richard, 1946. *Al-Kindi, Metaphysics*, quoted in "Arabic

Transmission of Greek Thought to Medieval Europe." Bulletin of John Rylands Library 29 (1945-1946).

Weiss, Dieter, 1995. *Ibn Khaldun on Economic Transformation,* International Journal of Middle East Studies 27(1), pp. 29-37.

Whinfield, E.H. and Kazvini, Muhammad Mirza, 2010. *Flashes of Light.* (Translation of *Lawaih of Nur addin Abdur Rahman Jami*), Golden Elixir Press, Mountain View, CA.

Wiet, Gaston, 1937. *Les Pays* (Tranlation of *Kitab Al-Buldan* of Al-Yaqubi), L'Institit Francais d'Archeologie Orientale, Cairo.

Wood, Michael, 2007. *India,* Basic Books, New York.

Young, M.J.C and Serjeant, R.B., 1990. *Religion, Learning and Science in the Abbasid Period* (Ed. Young, M.J.C and Serjeant, R.B.), Cambridge University Press, United Kingdom.

Zaman, M.Q., 1997. *The Caliphs, the Ulama, and the Law: Defining the Role and Function of the Caliph in the Early 'Abbasid Period,* Islamic Law and Society, 4 (1), 1-36.

Web References

WR1:
http://plato.stanford.edu/entries/aristotle-natphil/#5 11/07/2016

WR2:
http://plato.stanford.edu/entries/ibn-sina-metaphysics/#CauCha (section 5.3) 11/07/2016

WR3:
Andalusian poetry: http://www.islamicspain.tv/Arts-and-Science/andalusi_poetry.htm Unity Productions Foundation, Potomac Falls, VA , USA 13/07/2106

WR4:
Davis, Frederick Hadland The Persian Mystic: Jami. p.61 https://bo

oks.google.com.au/books?id=3C-KqscmXGEC&pg=PA61&lpg=PA61&dq#v=onepage&q&f=false 26/01/2017.

WR5:
William Montgomery Watt (2004-04-14). "Al Biruni and the study of non-Islamic Religions". http://www.fravahr.org/spip.php?article31 12 /07/2016.

WR6:
Science and Technology By Cole Brandser. https://safavid project. wikispaces.com/Science+and+Technology 22/08/2016.

WR7:
The Book of Knowledge of the Ihiya Ulum Ad Din Book 1, section III. p.67 http://www.ghazali.org/works/bk1-sec-3.htm. 25/ 08/2016.

WR8:
Rethinking Islamic Education with Shaykh Abdal Hakim Murad https://www.youtube.com/watch?v=bI8y3Q_FpD4 24/01 /2017.

WR9:
Kak, Subhash. 2010. Pythagorean Triples and Crypto graphic Oklahoma State University, Stillwater. http://arxiv.org/ftp/arxiv/papers/1004/1004.3770.pdf 26/01/2017.

WR10:
http://Qur'an-only.com/ḥadīth-Were-NOT-Written-200-300-Years-Later.php 26/01/2017.

WR11:
https://books.google.com.au/books?id=kzADhC7J1hYC&pg=PR2&lpg=PR2&dq=Orientations+pour+un+dialogue+entre+chr%C3%A9tiens+et+musulmans&source=bl&ots=GUgFFMY_GR&sig=hoy5iBJIj WUTwj8qw38veyKV0HM&hl=en&sa=X&ved=0ahUKEwjHu67sm-3PAhXJW5QKHZLQA90Q6AEIWTAJ#v=onepage&q=Orientations

%20pour%20un%20dialogue%20entre%20chr%C3%A9tiens%20et%20musulmans&f=false 15/10/2016.

WR12:
The Muslim Influence on Philosophy—Murad, Abdal Hakim https://www.youtube.com/watch?v=P9gQi6KKw28 20/10/ 2016.

WR13:
http://ilaahimasjid.webs.com/culturescience.htm 25/10/ 2016.

WR14:
UNESCO—The Medina of Fez. http://whc.unesco.org/en/ list/170 10/10/2016.

WR15:
Guinness book of world records http://www.guinness worldrecord s.com/world-records/oldest-university 11/10/2016.

WR16:
The Secular and the Sacred in Higher Education with Shaykh Hamza Yusuf & Dr. John Sexton. https://www.youtube .com/watch?v=oQJnj fq_aMk 15/10/2016.

WR17:
Centre for Islamic Sciences. http://cis-ca.org/voices/b/ bucaille-mn.htm 17/10/2016.

WR18:
www.thefreelibrary.com/Fakhr+al-Din+al-Razi+on+physics+and+the+nature+of+the+physical+world%3a...-a012860 6463. 12/10/2016.

WR19:
Sardar, Ziauddin. 1998. "Science in Islamic philosophy", Islamic Philosophy, Routledge Encyclopaedia of Philosophy. http://www.mu slimphilosophy.com/ip/rep/H016.htm 26/01/2017.

WR20:

Yahya, Asim. Imam al-Ghazali verses Ibn Sina. https://www.youtube .com/watch?v=9QhDDjP-Rf4 5/02/2017.

WR21:

Yusuf, Hamza. https://www.youtube.com/watch?v= g6LU8SFVBSg9/ 09 /2017

WR 22:

Chaney, Eric (2016). Religion and the Rise and Fall of Islamic Science . https://scholar.harvard.edu/files/paper.pdf 18/09/2017

WR 23:

Can Muslim womem acquire knowledge? Philip, Bilal.https://youtub e/cD2GARjKKkk 20/12/2017

WR 24:

Re-thinking Education in Islam: Reviving the Legacy of Muslim Scho lars. Quadi, Yasir. https://youtu.be/SE2ufcIhhlk 5/01/2018

WR 25:

Yasir Qadhi. https://www.youtube.com/watch?v=-rQLUlRpfgU 28/06/2018.

Index

www.ingramcontent.com/pod-product-compliance
Lightning Source LLC
Chambersburg PA
CBHW020742100426
42735CB00037B/178